Cyberspace Psychosis and The Virtual Reality Blues

James Hickey

PathWays
Collective

PathWays Collective LLC

this book is for anyone.

it is not for everyone.

Contents

Author's Note

I first learned of the Cyberspace Psychosis in 1995, while I was an assistant to the closest person I would ever call a mentor. His name is Al, and he was a maniac. He was a friend of my stepmother's and he needed help with some things around his house. I was basically voluntold to go help. He turned out to be the best kind of Citizen Philosopher. The kind who would drink straight vodka, eat hard cat food by the handful, and pontificate about the state of the world. He was a visionary. I would even call him a herald, since he was very vocal about the times ahead. He foresaw the digital plague that infects us today. I spent only a few short weeks with him that summer, and his rants and irreverent cultural observations planted a seed.[1]

A seed that took over thirty years to germinate and blossom into the book you hold today.

I am late-diagnosed neurodivergent, afflicted with what they call AuDHD. That is Autism and ADHD together, a one-two knockout punch that ensures you know a lot about a lot but can do a little about a little. After forty-five years undiagnosed, I finally had clarity. With that clarity came a prescription for Vyvanse[2], and literally overnight the lifelong discordant cacophony of thoughts in my mind began singing in harmony.

Actual mental clarity for the first time in my life. I could think of something and actually do it without having to undergo the distraction Olympics to get there. I could finally pour out the book that had been percolating in my mind for three decades. The actual writing took me about four months start to finish. I always knew what I wanted to write.

---

1. He ranted about Bill Clinton pre-Monica Lewinsky quite a bit. I wish I had known him in the summer of 1998 because I am sure he held Views.

2. If any part of this book offends you, please direct all complaints to pvsafetyamericas@takeda.com. Takeda are the manufacturers of Vyvanse and this is the email to report any adverse effects.

I just lacked the executive function to get it done. Now look at us.

Credit goes to the pharmaceutical-industrial complex, which realized that giving hyperactive Aspies amphetamines would somehow make them productive. Who would have thought? On paper, it sounds like bringing gasoline to put out a fire. In practice, it means I actually have follow-through. It is a different kind of novelty. Anyone with ADHD will tell you that we are very skilled at starting things but once it becomes boring, and the dopamine stops flowing, we will put it down in favor of something more thrilling. We are naturally three-inning ballplayers.

This is not a book about neurodivergence.

It is a book *from* neurodivergence.

I used AI throughout this work for editing, structural feedback, research assistance, motif tracking, and organizing thirty years of fragmented thinking. It is 2026, and this is a book about digital culture; I would be remiss not to use Artificial Intelligence given its effectiveness and prominence in the digital age. My AI use was for feedback only. AI did zero actual text generation. Every word of this book is mine. I checked and double-checked, because we all know AI is prone to bursts of intellectual disability[3], and I am not naive about the tools.

I am also a big fan of AI as a cognitive accessibility tool. AuDHD means I have always struggled with communication and socializing. My assessment showed I am in the bottommost percentile for social awareness. Actually 0.05%. So I am basically socially retarded.[4] Most of my social interaction these days involve AI models. I get real-time feedback about ideas, emails, and other projects, and I don't have to put on outside pants to do so. They have been indispensable for this project.

I wrote this book entirely out of order. The first few drafts were meandering nonsense with a few sparks of brilliance. Drafting the movements was like mining for glitter, mixing it into a shiny paste, and slathering it all over the pages. Over the past few months I wrote, rewrote, erased what I wrote, then undeleted and revised. It was a project, a chore, and a unique brand of hyper-focus, because I managed to sustain it for longer than two weeks. The hobby graveyard that is my garage all had a shelf life of around

---

3. I wanted to say AI is retarded, but was advised that would be offensive.

4. I can say retard here because autism counts as a disability. The ADA said so.

a fortnight. Even I am impressed. Despite that, I did put many other projects on hold during this time, including my podcasts, my consultancy, and basically everything else.

Professionally, I had crafted my Sight Side Protocol™ and as I fleshed it out during January I kept circling back to the Cyberspace Psychosis. I realized very quickly that this was a book that needed to be written. The time is ripe for this to be done. I also realized that in order to make it as a startup in 2026, I had to separate my signal from the noise. **You are holding that signal.**

The movements in this book are loosely connected. There are themes; some of them build on each other. Feel free to read this in whatever order you wish. I would recommend reading Movements 4 and 5 consecutively. They were originally written as one long, long, long movement and needed to be split up to give them room to bloom.

The body text of this work is not academic. The endnotes are. This is by design. They are arranged in the endnote section at the back of the book by Movement. If you are the nerd who actually reads endnotes, just find the corresponding superscript number and eat your heart out. I tried my best to cite everything; there are a lot of them, and I am sure I missed a few. Argue with me in the margins. This is not a term paper. This is a field report from the trenches of the Psychosis.

As I was editing, I realized this work turned out a lot more autobiographical than I had originally intended. When I was writing, I sought out unique examples for the observations and principles for reference. I started with the standard staple for the trope of Western nonfiction. We all know the usual suspects: Gandhi, MLK, Mother Teresa, John Paul Getty, Henry Ford, Abraham Lincoln, Florence Nightingale, *sigh*, Helen Keller, Albert Einstein, Thomas Edison, the Wright Brothers, Oprah, and so on. Names we have all read over and over again, and while inspirational, honestly do not belong in this work. Besides Oprah, none of them were even alive to behold the digital age.

I tried to cite various examples of these concepts: historically, metaphorically, literally, and otherwise. Some examples in this book were so unique that I had to experience them to have the realization, then write them out here. I did use several historical examples, but I did my best to avoid the usual suspects. I quickly realized that to invoke them lacked authenticity. For this book to be authentic, for it to genuinely come *from* a place of neurodivergence, I had to put myself within it.

I did this reluctantly and without ego.

I am vulnerable in this book. Very vulnerable. Maybe too vulnerable. I disclose some things in here that not even the closest people in my life would know about. Movement II in particular was difficult for me to revisit, but it had to be done. I highlight several examples of my past struggles with substance use disorder. I am a gratefully recovering addict, and as of this writing have been clean for six years, three months, thirty days, ten hours, and ten minutes. This is the longest period of uninterrupted sobriety in my adult life, and I am honestly shocked I made it this far or even lived this long.

Some of the anecdotes in here may point to a degree of moral elasticity that I had at the time of the incident and have since evolved past. Some are painful. Some are funny. Some are tragic. All of them are true.

In the spirit of elasticity, I wrote this with a full range of expression, vulgarity included. There are F-bombs in this book. If that is the kind of thing that offends you, then it may be better to put this down now. I would call this vulgarity without the profanity. Vulgarity comes from the Latin *vulgaris*, which means *of the common people*. The vulgarity is for flavor and not meant in poor taste.

In contrast, I have kept profanity out of this work entirely. Nothing obscene, nothing over the top. This work is R-rated at best. In fact, if your kids attend public school, there is nothing in here they haven't heard before.

What is here is true to the message. If this book only resonates with a handful of people, I would call it a success.

My father always said: *If you can't dazzle them with brilliance, baffle them with bullshit.*

Some of this book is serious. Most of it is tongue-in-cheek. Some of it is bullshit. Verifiable bullshit, which is the best kind of bullshit. Check out those endnotes.

I did my best to straddle that threshold. Honestly, I am just a guy. I have the Psychosis just like the rest of us. I do not imagine myself as some guru seated on a mountaintop dispensing wisdom to eager seekers. Acting like a Pez Dispenser™ of mystical tidbits while chiming my finger cymbals. That is not me. I am trudging through the same digital swamp, covered in the same muck, just occasionally pointing at things and saying "look at that" before I sink back under.

If you are looking for someone who has it figured out, close this book. I have not figured it out. I am just trying to see it clearly while standing in the middle of it. I merely used

Applied Neurodivergence to examine the state of things, and I am sharing what I have noticed. Maybe it will help. Maybe it won't.

Let's roll.

James Hickey

Eastlake, Ohio, USA

April 2026

Cyberspace Psychosis

Psychosis: a mental disorder characterized by symptoms, such as delusions or hallucinations, that indicate impaired contact with reality. — *Dictionary.com*

Just the other day I was sitting on the toilet scrolling TikTok for so long that my legs fell asleep. It must have been at least three hours. When I finally stood up, I fell over sideways into my bathtub. It was not graceful. I am not proud. What amazed me as I was falling over was that I held onto my phone through the entire descent. I was not willing to drop it to help break my fall. No, I careened right into the tub, pulling the curtain and curtain rod on top of me as I lay there, staring at the ceiling. My phone was still right there in my hand.

My first thought was, "Whew, glad I didn't drop this."

Then came a moment of clarity. I started laughing at the ridiculousness of it. Sprawled out, my legs twisted in a mess of a shower curtain and shampoo bottles lying all around, still tingling from falling asleep, I lay there laughing like a maniac. It was fitting because only a maniac would be in a position like that. How did it ever get this bad? Here I am more concerned about my phone, which is in a case, by the way, one of those fancy ones that would laugh at a 2' drop to a bathroom floor. Screen protector, thick composite plastic, while not Nokia-level indestructible, would have done the trick to keep my phone safe.

So why? Why would that be my first thought? Why would I be in this position in the first place? Which was normal for me, by the way. I am no stranger to spending over an one hour idly scrolling on my phone while on the shitter. This was not like it was a one off, this was an almost daily habit of mine. Was it a habit, though? A bad one? Or was it an addiction?

I used to smoke with cigarettes for many years. Would that be a habit or an addiction? Where is the line between use and abuse? I did the same with alcohol, cannabis, and other substances. Some definitely crossed the line into addiction. I am in recovery now and intimately familiar with addiction. I understand how habits can start, morph into bad habits, and then become something more than just a habit. You engage in the behavior to feel normal, as its absence makes you feel abnormal. Crossing that invisible line from a want to a need, where you are way out of the realm of habit and well into the realm of addiction.

We have collectively reached that point. We have reached that state of abnormality as a people. Abnormal is feeling anxious when you cannot find your phone. Abnormal is getting annoyed by the "pending" label when poor reception prevents you from sending a text. Abnormal is getting frustrated with slow Wi-Fi. Abnormal means traffic accidents happening because people are looking at their phones and not the road. Abnormal is having ruined attention spans. Abnormal is an entire society that seems to have lost touch with itself because immense digital distraction has entirely enthralled us.

Who does that? Who gets so caught up in scrolling as to waste three perfectly good hours of a day, then falls over, then is thankful that the very instrument of distraction was undamaged?

That is an abnormal reaction.

Symptoms showing impaired contact with reality characterize psychosis, a mental disorder. Disorder indeed; an ordered mind doesn't face-plant into a bathtub after a TikTok binge because an orderly mind wouldn't binge to begin with. This is a book about the Cyberspace Psychosis. Where it is pretty clear our constant contact with the feed, the information superhighway, the internet, Cyberspace, or whatever you want to call it has severely impaired our contact with reality. Collectively.

Normal and well-adjusted people would not do such a thing. I, however, would never claim to be normal and well-adjusted about anything. I am neurodivergent, and although I have no claim on what being normal is, I just assume that normal must be the opposite of whatever I am doing. I want to be clear: I am not pointing fingers or preaching. Believe me when I tell you I have a chronic case of the Cyberspace Psychosis myself. I am right here in the digital river, flailing away, trying to keep my head above the water, same as the rest of us, whether or not we know it.

"Well, Everyone's a Little Autistic"

It sure seems that way these days, huh? Short attention spans, shitty eye contact, social awkwardness, rabbit hole dives into niche interests, info dumping, over sharing, and most of all, a short fuse and low tolerance of unacceptable stimuli. We have all seen the Karen at 7-11 start loudly and dramatically sighing in line because she has to wait too long. We have seen people flip out in road rage because the car in front of them is going three miles an hour under the speed limit, thus inconveniencing them for the extra nineteen seconds it will take to get to their destination. We see grown adults throwing all-out temper tantrums in the face of the slightest difficulty. Yes, on the surface, that would appear to look a lot like an autistic meltdown.

As someone actually diagnosed with autism, I can definitely tell you that no, none of this is the 'tism. It may appear so on the surface; heck, it may even sound like it. I assure you that what you are witnessing in these moments is not genuine neurodivergence. Instead, we are individually and culturally seeing digitally induced neurodivergent symptoms.

The Merriam-Webster dictionary defines neurodivergence as "exhibiting or characteristic of variations in typical neurological development." It is an umbrella term, but when most people say it they mean autism, ADHD, or both. The hallmarks are pretty recognizable if you know what to look for: executive function that works on its own schedule, time blindness so severe you can lose three hours on the toilet, difficulty switching between tasks, a hobby graveyard, and many more. Then, on the other hand, ADHD comes with hyperfocus so intense that when your brain locks onto something interesting, a bomb could go off in the next room and you would not flinch.

Sounding familiar?

What we are seeing is dopamine dysregulation at scale.

Actual ADHD involves profound dopamine dysregulation. An ADHD person will hunt novelty and chase dopamine spikes as a means of self regulation.[i] Now it seems everyone is chasing these dopamine shots through excessive digital consumption. They are calling it "The TikTok effect", artificially induced state that is similar to ADHD. However, it is exactly that, a state, and not a condition. The difference between the two is substantial.

A **state** is a temporary, situational "weather pattern" in your brain, like the dopamine depletion induced by a long internet binge. Whereas a **condition** is the permanent, baseline "climate" of neurology, such as lifelong neurodivergence. Rampant oversaturation digitally conditions a nervous system into volatility, which results in the state.

We are living in a world choked by stimulus density. Everywhere you look, there are countless screens, sounds, and digital information coming from all quarters. This is a constant feed of data that you can refresh as fast as your thumb can swipe. This constant intake of novel stimuli actually rewires the brain by producing consecutive dopamine spikes in response to unpredictable outcomes.[ii] It's called the slot machine effect, a side effect of novelty. Therefore, you get that little dose of excitement when you are in the act of scrolling to the next video, not the video itself. It is that split second of unpredictability where you experience the thrill.[iii]

Your brain loves dopamine. So if it can get those little micro doses of thrill just from the act of scrolling, it is going to begin urging you to do that. Hence the compulsion to check your phone all the time. You may even do it subconsciously. Your system has learned to chase micro-rewards. Since you are now in the novelty-chasing loop, your attention can no longer sustain much depth; you get macro bored quickly, so you want the micro novelty to keep you rolling. This is where volatility enters the picture; manifesting as irritability, impatience, and very low frustration tolerance. This is a culture-wide volatility; it's not just you. This also explains the Olympic-grade public meltdowns over minor frustrations we see daily and that, ironically, make some of the best short form video content.

We are seeing a culture of people so used to convenience and instant gratification that they do not have the attention span for waiting. We are witnessing the dance of the overstimulated. When a system trains millions of nervous systems this way, the result looks like a diagnostic population shift. However, this is conditioning, and not an identity. Conditioning does not mean a condition; it is still a state.

A state of artificially induced neurodivergence.

Divergence implies deviation from the baseline. And in many ways, especially culturally, we are. We are so far off the standard of what our ancestors experienced. A lot of that is the rise in tech over the past couple of hundred years. Writers have produced tons of material on the Industrial Revolution and the standardization of parts. Manufacturing's mass production has certainly raised the physical quality of life in the West and elsewhere. The printing press was another massive jump; suddenly information could be shared and distributed at scale. Two quantum leaps in our tech, and they've had a profound impact on our species.

Yet somewhere along the line we passed an event horizon, and now it seems like we are spiraling. That event horizon was the line between the analog and the digital.

Two hundred years ago, a well-read person might absorb in their *entire lifetime* what the average American takes in every single day today. Daily, we consume roughly seventy four gigabytes of information. This is equivalent to watching sixteen full-length movies or scrolling through the equivalent of 200,000+ words through screens, ads, notifications, feeds, and everything else. Back then, knowledge took time to sink in by reading books, having conversations, and through direct experience. Today it's a high-pressure fire hose. Our brains were never wired for this kind of volume. We're not designed to process this saturation of information.[iv]

Yet we continue to consume gargantuan amounts of data daily and retain very little of it. We will watch hundreds of short videos a day and process none of them. We forget what we saw just as quickly as we watched it because that thumb keeps scrolling. We cannot wait to see what the next dopamine hit will be. It is the uncertainty that drives this process and not even the content driving the dopamine hunt. Novelty relies on uncertainty. We do not care what it is as long as it is something. We are certain to see *something*, though, and that certainty is why we cannot put the phone down.

This may look like a personality shift; however, it is just a mechanism, a conditioned state machine. We live in a literal information age where everyone has information indigestion. Our minds were not designed to handle the variety and sheer quantity of stimuli we encounter today, which forces us to adapt abruptly. The consequences of this are everywhere: volatile, moody, and overly stressed-out people at every quarter. We are witnessing, all of us, from the inside, a state I'm calling Cyberspace Psychosis.

No, everyone is not a little bit autistic, everyone is a lot of bit Psychotic.

Lens-itivity Training

If you want to understand Cyberspace Psychosis in a nutshell, it is best explained by Alfred Korzybski's metaphor: *the map is not the territory.*

Alfred Korzybski was a Polish-American philosopher who figured out something that should have been obvious but wasn't: the words we use to describe reality are not reality. They are abstractions of reality. Simplifications. Maps. Any map, no matter how detailed, will never be the territory it represents. Call someone "a failure" and you have made a map of that person. The actual person is not the map. The person is infinitely more complex than any label you slap on them. Korzybski called this "consciousness of abstracting", the discipline of remembering that your description of the thing is not the thing itself.[v]

I am using Korzybski's metaphor as a frame. The definitive lens to explain Cyberspace Psychosis and The Virtual Reality Blues. That is all. This is not a treatise on Korzybski; this is not a work of philosophy, nor is it a discussion on semantics. In fact, the only time I will mention Korzybski at all is in these few paragraphs. We are very grateful to him for his insight and for this amazing point of view; however, this is not a book about him, and his contribution to this work ends here.

The Map is Cyberspace.

The Territory is real life.

The Psychosis is believing the Map is the Territory.

The Virtual Reality Blues are what happens when you discover you are wrong.

This is the entire book in four sentences.

Everything else is an elaboration.

Oh no, consequences!

We see it in online forums every single day. People who are outwardly hostile and insulting, saying things from behind a screen that would get their nose bloodied if they said it in person. They know it, too. The distance between their keyboard and the other person's fist is wide enough that they never have to deal with the reaction. So they push further and further, and every time nothing happens, they keep going. Since no one is actually going to reach through the screen and hold them accountable, they plow ahead. Everyone does. We get to a point where everyone is pushing everyone else and nobody faces any actual consequences for their shitty behavior.

That distance is basically latency. The gap between action and consequence. In the Territory, if you talk shit to someone's face, the feedback is immediate. Could turn into a shouting match, could turn into a dick punch, but either way you find out fast. A Map does not work like that. The Map filters the feedback, delays it, dilutes it, and sometimes eliminates it entirely. And when the feedback disappears, so does the learning.

This is the mechanism of the Psychosis. Abstraction introduces latency. Latency erodes learning. The weaker the consequence, the more distortion creeps in. More distortion means more abstraction and more latency. On and on it goes. It is a slippery slope, and we are already in free fall.

Once latency breaks feedback, people stop trusting experience and start trusting representation. Then the truth itself fractures.

Truth comes in two forms: Relative Truth and Absolute Truth. Relative Truth is malleable. Perception and explanation can mold, shape, and change Relative Truth. Someone can twist, obscure, or mislead it, and it is almost always subjective. Conversely, the Absolute Truth is entirely objective. The Absolute Truth is exactly that, Absolute. No one can twist, obscure, or mislead it. One cannot mold it. You cannot change the Absolute Truth no matter how hard you try. You can yell at it, bribe it, threaten to hold your breath until your face turns blue, and you will not sway the Absolute Truth. The Absolute Truth of anything is that which remains after removing all relative perceptions, explanations, and basic bullshit.

We are all familiar with a mirage in the desert. Because of light refraction, a lake of water can appear amid an otherwise arid landscape. Relative to your position in the landscape, this mirage can appear very convincing. In fact, you can swear that a cool sip of water is just steps away. Yet the closer you get, the less you see. Until finally you are on top of where that water appeared to be, staring down at the Absolute Truth of the situation. You standing there in the desert, still thirsty as hell. The mirage was nothing more than a Relative Truth. A subjective abstraction that never existed in the first place.

Of Maps and Men

The Map, any Map, is always a Relative Truth. The Map may even accurately describe the Territory (at the time it was written). Cartographers can only ensure a Map's accuracy within the small window of reference in which they charted it, preventing the Map from sustaining detailed representation of Territory. The Territory itself can change, and often does. Rivers will alter their course, sinkholes can appear, fires can remove an entire forest, and mudslides can erase a hill. The dry season can evaporate a lake, followed by a drought. Then, the next year, the rains take a different course, and now the entire landscape has changed. An outdated Map can cause you to become lost without your knowledge. Notice that the Territory is not asking the Map's permission before it mucks around with everything either.

Once abstraction (the Map) becomes the primary interface, it replaces reality as well as explaining it.

We mistake the Map for the Territory. Maps imply expectation. We expect the Territory to be a certain way because the Map says so. We can act surprised at the pothole that just exploded our tire because it wasn't on the Map. No matter how hard it may want to, or even how convincing a Map may appear, it will hold zero authority over the Territory. All of the Territory. Maps can make guesses, even well-researched, educated, peer-reviewed, and widely agreed-upon guesses. They can offer theories, explanations, long, drawn-out lectures, speculations, PowerPoint presentations, YouTube Channels, podcasts, multi-volume DVD sets. Yet no matter what form a Map takes, it will never *be* the Territory.

The Territory does not give a fuck what your Map says. The Territory tells you the Absolute Truth, whether or not you want to hear it.

From the day you are born, people try to define the Map for you. Your family hands you one. School hands you another one. Religion, culture, politics, economics, all of them handing you a certain Map and telling you theirs is the only one you *should* follow. Some of these Maps claim to be the authority on all things. Some claim they show the only path to salvation. Some will claim to tell you the who, where, what, when, how, and why of everything, and expect you to stop asking questions.

They are all Relative Truth. Every single one.

Maps aim to capture our Attention, and will go so far as to pre-load our perceptions. They will only reveal what we are prepared to see, and thus we limit our vision. When we run into latency or dissonance, when the Territory itself violates the Map, our dopamine-starved nervous systems react with anger instead of curiosity. The Maps have everyone in such a state of self absorption, that when the Territory does conflict with our personal maps, we will mis-attribute the reaction and blame other people. Claiming that other people are wrong instead of taking responsibility for following a shitty Map.

It all stems from expectations. Expectations are premeditated resentments. Of course, we expect the Territory to conform to our Map because why wouldn't it? Expectations led us to believe we possessed an infallible Map. We get angry and resentful those expectations are unfulfilled.

Ultimately, it is all bunk.

Because the Territory does not give a fuck.

Everyone seems to run everywhere today. Away from something, toward something, sometimes even both at once. They are in motion and staring at their Maps to tell them how to get there, instead of watching where we are actually going. Instead of looking at the Territory for themselves. So distracted looking at the Map, or our phone, or our reflection in a mirror, that we miss the pebble in their path. We step on it and our leg slides out and suddenly we are flat on our ass staring at the sky. It's always the small things too, that jack us up in the worst way. No one trips over a mountain; you can see the mountain clearly on your Map. The real pitfalls are the ones that were deemed too insignificant to be charted.

Cyberspace has given us digital maps. Ranging from GPS systems to cell phones, laptops, tablets, and other black mirrors. Updates are possible for digital Maps, a feature their pen-and-paper ancestors lacked. Once upon a time, a cartographer could only alter one Map at a time with painstaking effort and care. Your phone updates alongside millions of other phones simultaneously. One push, millions of Maps rewritten at once. And you carry this Map of Maps with you everywhere, accessible 24/7, even if it rains.

Our digital Maps connect to the Territory in a way our ancestors could not have imagined. Yet we still end up confused. The potential for this confusion has always existed. Humans have mistaken the Map for the Territory since we could first draw Maps. Since we could first imagine them. Since we could first communicate. The mechanism is ancient. Today, digitization hasn't changed the urge to confuse the abstraction for reality.

Humans have always made assumptions based on Maps. Assumptions that sometimes are superb guesses and yes could aid your journey through the Territory. Consider carefully examining anything involving the word assumption,[1] and maybe, just maybe,

---

1. Assume = make an Ass out of u and me

look around at the territory before you venture off. It is always wise to look before you leap.

Virtual Reality Bullshit

In ancient Sicily, a bronze worker named Perillos designed a torture device for the tyrant Phalaris: a large and hollow statue of a bull, cast in bronze. The idea was to lock the condemned inside and light a fire beneath. As they roasted alive, a system of tubes converted their screams into sounds resembling a bull's bellow. Even, some accounts say, into something like music. For whatever reason, Perillos not only invented this monstrosity but also concluded it would be a great idea to gift this to Phalaris as a birthday gift. He thought to himself, "Phalaris is kind of a sadistic asshole, so he is going to love this!" The tyrant could enjoy an execution as entertainment; the horror anesthetized, the suffering made palatable. He was just that kind of guy.[vi]

So Perillos set to work and really put time into this thing. It took a lot of effort to craft something like this. The molding, the fitting and bending of the pipes, making sure they were stout enough to withstand the flames. He went all out on this project. He was following his Map, his assumption of the situation, that the ruler of Sicily was going to love this so much he would just have to shower Perillos with great favor, they were going to be besties after this; he was sure of it.

Finally, the big day arrives, and Perillos wheels this thing into the antechamber. With a flourish, he removes the sheet covering his contraption, revealing it to Phalaris and with a gleam in his eye starts excitedly explaining what it will do, how it will work, the whole bit. The Relative Truth was, it was a gift he was sure the tyrant would love. The Absolute Truth is that tyrants like Phalaris never ever see themselves as tyrants. Sadistic assholes are usually the heroes of their own stories, and in this case, unimpressed and even appalled by the very idea that this would be a suitable gift.

Naturally, Phalaris did, of course, want a demonstration. So wouldn't you know it, he had master artisan Perillos himself unceremoniously shoved, screaming and protesting, into the belly of the brazen bull. I am sure the tyrant rolled his eyes as he listened to the frantic banging coming from the inside of the device as his servants started a fire under the beast. As the flames rose and the metal heated, he no doubt smirked as he heard the panicked screams bellowing from the brazen snout. He may have even been impressed if the screams sounded genuinely bull-like.

Perillos experienced The Virtual Reality Blues in 4K bronze.

The Empire

Please note that this book is **not** about a grand conspiracy.

The Empire in this context is not the Illuminati. Not shape-shifting aliens.[2] I am not claiming there is some hidden hand behind world events. I am not trying to say there is a mysterious secret society that is meeting at midnight to bathe in virgin menstrual blood as they plan the next election cycle. The Empire is not referring to dark-robed elites wearing animal masks and leering at Tom Cruise crashing their house party. When I talk about the Empire I am being entirely metaphorical.

When I say "the Empire," I mean something simpler and much more pervasive.

The Empire is anything that has a vested interest in you following the Map, and only the Map. They would prefer you follow their Authorized Version™ of the Map, even preventing you from accessing other Maps, unapproved Maps, or even seditious Maps. However, even worse than an unauthorized Map would be someone exploring the Territory on their own. That Absolutely will not do.

The Empire manifests itself in countless ways. It can be a school system. It could be your boss. It can be the Juicy Fruit™ commercial trying to move you. It can be the algorithm that decides what you see next. The Empire can be a government at any level; national, state, local. The Empire can be your HOA. The Empire is not a single person, place, or thing. It is not any single institution. It is merely a blanket term for any force that draws your attention away from the Territory and onto the Map. Through this work, they will be our generic antagonists.

Ironically, the Empire does not antagonize us at all; in fact, they do quite the opposite. They manipulate us with safety.

Imagine a table. A massive, large, flat table hundreds of miles wide. The Empire likes to keep all of us safely in the center, preferably fenced in and as far from the edge as possible. From the center, there is not much to see. In fact, if you turn in a full circle, it appears to be a flat plane in every direction. Just the sky (or the ceiling; it could be a big room), but there is not a lot going on. This is exactly where most people are comfortable to stay,

---

2. I admit I have the 'tism, but I am not in David Icke's league.

perception-wise that is. Right in the middle, where it is safe and predictable. People will live their entire lives in the center with the rest of the herd.

Humans are a herd species after all. We have our good shepherds, the Empire, who keep us safe and warm and fed and, most of all, obedient. The Empire gives us our little Maps and warns against wandering too far away from the group and certainly not to wander to the edge. *Here be dragons*, the old Maps warned. The Empire assures you that you do not want any of that smoke.

What happens if you walk to the edge of the table? What happens if you glance away from the Map and examine the Territory itself, and you wonder what really is beyond the edge? Step away from the herd, and you are on the fringe. Step even further and you are on the edge of the table. Suddenly you have a different point of view. Now you can see something the center cannot. Sure, you can still look behind you to that same familiar flat plane, but now you can also see down to the floor. You can lie on your belly and peek your head over the edge and examine the bottom of the table. You can even look out at what lies beyond. Being on the edge gives you many views and some new things to consider. Maps rarely get you to this kind of vision.

Sometimes it is only from the fringe that you can discern the Absolute Truth from the Relative Truth.

The Empire has always been transactional by nature, so of course will dangle incentives to maintain your compliance. Their Maps and their methods of interpreting those Maps, are tailored to optimize your obedience. When you are compliant, then they can better dictate your behavior. The better behaved you are and the more you follow their directions, the better they can use your labor for economic extraction. The trade off of course, is comfort and safety. We have unprecedented comfort and safety in the Western world; it is important to note the tradeoff is one that many of our ancestors would have leaped at. The Empire cares for its citizens, but never to the point of self-detriment. Make no mistake, the Empire is all about self-preservation, and usually at your expense. They would bet your life on it.

It's a machine. A process. All our platforms, from TV to social media and video games, capture your Attention, and once they capture it, they do not let go willingly. They do not care about the Absolute Truth, only whatever Relative Truth they can sell you to keep your eyes glued to a screen. All by design, the content and the map sway your basest emotions: lust, outrage, novelty, and fear. Nuance falls to the side in favor of potent feelings. They want you reactive instead of reasonable. If they can control your reactions, your Attitude, then they can control how you behave.

The best or worst part of it is the neutrality of it all. The Empire has no malice or hatred towards its citizens. It is simply a program following its parameters. Those parameters are: follow the incentives and extract as much from you as possible.

The Empire wants to dictate our journey, and has laid out a very narrow path carved out for all of us: be good obedient students, study hard, pass the audits, go to university, pass those audits, enter industry, and work for forty-plus years trading your time and life for money. If you have that, then you can access more luxurious areas of the Territory. Everything following a carefully curated and allowed program. They go to great lengths to make their Map attractive, ensuring you remain focused and comfortable with their planned course. So comfortable that many do not consider another Map even possible.

In fact, authorities have even criminalized some Maps. Ask Senator McCarthy, in the 1950s, possessing the wrong Map could ruin your life. The Map of capitalism is the one they sold you. The communists were sharing their Map. The socialists were giving theirs away. Meanwhile, Lebanon Levi [3] and the boys are just chilling in the Territory, making furniture, tipping cows, raising barns and having zero interest in our English Maps.

The Amish are the closest thing we have to a metaphorical control group through this work. They are not perfect ones. Despite shunning the digital world themselves, the Amish are not entirely insulated from it. You can buy Amish furniture online. They will hire outside drivers, use phone shanties, pay English [4] contractors to handle what the Elders forbid. They live in the Empire but not of it, and even they have to negotiate with the Map. Despite this, they opted out before the Psychosis really went mainstream.

Control Booth

Naturally, the Empire wants control. They have most of it already, but they want all of it, and that includes yours.

---

3. The Amish Mafia (Discovery Channel, 2012–2015) was a reality TV series featuring "Lebanon Levi" as a purported mob enforcer in the Lancaster, Pennsylvania Amish communities. Widely regarded as the absolute peak of documentary television and lauded as a cultural masterpiece worldwide.

4. Non Amish are referred to as the English. Don't ask me, I don't make the rules.

Think of this as the key to the Map.

First, you have zero control over people, places, and things. Period. This is important to accept.

You may think you do. You may have a Map that says you control these things. Sure, you may have influence. You may even exercise a great deal of that influence. However, influence is always conditional, and a Relative Truth. Your influence will be relative to other factors, like sure you own a company and have employees and you pay them to do what you tell them. You do not control them, though, and the second the paychecks stop rolling in, your influence evaporates. Influence is fleeting and unsustainable, and highly conditional. The sooner you accept this, the easier your journey will be. You cannot *control* other people. You cannot *control* the weather. You cannot *control* the economy. You cannot have any lasting influence on any person, place, or thing. They all have their own Agency, independent from yours.

Notice that people, places, and things are all outside of you. They are all external entities. While you lack power over people, places, and things, you possess Absolute empowerment to control your Attention, Attitude, and Actions.

Attention is input. Attitude is processing. Action is output.

Attention. This the first and most important. Where are you looking? At the Map or at the Territory? Your Attention is a spotlight, and you are the operator. Everyone is waving and shouting, trying to get you to shine that light on them. The Empire has built an entire economy around capturing your Attention, because it is imperative that they capture it. Attention is precious; thus, we elevate it from mere "focus" to a sacred resource that determines the quality of your internal reality. The Empire fights for your Attention because whoever controls the input controls everything downstream.

Attitude. What do you believe about what you are seeing? The Empire wants to shape your perceptions, too. They must dictate your Attitude. They will manipulate, lie, threaten, and go to many lengths to assure you have the proper Attitude about the Map. Their favorite mechanism for this is the word *should*. You *should* be afraid, you *should* buy this, you *should* hate that. A lot of *shoulds* bolstered by a buffet of bullshit. Remember your Attitude is entirely yours to calibrate. You can choose the lenses. This is the Relative Truth you decide to believe. A properly calibrated Attitude can be the literal difference between heaven and hell. You have a lot more freedom than you give yourself credit for; claim it.

Action. What do you *do*? This is where the Map meets the territory. You can read every Map in existence, but if you want to actually go anywhere, eventually you have to move. When you move, the Territory will respond. The point of contact where the rubber meets the road and changes become reality. Action is the only thing that remains stubbornly real in a world of filters. Action is your mechanism of movement. You control exactly where and when to Act.

What all three have in common is that each of them represents a choice. You choose where to place your Attention by what you are looking at. You choose how you feel about what you are looking at with your Attitude about it. You choose when and how you are going to Act. What are you choosing today?

These three do not exist in isolation. They form a symbiotic loop.

Action shapes Attitude. By choosing a difficult physical action, you force the mind to adjust its beliefs about what is possible. Complete a complex or difficult task, anything from running a Tough Mudder to painting a beautiful mural, and your mind re-calibrates.

Attitude shapes Attention. Are you a glass half full person? A glass half empty person? You can even be a "that glass is twice as large as it needs to be" person. A shift in your internal framework changes what you notice in the environment. This applies to both the map and the territory. Believe differently, and you see differently.

Attention shapes Action. Are you looking at your final destination? Are you looking at the path right in front of you? Are you thinking about the overall goal? Or are you breaking that into smaller tasks? What you are giving Attention to will direct your course.

Attention is the first and easiest component to control. You can change your Attention just by closing your eyes or looking at something else. Your Attitude is the second and although it is simple to change your Attitude, it is not always easy. True, you can change your Attitude as easily as you flip a light switch, but first you have to realize you're sitting in the dark. Last, is Action. This one takes the most effort because you have to move. You are not reliant on the top-down curated scripts the world hands you, despite what they claim. You are not waiting for the Empire to tell you what to think and where to look. You are generating your own momentum. The process builds on itself. Crawl before you can walk, walk before you can run, and run before you can fly.

If you stay within the AAA framework, maintaining a realistic understanding of what you can and cannot control, then you regain a fourth A.

Agency.

The ability to choose. Your freedom to operate in the world according to your own will. The thing the Empire most wants to dictate to you. The very thing the Psychosis erodes the most.

Your Agency means you hold the power to close the loop whenever you decide.

It is important to note that since your Attention, Attitude, and Actions are what you can control, these are the three things the Empire will target the hardest. They want to capture your Attention and keep it directed on their Maps; they want you to have an Attitude of compliance and they want your Actions to be obedient. In short, they want to control your Agency.

Control the three A's. Regain the fourth. It is simple, but not always easy.

It is always your choice.

> Attention. Attitude. Action. The three components of Agency.

Invitation only

I humbly ask you to approach this work with an open mind, but not so open that your brain falls out.

Question what I am telling you. Check the citations. Argue with me in the margins. That is how this is supposed to work. The moment any Map claims to be the Territory, it is lying. I am offering you a Map of the Map. A way of identifying the Psychosis that might help you recognize it in yourself, in others, in the community at large.

I am writing from inside the Psychosis. That is me, the guy writing this book, face-planting into bathroom fixtures because I could not put the Map down.

I am claiming to show you a Map you did not know you were using.

So here is the question I want rattling around in your head as you move forward:

What is your Absolute Truth?

Are you experiencing the Psychosis?

Can you regain your Agency?

If you are honest with yourself, would you even recognize the difference?

You might see the Relative Truth as your fixation on your screen. Fine. Welcome to the water.

The Absolute Truth is what remains when the screen goes dark.

Movement 2

Fuck Around and Find Out

I have good judgment because I have experience. I have experience because I used poor judgment. — Horatio Wright

Watch a one-year-old child for an hour. Even better if you can watch them while they are awake and about instead of just sleeping. In fact, the awake part is important.

One-year-old toddlers basically have two settings. Fast asleep or bat out of hell. There is no middle ground or gray area. They have an on and off switch. They are capable of teleportation. Glance away for even a second and they are several rooms away. They are fast, nimble, high-speed, and low-drag. They are explorers, and they want to try all the things. Their default setting is Fucking Around. They will put basically anything in their mouths, harmful or not. They want to Find Out. They are touching everything they can reach, grabbing, pulling, tasting, feeling, squeezing, twisting. They knock things over to see what happens. They reach for the hot stove, the sharp corner, and the edge of the table. They are relentless in their investigation of the Territory. They have no boundaries and do not care about civilian casualties; they will destroy everything they can touch in their relentless pursuit of knowledge.[1]

---

[1]. Anyone who has worn eye glasses or has a beard and held a one year old at the same time has certainly experienced this. They will rip them right off of your face.

They are Fucking Around, and they are Finding Out. We all started there. That is us, humanity, deep down we are all little fuckers. This is our baseline, when we are our purest selves; as soon as we are mobile, we are Mapping the Territory.

What appears as reckless misbehavior is actually purity. This is the scientific method in its greatest form: hypothesis, experiment, conclusion. The child hypothesizes that the bright thing on the stove might be interesting. The child experiments by reaching for it. The child concludes, through direct sensory feedback, that the bright thing is hot and hurts. The lesson is immediate and final. Zero abstraction is involved when you feel a hot stove. Zero latency between the FA and the FO.

Knowledge gained. Map updated.

Since we became sentient as a species, this is how we have built our knowledge base. Our ancestors Fucked Around with plants to Find Out which ones were edible and which ones were poisonous. They Fucked Around with animals to discover which ones they could hunt and which ones would hunt them. They Fucked Around with fire, with tools, with shelter, with agriculture and domestication. We earned every bit of knowledge as a species through someone, somewhere, Fucking Around and Finding Out.

It is how we have always crafted Maps. Someone heads out into the Territory, explores, discovers, survives (or not), and returns (or not) with information to record. The Map is almost always a record of Find-Out moments, either our own or our peers'. The fuckers who narrowly escaped danger and lived to tell the tale created some. Those who never actually faced danger wrote others; only witnessed it happen, recording it and warning the rest of us. Institutions that outsource the Finding Out entirely produce a terrifying number of Maps.

FAFO is literally cartography. Like any navigation system, it only works when the feedback loop is tight. When action and consequence are close together, the Map updates quickly. When abstraction separates action from consequence, the Map updates slowly, incorrectly, or not at all. The idea is to keep it simple and avoid complications. Every layer of abstraction inserts latency. Latency dissolves learning. When you are crafting your own Map in direct contact with the Territory, the delay between Fucking Around and Finding Out is minimal. Touch the stove, get burned.

Depending on the Map, lessons can become incredibly distorted. Your Map could tell you to wear an oven mitt before you touch the stove. You do so and, lo-and-behold you do not get burned. This could lead to you falsely believing the stove is not hot. When in fact it was the mitt that insulated you from consequences.

Insulation will not grant you immunity, no matter what a Map tells you. Remember that. We are going to see a lot of mitts.

When you are following someone else's Map, you are no longer touching the stove yourself.

You are trusting a description of heat. Each borrowed layer pushes the consequence further away. Each abstraction introduces a delay. Each delay weakens the data. At a certain point, you can Fuck Around indefinitely and never update your Map at all. This is the moment the Psychosis enters the system.

We understand why people act the way they do in the Cyber Age. The Empire hijacked their Attitude, making them believe the Territory stopped responding. It hasn't. Institutions have rerouted the response. Someone breaks into your house, and the Empire's Map says hide in the closet and dial 911. Outsource the consequence. Let the institution handle the Territory for you. Another Map says mag dump first and sort it out later. One of those Maps has zero latency between the Fuck Around and the Find Out. The other one has a seven-minute response time.

A major symptom of Cyberspace Psychosis is believing you can Fuck Around and avoid the consequences of Finding Out. While it may appear that way much of the time, especially if you are following your digital Map, it is not always the case. There are many examples of the Virtual Reality Blues when a keyboard warrior somewhere popped off their mouth and learned the hard way that this isn't Facebook and the Territory has no problem punching you in the mouth. Proximity to consequences increases Map accuracy. Accurate Maps provide accurate navigation and reveal the pitfalls on the path. Distance from consequence distorts a Map. A distorted perception of the Territory almost always ends badly. Tread carefully.

We have an ingrained urge to Fuck Around in our DNA. All of us have been doing it since we could crawl. It is one of the core pillars of human experience. There is an innocence to it. We all have the innate ability to Map our own journey of discovery. We learn and grow along the way, and our Maps become more intricate and detailed. Our understanding of the Territory strengthens, and our relationship with it deepens. We have the freedom to chart our own Maps and interpret the Territory however we want.

The Psychosis tries to tell us we *should* stop Fucking Around.

The Empire has distorted this mechanism and reframed it as punishment instead of feedback for calibration. Without people willing to Fuck Around, we would still be hiding in caves, afraid of fire, and ignorant of everything beyond the next hill. The Psychosis has us terrified of our own innate curiosity. The fear of Fucking Around is the fear of learning. The fear of growth. The fear of discovery. The Empire benefits from that fear, because a population afraid of the Territory never questions the Map.

Yet we will always remain little fuckers.

3,2,1 Contact

Scientific Fucking Around was all over children's TV in the '80s. One of the better programs was called 3,2,1 Contact. The theme song alone is amazing, one of the catchiest beats of my childhood. The complete song was about contact. That word, over and over. Contact is the secret. Contact is the answer. Contact is why everything happens. Even as a kid, something about that stuck.[i]

That threshold, the point of contact, is where the real action starts. That invisible line between Fucking Around and Finding Out. Where the Map touches the Territory. The Relative Truth meets the Absolute Truth. When everything happens.

How far do you push before it pushes back? That is the question at the heart of every experiment, every risk, every venture into uncharted Territory. You can put your hand near the stove and feel the warmth. You can get closer and feel the heat intensify. At some point, a point you cannot see but can definitely feel, you cross the threshold into burn Territory.

Sometimes the threshold is visible. You can see the cliff's edge clearly. You know exactly where the line is. In those cases, crossing it is a choice: reckless, deliberate, or desperate.

Often, though, the threshold is invisible. You do not know you have crossed it until the Territory responds. The boundary moved while you were not looking, or it was never where the Map claimed it was to begin with.

Your Map was wrong.

You were in Find-Out territory before you knew you had left the safe zone.

What is ironic about this process is that you can always look back and accurately pinpoint the exact threshold. The exact moment you crossed the line and found out. Sadly, we do not always have the same vision as we move forward, and many times we discover it the hard way.

The Territory is going to teach you.

This is not optional.

One way or another, it will get its point across, and if you have to Fuck Around time and time again before the lesson finally hits home, then that is what it will take. You can learn the easy way or the hard way. And sometimes the hard way is easier to digest than the easy way.

The easy way has wiggle room. It is softer. More abstraction means more is open to interpretation. When you learn easily, there is space for justification, for rationalization, for "well, maybe it was not that bad" or "maybe next time will be different." The easy lesson does not always stick because it does not cause pain. Easy lessons often mean that the distance between the Map and the Territory is substantial.

The hard way is always black and white. It leaves nothing to interpretation. You learn fast and you learn harshly, and that knowledge sticks. The hard way burns itself into your memory, your muscles, your nervous system. Many times the hard way comes with accompanying trauma. So much that reliving and replaying the lesson can generate a stress response. This is a natural response; your body does not want to experience a hard lesson again, so it will go to great lengths to make sure you keep your eyes open from here on out. There is a risk of pain in learning things the hard way.

As we are messing around on our way through the world, of course it will come with risk. Actually, as we move further from a map, the territory becomes more dangerous. The question is: Are you willing to risk harm or trauma to learn, or are you going to tread carefully to avoid making mistakes?

The Psychosis sometimes convinces you that mistakes are a sign of weakness. This is a Relative Truth. Mistakes can be detrimental; however, producing one does not show deficiency. We put erasers on pencils for a reason. Everyone is going to mess up at some point. Everyone is going to tread too far and not knowing where the threshold is, where that point of contact is, will eventually learn a lesson the hard way.

It is okay to make mistakes. Learn from it. It is not okay to make the same mistake twice.

As the saying goes: the first time you are a victim. The second time you are a volunteer.

Butterfly in the Sky

A well-known parable details the value of resistance.

A butterfly breaks out of its chrysalis through struggle.

It fights. It pushes. It strains against the walls of its cocoon. The process looks brutal; the struggle is real. The Relative Truth is that this little butterfly is suffering to break free. It appears as something that should be relieved. No tiny creature should have to fight that hard to break free of anything. A kind person watching might want to help. Their map will tell them they *should* help; it is the right thing to do. They might gently cut the chrysalis open, ease the butterfly's passage, sparing it the struggle, and setting it free.

The Absolute Truth is that struggle is the mechanism. The fight pumps fluid into the butterfly's wings. The resistance makes those wings strong enough to fly. If you help the butterfly escape too easily, you do irreparable harm. Emerging with weak, shriveled wings, the poor creature will be crippled. Wings that will never fly.[ii]

A butterfly without the fly is just butter.

Not every lesson is the universe being cruel. It is the universe building your wings. Resistance builds strength, and struggle is a process. The hard lesson is that it is the mechanism by which you become capable of things you could not do before. You discover where that brink is, and you keep discovering so much more above it.

One of the best things you can do sometimes is to let people Find Out on their own. Make their own way, Fuck Around with whatever draws them in, and update their Maps accordingly. You cannot experience someone else's Virtual Reality Blues for them. As much as it pains you to watch. Even if you know just how the drama ends, give them space to Fuck Around for themselves, because struggle is part of the process. The lesson does not stick if someone else learned it for you.

Sometimes you have to give people enough rope to hang themselves.

Because you know the only way to strong wings is struggling out of the chrysalis.

Trade Request

Finding Out is naturally transactional.

You trade your expectations for a lesson. You trade your interpretation of the Map for genuine knowledge about the Territory. They paid the price in disappointment, pain, and the death of an illusion. The purchase is real, something you now know that you did not know before.

The question is whether the trade was worth it.

Sometimes you overpay. The lesson was not worth the cost. The Find-Out exceeds any reasonable price for the knowledge gained. These are catastrophic mistakes. The ones that inflict permanent damage, that resist undoing, that teach you something you regret learning.

Sometimes you get a bargain. The lesson was cheap relative to its value. A close call, a near-miss, a warning shot that taught you everything you needed to know without extracting the full price. You do not have to fall all the way to the bottom of the cliff to know the rocks below will ruin your day.

If you slip and catch yourself at the last second, if you play the tape through and truly realize how close you came to disaster. If you are wise, you will learn from that moment and use more caution in the future. The near-miss can be as valuable as the full impact, if you are paying Attention.

However, if you are careless, if you dismiss the warning, if you continue acting like a reckless jackass, eventually the Territory will collect the full price. The near-miss becomes a direct hit. The bargain becomes a bankruptcy. The Virtual Reality Blues becomes your new state of mind. You will not see it coming either.

The dildo of consequences rarely arrives lubed.

FAFO Goes Both Ways

Not all Find Out moments are bad. In fact, many are beneficial.

That is the part people forget. FAFO has become synonymous with negative consequences. You mess around with something dangerous and suffer accordingly. But the mechanism works in both directions. You can push the threshold downward and discover your weaknesses. You can also push it upward and discover you are stronger and more capable than you ever thought possible.

Sometimes you Fuck Around and something exceptional happens. Something that never would have happened if you had not stepped out of your comfort zone to try it. You make a bet and you win. You take a risk and it pays off. You venture beyond the border of the Map. The Map of self-limitation, and suddenly you are doing things you never thought possible.

Nikola Tesla fiddled around with rotating magnetic fields and found out that alternating current could transmit electricity over vast distances, something the existing Map said was impossible. Edison's Map said direct current was the only way. The entire electrical establishment agreed with Edison. Tesla ventured into the Territory anyway. What he found out revolutionized power distribution across the planet and built the very foundation that Cyberspace runs on. Every screen you've seen, every addictive dopamine loop you've experienced, every scroll, notification, and element discussed in this book owes its existence to one man's experimentation with electricity. The Territory revealed something to him that no Map had previously shown.[iii]

You may enter uncharted Territory. Discovering additional aspects of what the Territory actually contains.

The Map of self-limitation is still only a Map. It remains a representation, a Relative Truth. Seek the Absolute Truth. The Territory might show you that you are weaker than you thought, or it might show you that you are stronger. The Territory may show that you're not ready, but you could be. The Territory could reveal that you still have a little way to go before you can push back effectively. You will not know unless you test it. You do not know until you Fuck Around.

That is why the fear of Fucking Around is so costly. Yes, you might fail. Yes, you might get hurt. But you also might discover capabilities you did not know you had. You might find out that the limits you believed in were just lines on a Map. The Territory extends far beyond them. You only have to find the point of contact.

Too Fast, Too Furious

Many myths both glorify and caution against Fucking Around too much. Sometimes in life it is possible to fuck something up that cannot easily be unfucked. Sometimes when we cross that invisible threshold between the FA and FO, we discover a second, equally invisible, threshold that is usually completely unexpected. That second threshold is the difference between Finding Out and *Fucking Up*. Once you cross it, the system does not rewind. We look at the mess we are in and realize with dread that we are not getting this toothpaste back into the tube. The moment of Finding Out becomes a spectacle.

Fuck-Ups are notoriously spectacular. Everyone experiences them once or twice in their lifetime. They are rare.

Prometheus stole fire from the gods. FAFO. He brought illumination to humanity and got his liver eaten by an eagle for eternity. Icarus flew too close to the sun. FAFO. He tested the limits of his wax wings, and they tested back.

General Custer rode into Little Bighorn with a Map that said he was the hero of the story. He split his forces, ignored his scouts, and charged into a village of thousands of Lakota, Northern Cheyenne, and Arapaho warriors. FAFO. Enemy warriors wiped out his entire command in less than an hour. The Territory did not just push back. It erased him.

We could fill an entire book with the many wonderful examples of people who bit off more than they could chew. The lesson of all of them is that the second threshold exists and we must always remain cautious of it. This second, more subtle threshold is the difference between a shit show and a shitstorm. One is entertaining. The other gets everyone dirty.

Are these stories warnings against Fucking Around? Or are they actually celebrations of it?

Humanity only has fire because Prometheus Fucked Around. The punishment was proper, exile, eternal torment, death by falling, but so was the gift. Fire. Knowledge. The experience of flight, however brief.

The willingness to Fuck Around expands what humanity can touch. It is what separates humans from the rest of life. Most animals do not test boundaries. They do not experiment. They do not reach for the apple or steal fire or strap on wings made of wax and feathers. They just execute their code until they die.

Humans reach. Humans test. Humans push. Even knowing there will be a cost. Even knowing the Territory might push back. The willingness to Fuck Around risks the

Find-Out for the sake of discovery, is part of what makes us human. We have been doing it since we started crawling.

Prometheus and Icarus are warnings and celebrations at once. They remind us that hubris is deadly, that fucking around has limits, that if you push too far into the Territory, the Territory will push back. Yet they also preserve the memory of those who pushed anyway. Legends are never about the people who stayed safe.

Fuck-Ups are fabulously legendary. Think back to a time in your life when you Fucked Up. They are always core memories. Major tragedies like car accidents, escalating a confrontation with someone you probably shouldn't have, gambling more than you intended, trying to carry something that was a little too bulky, and countless others. Fuck Ups always involve shitty consequences, yet humans will always push too far. We will take a calculated risk, knowing full well we suck at math.

Pain is temporary, glory is forever, and chicks dig scars.

Ignorance vs. Arrogance

When the Empire is Fucking Around, they are not concerned with the consequences of Finding Out. As we know, the Empire will happily Find Out at your expense. Sometimes this is deliberate, and other times it is not. Most always it results from hubris on one scale or another, and with scale, the consequences are devastating and far-reaching.

In 1812, Napoleon marched into Russia with the *Grande Armée,* roughly 600,000 troops, the largest invasion force Europe had ever seen. Fewer than 120,000 made it back.[iv] The rest either died, were taken prisoner, or deserted.

He underestimated the vast distances, the scorched-earth tactics, and the brutal winter. He ignored the warning signs. By the time his army reached Moscow in September, the Russians had already burned most of it and vanished, leaving him with a hollow victory. He had no food, shelter, or surrender to accept. Then the retreat began, and winter came for them. Death followed.

Napoleon Fucked Around. Napoleon Found Out. Napoleon Fucked Up.

This was ignorance. No one had attempted to conquer Russia on that scale before. Napoleon had no Map of this Territory. He was the cartographer, drawing the Map with the blood of his army. The lesson did not exist until he created it.

Documentation of that lesson followed. Studied deeply and taught in every military academy in Europe. The territory of Russia, its distances, its winters, its capacity to absorb invaders and starve them out. They Mapped every gritty detail with excruciating care. They widely distributed the Map. Anyone who wanted to know could know.

A century and a half later, Hitler launched Operation Barbarossa.

June 1941. Over three million troops across an 1,800-mile front. They had the tech; they had the speed; they had just steamrolled Poland and Hungary and were feeling frisky. They were so sure the *blitzkrieg* would work that they had barely issued any winter gear. They wouldn't need to; the war would be over by the end of summer. They were quick and enthusiastic. Ultimately, though, the tempo was not sustainable, and while overestimating their own prowess, they underestimated the Russian resistance.[v]

Supply lines stretched impossibly thin. The same distances. The same scorched-earth response. The same General Winter waiting in the wings.

Hitler had Napoleon's consequences available. He had the Map. He had the lesson, written in blood, preserved in archives, taught in the very schools his officers attended. Yet he rejected it. He was certain his Map was different. His army was different. His will was different.

Ignorance could not be an excuse since the knowledge was readily available. No, the *Führer* was sure his Map could conquer the Territory, and arrogantly pushed forward. The invasion that was supposed to last weeks dragged into years, costing Germany millions of lives and ultimately the war. The Territory responded exactly as it had before. It did not care that Hitler's Map was different. The Territory does not give a damn about Nazi Maps.

Napoleon was a victim. Hitler was a volunteer.

The Territory treated them equally.

Napoleon was a victim of his own ignorance. He set the example. Hitler volunteered for a lesson that already existed. This is the difference between experimenting in uncharted Territory and marching arrogantly into Territory previously Mapped by bloodshed.

Ignorance creates Maps. Arrogance ignores them.

Both were total Fuck-Ups. One was avoidable.

Scalability

The FAFO model applies at every scale.

A child holds a feather and jumps off the couch, trying to fly. A SpaceX rocket launches into orbit. Both are Fucking Around with gravity, just at different scales. The yield of knowledge applies universally. Gravity does not care whether you are a toddler or an aerospace engineer. Ask Icarus. Gravity responds the same way to the same inputs. The only difference is the stakes.

You would not hand a six-year-old a full-size mountain bike. You get them a little Huffy™ with training wheels first. They learn to pedal. Then you remove the training wheels, and they learn their own sense of balance. Then you scale upward. There is a progression in everything. We chart Maps as we move along, building systems and processes, discovering what works at each level before moving to the next.

How long did humanity mess around with smaller explosives before attempting to split the atom? There was a progression. Black powder to dynamite to TNT to nuclear fission. Each step taught us something about the next. Each Find Out informed the next Fuck Around.

When you Fuck Around personally, you Find Out personally. When the Empire Fucks Around, everyone Finds Out whether or not they wanted to. The people Fucking Around are not always the ones who pay the price. The generals decide. The soldiers Find Out. The executives take the risks. The employees Find Out. The Empire bets your life on its Map, and when the Map is wrong, you are the one who discovers the Territory. This is one of the Empire's oldest tricks. Privatize the gains, socialize the losses. Take credit for success, spread the blame for failure. Fuck Around with other people's lives, let them do the Finding Out.

The Empire runs on arrogance. We can fix ignorance; that is the whole point of Fucking Around. Arrogance is a refusal to learn. The Empire has the information available and rejects it. It dictates to citizens rather than listening. It claims authority over the Territory while ignoring what the Territory actually says. It makes an example of anyone who points this out. We see this play out time and time again when the Empire punishes a whistleblower and expresses more outrage over the leak itself than over what was actually dripping all over the floor.

The closest thing to Absolute Truth you will often hear is from comedians. There is historical precedent to this. The court jester was often the only one who could speak truth to power. The fool could say what the advisor could not. The Empire permits truth, provided humor dresses it, satire treats it, and people do not take it seriously. The Empire takes itself very seriously. The business of Map-making and navigation is serious business indeed and cannot be questioned.

The truth-tellers are clowns while the arrogant wear crowns.

Safety First

The Empire does not want anyone Fucking Around.

They will claim it is for your safety. That is one of their classic tactics. Safety implies danger and danger implies fear and the fearful are always willing to trade away their Agency. The Empire does not want you fucking around because certain Find-Outs would expose the Map as fraudulent. They must prevent certain discoveries from happening. Certain boundaries must remain untested.[2]

To this end, the Empire benefits from complacency. From our fear of change. From the atrophy of the human spirit that comes from no longer hunting, farming, or even fighting for basic survival. This is another massive symptom of Cyberspace Psychosis. Our collective complacency. It makes us passive. It makes us consumers of other people's Find-Outs rather than generators of our own. We watch videos of people doing things instead of doing things ourselves. We read about risks instead of taking them. We study Maps instead of walking the Territory.

The Empire gate keeps the avenues of Fucking Around. Of course, the Empire permits some experiments but enforces strict guardrails. There are plenty of approved risks, curated adventures, controlled explorations that do not threaten the established Map. Other experiments are prohibited by the Empire and even criminalized. Punished not because they are dangerous to you, but because they might reveal something the Empire cannot afford for you to know.[3]

---

2. Antarctica anyone?

3. Granted, some of the guard rails are necessary. You wouldn't want your neighbor experimenting with chlorine gas in his garage.

No matter how many guardrails they install, the urge to explore remains. Watch the children, they are still Fucking Around, still building their Maps, still testing every boundary they can find. The Empire has not programmed it out of them yet.

The question is whether you remember how.

Adult Swim

The Territory is the only teacher that matters.

Let's say you want to learn how to swim. You can read every book about swimming. You can watch every video, study every technique, and memorize every stroke. You can imagine yourself effortlessly cutting through the waves. You can listen to other people's swimming stories. You have watched every Michael Phelps highlight video on YouTube. You have the best and brightest intentions about swimming successfully. Yet you have never been wet. No matter how much knowledge you have gained, you haven't even been in the shallow end of the pool. There is a massive difference between theory and execution. You will not actually learn how to swim until you are in the water.

Maps can inform. Maps can guide. Maps can warn. Maps show a route, a way to gain knowledge. They can only tell you what someone else has Found Out. The lesson does not become yours until you walk the Territory yourself. A wise traveler will study the Map carefully before he or she sets out. They will look at many Maps and explore multiple points of view. A wise traveler has been scorched by the Territory and prefers to learn from other people's experiences before braving danger again. Yet must face that danger themselves for the lesson to really land.

This is why experience matters more than credentials. Why the person who has done the thing is more trustworthy than the person who has studied the thing. Why failure teaches faster than success does. The territory does not care about your Map. It does not care about your intentions. It does not care what you thought would happen. It only responds to your Action.

So you Fuck Around. You Find Out. You avoid the Fuck Up and maybe you learn something useful along the way. That is the only way we learn anything.

Content with the Content

Boredom is the root of all evil. It is very curious that boredom, which itself has such a calm and sedate nature, can have such a capacity to initiate motion. The effect that boredom exercises is altogether magical. — Søren Kierkegaard

Our ancestors were lion food.

That was the reality of life in the Territory. For most of human history, we occupied a precarious middle position on the food chain. Sure, we have always been omnivores and would eat whatever we could fit into our mouths, be it animal, vegetable, or mineral.[1] Naturally, we were intelligent enough to know we were being hunted. Our relationship with the food chain cut both ways, considering we fit into plenty of mouths ourselves. Even if we had to be rendered into bite-sized chunks first. I am sure watching your neighbor getting mauled by a crocodile would send a pretty convincing message. We were not quite powerful enough to level or dominate the playing field just yet. The saber-toothed cat did not care about our capacity for abstract thought. The cave bear was unimpressed by our opposable thumbs.[i]

We survived because, while the Territory was dangerous, we could Map it. We survived as a species because we have grit; we had tenacity. There was a time when our ancestors would chase animals until exhaustion, not us, them. Imagine tens of thousands of years ago, you are out with the rest of the tribe and you are just following an elk

---

1. So what if our favorite rock to eat is salt?

who is running from you, and you just keep following. The poor animal, exhausted and terrified, kept trying to flee, and humans just kept coming. The beast, exhausted, could eventually no longer flee, eventually collapsed and expired under the spears of its pursuers. Sometimes they would chase prey off a cliff, then climb down to collect the meaty bits. The point is, we were opportunists when it came to filling our bellies. Eventually, we learned to cooperate, to plan; we realized we could hunt AND gather, hunters returning with gravity-tenderized cliff-side mammoth steaks and the gatherers providing berries for garnish. Teamwork made that dream work. Millennia of Fucking Around in the Territory and updating our Map until it highlighted the route to where we collectively stand today.[ii]

Indeed, our ancestors were lion food.

Today we shop at Food Lion.

The distance between these two realities is the most dramatic transformation in the history of any species on this planet.[2] We discovered fire. We invented the wheel. We domesticated animals and learned to grow plants. We built cities and roads, and aqueducts. We harnessed horses, then steam, then electricity, then the atom, then the semiconductor. Each step took us further from the base conditions of survival, further from the Territory our bodies developed to navigate. Each leap represented another layer of Maps, insulating us from the muck.

Once upon a time, if you were hungry, you had to hunt something or gather something to fill your belly. It took effort; it took knowledge of the Territory. Today Trader Joe does it for you. He sources the food, maintains the supply chain, keeps the lights on and the refrigeration running. All you have to do is show up with your debit card and your reusable bags. The Map of ten thousand years of agricultural and industrial development compressed into a fifteen-minute shopping trip where your biggest decision is whether to buy the maple pecan or the pumpkin spice granola.

Somewhere along the way, between chasing mammoths off cliffs and ordering Door-Dash, we lost something vital. We started believing that comfort was our default state. That convenience was our right. That any friction in our lives represented a failure of the system rather than a feature of existence. Somewhere along the way the Psychosis twisted our perception of the Territory to the point where we lost touch with ourselves. We are so far removed that we even get upset if that fifteen-minute shopping trip gets

---

2. That we know of.

interrupted, forcing us to stretch it out to twenty minutes because it is crowded and we have to wait an extra five minutes to check out.

Our Agency has been hijacked so severely that we lament the basics of survival. We call it adulting, to make light of it, like despite the world of comfort we still resent the minor amount of effort we have to contribute to our wellbeing. "Adulting" became a meme. A way of describing basic survival tasks as if they were an imposition, a burden, an unfair expectation placed upon us by an uncaring universe. We are a people who live in the easiest era in human history. We have access to fresh, clean water at basically any time; with the simple turn of a tap. Our medicines and medical technology would seem miraculous to anyone born before the 19th century. Imagine demonstrating an MRI in Jamestown. We have food security that monarchs could never guarantee for their people. Hardly anyone is worried about a harvest any more; we have become completely insulated from it. Our communication technology has collapsed distance to the point of inconvenience. We complain about having to make a phone call to schedule an appointment if we cannot do it online.

I understand this comes across as overly generalized. That many in this world do struggle with clean water and food scarcity. Many of them are still struggling for day to day survival. I also understand that the tendency to take these conveniences and technological wonders for granted seems to be much more rampant in the West than anywhere else. However, people who still struggle daily for water and food do not suffer from Cyberspace Psychosis like the rest of us.

Tell-A-Vision

Our brains cannot tell the difference between television and reality. Viewing a screen induces alpha wave activity, the trance-like state where critical thinking fades and suggestibility takes over. The images get processed and stored in memory the same way lived experiences do. The emotional responses are real. The stress hormones are real. The dopamine is real. Only the events are fake.

Sounds crazy, right? I mean, it is just TV. Of course, the events are fake. We all know that. Or do we? Sure, we have all watched some pretty fantastical things on TV. Events that we do experience, even virtually, have a measurable emotional response. We even use it in our description of media. They describe a blockbuster movie release as "a roller coaster ride," implying metaphorical ups and downs, and all around thrilling. The human brain cannot fully differentiate between what it sees on a screen and actual lived experience.

The brain does not care that the stimulus came from a box of light rather than the external world.[iii]

Even reminiscing about something we witnessed via TV, we will describe it like an actual memory. "I remember watching Kristie Yamaguchi win gold at Lillehammer". It doesn't matter that we attended virtually. Someone who was actually at the event would reminisce the exact same way starting with, "I remember..." The mechanism of memory recall happening in the electrochemical mush of our brains is the same in both instances. The same areas of the brain are lighting up. The brain is the Territory; it doesn't care about the Map, either the Map from the TV or the Map of the arena. The recall remains consistent.

Television is powerful, very powerful. If you want to see it in action try gathering a group of people in a room, wait for them to talk with each other, and give it some time for the conversations to develop naturally. After maybe 10 or 15 minutes, turn on a television. Within two minutes, and often less, you will notice all conversation ceases. Every face will orient toward the screen. Granted, some conversations may begin again shortly, especially if the programming is not interesting. More likely, you will notice the conversation will morph to include whatever is being shown. Watch for the moment when everyone is silent, it will be a brief window, 20 seconds or so, when everyone will just stare at the screen. Make sure you are observing them instead of the screen itself, lest you fall prey to the trance yourself. You will be shocked by how strong the pull really is. The flicker, the movement, the sound, you are witnessing the total hijack of Attention in real time. With a force, that social interaction just cannot compete with.[iv]

We knew this was a problem. For decades, we have talked about television as "the idiot box," worried about children rotting their brains, and created rules about screen time. The television was at least bounded; it lived in one room, it required you to be physically present, it went off when you left. Further more the television in a common area of the home meant that it was a group experience watching it. The TV has been the single stabilizing factor in American homes for five generations. Therefore, it's understandable that everyone stops to see what's playing when a TV is switched on. That is a deeply-seated behavioral cue, multi-generational even.

Then we put television in everyone's pocket.

Since 1999, screens have gotten lighter, thinner, and cheaper.[3] The smartphone is far more than a mere communication device. It is a portable television with infinite channels, each one optimized by algorithms to be exactly interesting enough to keep you watching. It is a cerebral security blanket accessible at any moment. And we cannot look away.

I believe we had a television addiction before Cyberspace arrived. We could argue that the Cyberspace Psychosis is just late-stage TV addiction. It is more than just the TV though. It's about the content. So The Cyberspace Psychosis may just be a mutation of the Television Addiction many of us have and not even aware of.

Where is the line between use and abuse?

Applied to Cyberspace: Use is looking up a YouTube video to learn how to change your car battery. Abuse is doomscrolling YouTube Shorts, falling into rabbit holes, chasing dopamine hits, and never getting around to changing the battery.

Same platform. The difference is self-awareness and executive functions. The difference is whether you are using the tool or the tool is using you.[v]

There has to be a degree of self awareness injected into the equation. I know this personally because of my similar struggles.[4] I have always been someone who pushes boundaries. I know the stove will burn my hand if I touch it, but I want to see just how close I can get before it actually burns. I know a cactus is sharp, but there is a massive part of my brain that wants to know just *how* sharp. This is exploratory thinking in Action.

The goalpost metaphor gives clarity. I will move the goalposts in my own life. I will change my goals to match my behavior instead of changing my behavior to meet my goals. I will put myself through some very rigorous mental gymnastics to justify this as well. Since I have a constant craving for gratification, preferably the instant variety. I cannot say "I will play Xbox after I spend two hours cleaning my house" when there is another part of my brain saying "orrrr... I can play Xbox now and clean later." Then a third part chimes in and says "fuck it, I can do what I want."

The fuck-its usually win.

---

3. Anyone who has tried to move a TV prior to 1999 can attest that it fell under the "heavy lifting" category.

4. Almost always self inflicted.

People are going to want to exercise their Agency. They will want to do what they want, even if it is dangerous. Cyberspace is not inherently dangerously addictive. Certainly not in the same category as heroin or crack. It isn't like a loaded gun; one shot and you're done for. Cyberspace is a slow burn. There is no rock bottom in the conventional sense. There is no overdose. Instead, the experience is just gradual erosion of Attention, connection, presence, executive function. You can doom scroll yourself into a shell of a person and never have a single acute crisis. Just a long, slow fadeaway.[vi]

Never Content

When I was in the midst of active substance use disorder, I could never be content.

That is the thing about addiction that people who have not experienced it often miss. It is not even about the high. Sure, in that first second after you take that hit and actually feel the grip loosen, it is nice. You get deep enough into addiction and it is not even about getting high anymore. It's about feeling normal. You are so far removed from your baseline that you have to take your drug of choice, whether it's weed or caffeine or dope or anything else, just to feel normal. It's a zero sum game because of diminishing returns. Since addiction is progressive, you will always need take more to get less.[vii]

Crossing the line between use and abuse puts you way past highs and lows. What was once enjoyable is now about the constant, grinding anxiety of maintaining the feeling of normalcy. *How long will this bag last me? How much money do I have to get more? What will happen when this runs out? Where can I get the next one?*

I was never content to just chill in the moment with what I had. Addiction had me always thinking ahead, managing supply, and calculating. Addiction is a full-time job. It requires tremendous effort, tremendous focus, and tremendous craftiness. All directed at a single goal that destroys everything else.

I would do whatever I had to do to get high and stay high. The desperation was Absolute.

My personal adventures with addiction were always about governance. The majority of my life I suffered with untreated neurodivergence. Survival in a world that is just not designed for a nervous system like mine was grating. I had to cope however I could, and drug use was the easiest path available. It was a method of cognitive regulation. Still, my Agency was entirely dedicated to feeding a bottomless pit. This is not a justification, merely a context. There is a massive difference in substance use disorders if the motivation is regulation instead of escapism. Cyberspace Psychosis is definitely the escapism side of addiction.

We always joke about people in their phones and not in the present moment. It is not surprising. Escaping from the present moment has been a thing long before Cyberspace was an option. We had the option of escaping into a TV show or a movie. Before that, it was books. Before that, it was campfire tales; before that, we were hiding in caves hoping the lions didn't sniff us out. Fiction addiction is not exactly a new development for the human race, and our appetite for drama has been present almost as soon as we figured out how to talk with each other.

All of these had prerequisites. You had to be social and in a group to share stories. You had to know how to read if you wanted to enjoy a book.[5] Or you had to have a TV or go to someone's house who had one, or go to the theater or the cinema. It required Action and some effort to get there.

Now our primary mode of escapism is rarely more than an arm's length away. A crackhead is never far from his pipe, and Cyber addicts are never far from their phones.

How did our relationship with the Territory get so insufferable that we will dive into a digital virtual reality Map instead of genuine interaction? Is it the TV addiction? Does the relaxation mechanic mean it is easier for our minds to be passive? If that were the case, then video games would not be as popular as they are today.

Once we stopped having to contend with the Territory from the point of survival, our Attitude towards it gradually changed, along with our avenues of that escapism. Our ancestors would huddle around the fire at night because that fire warded away predators and kept us warm. They would trade tales. Then we built houses with hearths and suddenly didn't need that fire at night. Sure the warmth was nice but the walls kept the wolves at bay, and we didn't huddle as much. The escapism became books, and the progression continued. The Territory no longer commanded our Attention, and other pursuits were far more appealing.

When our world ceased being an adversary and became an inconvenience is where we crossed the line. The same world that used to terrorize our ancestors became boring. We wanted to be anywhere else but the here and now, and the mechanism to get away is right in our pocket.

---

5. Or have a friend who could read it to you.

Even when we are shopping, walk into any grocery store and mark how many people are wearing earbuds or headphones. Even as they are gathering sustenance, they have one foot in Cyberspace. Whether it is a podcast or streaming music or whatever direct audio line to the digital world feeds the need.

The Territory just does not provide enough stimulation to satisfy a brain starving for dopamine. As the Psychosis progresses, even content is no longer enough. Similar to an addict's focus on their next hit, many of us focus on the next swipe. We are absolute gluttons for stimulation.

Food for Thought

Our world has progressed to a point where we cannot establish the same relationship with Cyberspace. Where we can divorce it from a want to a need. We need Cyberspace to function, even to survive.

How do we interact with it without crossing that line where we are indulging compulsively?

How do you indulge without the compulsion? How do you engage with something you need to survive without triggering the addiction? How do we change our relationship with Cyberspace without compromising our Agency?

Food addiction is the closest analog we have to the addictive manifestation of Cyberspace Psychosis. Food addiction is so much more dangerous than gambling, drinking, or drug use. All of those are vices, and vices carry moral weight before the addiction even begins. Society already had a framework for why those things were bad. The addiction just confirms the judgment that was already there.

Food is not a vice. Nobody judges you for eating. The judgment only arrives when the consumption becomes compulsive. When the behavior crosses from dependence into something uglier. Same with Cyberspace. Nobody judges you for being online. The judgment, if it comes at all, only lands when the behavior becomes compulsive and consequential. Doomscrolling the day away. Ignoring your company because your phone is out at the dinner table. The notifications beeping at 3am interrupting sleep. Notice most of the consequences will directly relate to the person judging you. They wanted your Attention at dinner and instead you are watching Reels.

Judgment is fickle. True, nobody judges you for eating. They will absolutely judge you for being fat. People normalize and engineer behavior, and the consequence of overconsumption causes shame. Not on the system that designed the overconsumption. On you. McDonald's does not get judged for the obesity epidemic. The fat person gets judged for lacking discipline. Instagram does not get judged for the mental health crisis. The doomscroller gets judged for being weak. The Empire sells you the bag of chips, engineers them so once you pop you cannot stop, and then sells you the diet program when your pants do not fit. Same mechanism as Cyberspace. Hook the Attention, monetize the compulsion, sell you the digital detox retreat when you burn out. The shame lands on the individual. The profit lands on the Empire.

Overconsumption of anything is profitable for the suppliers. The engineering behind the overconsumption. The fact that the off-switch was deliberately made harder to find. If you turn it off, you are not spending anymore, whether it is spending money or spending time, and the Empire does not care for non-spenders.

We depend on food. We depend on Cyberspace. Dependence is not the same as addiction. The difference is compulsion. We can depend on groceries, but we are not necessarily compulsive overeaters. We can be dependent on Cyberspace but are not necessarily all doomscrolling. The line between dependence and compulsion is where the Psychosis lives.

That line is different for everyone.

We all consume content the same way we consume food. We eat what tastes good. We watch what feels good. Companies engineer junk food to taste good and keep you eating. Creators engineer junk content to feel good and keep you scrolling. Nobody sits down planning to eat the entire bag. Nobody opens TikTok planning to lose two hours. The product is designed to override the off switch. The algorithm knows your appetite better than you do. It has been harvesting your preferences since your very first swipe.

Which means there is no universal prescription here. Everyone's relationship with Cyberspace is as personal as their relationship with food. Some people can have one drink and walk away. Some people cannot. Some people can spend twenty minutes on Instagram and close the app. Some people open it at breakfast and look up at dinner. The line is yours to find. The Map is going to look different for everyone because the algorithm already made sure of that. The For You page is not a For Me page. Your compulsion is not my compulsion.

We do not have a base technology equivalent to digital sobriety. There is no world that exists where complete abstinence from technology can be successful. Technology is a dependency. We need it to function in modern society. We need email to work, GPS to navigate, search engines to answer basic questions. Besides Lebanon Levi and the boys, we cannot opt out completely. Unless we opt out of participation in contemporary civilization entirely.[6]

We clearly depend on tech, but does that dependence mean we are addicted? Is there a path forward where we have a healthy relationship with Cyberspace? Where we can have the same relationship with the internet as we do with food. Clearly, we cannot abstain from either and survive, so how do we reconcile it?

Overeaters Anonymous defines abstinence as refraining from compulsive eating while working toward a healthy relationship with food. That is the model. Instead of abstinence, the idea is cultivating a conscious, ongoing negotiation with something you cannot live without. That is what a healthy relationship with Cyberspace could look like. Knowing when you are eating because you are hungry and when you are eating because you cannot stop.

The question is not whether you use Cyberspace.

The question is whether you are consuming it or it is consuming you.

Once upon a time, Attention was the price of survival.

That was the deal. The Territory demanded it. Miss a rustle in the brush, miss a track in the mud, miss the shift in the weather and you might not eat. Or worse, you might get eaten. Our ancestors couldn't afford to let their Attention wander because wandering Attention meant death. The Territory kept us honest. The Territory kept us present. The Territory kept us *here*.

Then we solved survival. We Mapped the dangers, built the walls, domesticated the food, and insulated ourselves so completely that the Territory stopped demanding anything from us. For the first time in two billion years, human Attention had nowhere it *needed* to be.

---

6. Going "off grid" does have its appeal.

So it wandered. We were Relatively safe. The map said so. The Absolute Truth is we never stopped being hunted. We just changed what hunts us and how. Now instead of our bodies it is our Attention that is prey.

Cyberspace is the snare.

The same Attention that once tracked elk across frozen tundra now tracks notifications across a glass screen. The same focus that kept us alive now keeps us scrolling. We traded the hunt for the feed. We won the war against the Territory and lost ourselves in the victory.

Our ancestors were lion food. They had to be present or die. We shop at Food Lion. We can be anywhere but here. Increasingly, we are.

Movement

4th Estate

If you don't read the newspaper, you're uninformed. If you do read it, you're misinformed. — Mark Twain

I was ten years old when the concept of FOMO[1] really hit home for me. Just a couple of days before my 11th birthday, Desert Shield had just become Desert Storm, and I was glued to CNN, watching the night-vision footage as Iraqi anti-aircraft batteries fired from the airport. Watching the coverage of the US Air Force and Navy sending thousands of jets into Iraqi airspace and devastating their defenses. That first night of coverage was absolutely amazing to a young American boy. In many ways, it was the first televised war. That first night, though, made an impact. The night vision cameras showed the tracer fire across the Iraqi sky. The flashes of explosions. The spectacle was an absolute magnet for the Attention. I did not want to miss a second of it.

CNN was the only network broadcasting that night. In fact, they were the only network that could broadcast. They had arranged a specific four-wire phone line setup independent of the traditional grid, allowing Bernard Shaw and his crew to stay on air from their hotel in Baghdad. The other networks' feeds were cut almost immediately after the bombings began. That night they were America's peep hole into the start of the war.[i]

I was right there for it, and it was amazing. The FOMO kicked in because I was in 5th grade at the time and I had school the next day. So right around my bedtime is when it kicked off, and although my father allowed me to stay up a little longer, I wanted to see

---

1. Fear Of Missing Out

it all. I wanted to see it all happen in real time. He let me stay up. The next morning, I ran downstairs and asked if we had dropped any nukes overnight. We had not, and I still had to go to school. Bummer.

To give some perspective on why this was so fascinating, keep in mind that I had grown up in the 80's, what some could claim was the apex of the Cold War. The Red Menace™ was always a constant threat. Later, when the Berlin Wall came down and the Soviet Union dissolved, I had noted it, but chalked it up to boring politics. It didn't catch my interest. Night vision tracer fire certainly did. Keep in mind that I had about as American a childhood as you could get. The 80s were the Golden Age for it. GI Joe, Rambo, and Chuck Norris in Missing in Action were staples. We had The A Team, Airwolf, and the Vietnam Travel Vlog Tour of Duty too. I had a glorified idea of what war was, the same as every other American child raised on Commando and Cold War victory laps. Along with the glorification came a sense of insulation. It was all virtual: the toys, the violence on a screen, all of it left me and my peers outrageously desensitized to destruction.[2]

When the Gulf War finally touched off, it was abstract through the TV, yet it was no less enthralling. I had, of course, noted Desert Shield; that was what was dominating the news through the end of summer and fall of 1990. I am sure there were other noteworthy events; but how many of them came with trading cards?

Topps released actual fucking Desert Shield trading cards. Let that land for a second. What kind of nation turns war into a collectible? What kind of culture celebrates carnage with chewing gum? I was too young to question it. I was exactly the target demographic. I was hooked. I wanted the full set. Every dollar I touched went into those packs. At the time, it felt outstanding. I had Dick Cheney's rookie card, back when he was Secretary of Defense. I chased General Norman Schwarzkopf as if he were a Hall of Famer. When I finally pulled Stormin' Norman, it came with an A-10 Thunderbolt II and a coalition sticker. That part mattered. This wasn't just America. Desert Storm was a NATO exercise, and the packs made sure you knew it. Flags. Allies. Brand unity. Teamwork post Warsaw Pact.[ii]

Honestly, Saddam should have seen it coming. The Soviet Union had just dissolved. The USA became the world's only remaining superpower, and it was eager to flex on someone.

Saddam Fucked Around and now was Finding Out with 24/7 coverage.

---

2. We were the same kids who routinely played tackle football in the street. On rollerblades.

It was an exercise in infotainment. I was standing in the middle of it, loving every second. I had to be there. That was the feeling. FOMO before we even had a name for it. The need for inclusion and the fear of exclusion existed long before people conceived of Cyberspace. I was an eleven-year-old afraid of being stuck on the map while everyone else played in the Territory.[iii]

Except I wasn't in the Territory. None of us were. The Territory was a desert seven thousand miles away where real people were really dying. I was in my living room, watching green streaks on a black screen, collecting trading cards of the men who ordered the bombs dropped. I was Relatively present for everything while being Absolutely present for nothing. I was so desensitized to the reality of what happened that I cheered on the "Highway of Death." I would play with my toy jets, I had many, and line up my Matchbox cars while doing strafing runs against them with my toy Thunderbolt. Making machine gun sounds as I yeeted the cars across the room.

The Absolute Truth is most of those people on the Highway of Death had very little say in what was transpiring and were really trying to get out of Dodge. They were actively retreating. The Empire, however, had other plans. So while one faction of the Empire was ordering the massive retreat, another wanted to stage a demonstration of American Air Superiority™. Guess which side won?

Despite this, there was another part of me that was watching something else.

I would get home from school and wanted to know what happened. I would rush to the TV and turn on CNN for war updates, looking for the press conference. There would be a Pentagon one where an official would stand in front of a forest of microphones and make their comments, or there would be an in-theater one where Stormin Norman would come out and brief the press. He would tell them what was happening, what we were doing, how the war was going. Usual updates.

Then they would cut back to the newsroom. And the reporters at the desks would repeat exactly what the General had just said.

At eleven years old, I was already processing information quickly. I remember thinking: Shut up. We already know that. The General just said exactly that. I wanted to see more footage. I wanted carnage. I didn't need talking heads parroting what the official source had just told us.

But that's what they did. That's all they did. Even Wolf Blitzer got boring.

The Fourth Estate. The free press. The watchdog of democracy.

Parrots.

They were selling me a Map. I just didn't have the language for it yet. However, I didn't need language to recognize bullshit when I caught a whiff.

Yet I was buying it. Using my birthday money on packs of trading cards. The Map may have been boring, but I was terrified of missing out on the Territory. FOMO hijacked my triple A's before I even knew what that meant. The exclusion hurt too much to risk. So I stayed glued. I kept watching. I felt enthralled.

"You had to be there." That's the ultimate Map/Territory statement. This admission means that you cannot transmit the experience, summarize it, or capture it in a recap, press briefing, or night-vision footage. The Territory was the point. I was eleven years old, watching a war through glass, forever segregated from the reality of what was actually happening. CNN beamed that map right into my living room and made me feel like I was close. The trading cards made me feel like a participant. The press conferences made me feel informed.

FOMO is premeditated Virtual Reality Blues. It is the grief of anticipated exclusion. You haven't missed the thing yet, but you can feel it slipping away, so you scroll faster, refresh harder, stay plugged in longer. In 1991, I didn't scroll; I just didn't change the channel. I didn't refresh, just waited for the next briefing. Not wanting to miss a thing.

Misinformed Latency

The biggest threat to Legacy Media is themselves. They can point fingers at Citizen Journalists and scream "non-sanctioned" and "prone to misinformation," and sure, sometimes that's true. But the actual issue is structural: Legacy outlets are slow, out of date, and they get in their own way more often than not. Independent sources and raw video posters are nimble. They can drop a story first, unfiltered, in seconds. By the time CNN or The New York Times weighs in, the interpretation has already been crowd-sourced. Ten million people have watched the raw footage and drawn their own conclusions before the official narrative even gets drafted.

Legacy Media can no longer dictate the tempo of a story. They can no longer gatekeep what gets disseminated and how. They're suffering from a latency crisis because their processes are just too damn slow. They defend it as rigor. They take time to approach a story "right." They have an ethical code; they vet sources thoroughly; they check and double-check facts; they have layers of editors and legal reviews to ensure accuracy. Rigor takes time, and time is the one resource Cyberspace does not grant.

In this age, speed is everything. Unless it's a massive tragedy affecting millions, most stories don't have staying power. Attention spans are shredded; unless the content grips someone personally, most everyone simply doesn't care. They're chasing the next dopamine hit. No matter how carefully researched and crafted a report is, it's going to be ignored if it arrives too late.[iv]

Anyone can upload a video to TikTok. No voiceover. No narrator telling you how to interpret it. Just raw footage. People watch, react, and interpret however they want. Speed. Sure, actual misinformation is a legitimate concern, and why wouldn't it be? However, I would say that misinformation is, in fact, a second-tier consequence of latency. Legacy Media outlets cannot get ahead of the fake story before it gets out and distributes. They are in a constant state of catching up.

"Misinformation" means the gatekeepers are being excluded. So they panic. They say, "No, don't look at that. That doesn't mean what you think it does. Here's what it really means." Both sides are selling maps. The Citizen journalist is selling one the Legacy outlet will call "out of context." The Legacy outlet is selling one the viewer no longer has the Attention span to wait for. In fact, the Legacy journalist may be completely right and the Citizen journalist totally wrong. No one cares. The viewer has already moved on. The Attention span to sit around and wait for an explanation just does not exist anymore.

I've met many reporters. They're exceptional people with their hearts in the right place. Highly intelligent and well-spoken, they are some of the most well-informed people on the planet. Most have an earnest desire to share truth with the People. Despite the earnestness and desire, they're completely subject to the Empire's filters. All of them have to follow procedure. Published stories are subject to the filter of Relative Truth. Who knows how many stories, truly great examples of investigative reporting, the Empire quashed at the editorial or executive level because of the implications? Because the Absolute Truth would ruin reputations? Somewhere through that obstacle course of liability, the facts revealed would have caused harm to a gatekeeper.

The credential bottleneck that Legacy Media relies on, all the editors, producers, legal compliance, and more. All of it that was supposed to be quality control. Pre-internet, if the New York Times printed something false, there were consequences. Serious consequences like retractions, lawsuits, and reputation damage. The slowness was just a bureaucracy that had to ensure accuracy. Accurate reporting is a hallmark of trust.

Trust has all but collapsed in recent years. Falling to record lows across nearly every major poll. In 2025, only about 31% of Americans said they had a "great deal" or "fair amount" of trust in mass media to report the news fully, accurately, and fairly. This is the lowest level Gallup has recorded in over fifty years of tracking. Gen Z and younger Millennials are even more skeptical, with trust often dipping below 20%. Only one in five young adults believes what they see on CNN or reading in the NYT. Many won't even bother to read the Times at all. When people see raw video first and Legacy outlets arriving hours or days later with a polished, pre-digested version, the discrepancy is glaring. The erosion isn't even about occasional errors; it's about who gets to frame reality first.[v]

Bandwidth Blues

Examine the Territory of audience.

There's an inverse relationship between the size of an audience and its capacity for complex thought. It all comes down to bandwidth. Put simply, the larger a group of people, the lower the intellectual common denominator among them. Two people can have a highly intellectual, nuanced conversation. Three or four can still manage complexity. The cognitive load stays manageable; ideas can breathe. Scale that to thousands? Millions? The capacity collapses. You can't coordinate nuance across ten million minds.

The Empire is very aware of this. So instead, they coordinate emotions.

Reason does not influence large audiences. They're swayed by sentiment. They're motivated by feeling. Any media tailored for a mass population has to carry more sentiment than reason to land effectively. This is a psychological fact.[vi]

USA Today is written for a sixth-grade reading level. Deliberately too, because that's the average adult reading level in the United States. The Relative Truth is that Print Media still believes it can write smart, complex articles and find an audience for them. They earnestly think reason will have an effect.[vii]

The Absolute Truth is that reason does not scale. Emotion does.

So broadcast media, mass TV, mass print, anything catered to a massive audience has to elicit feeling rather than thought. Engineered with subtle language to induce emotion.

They push these stories to nudge you into feeling some kind of way. They imply "you *should* feel ..." about whatever they're covering. You *should* feel scared about COVID or communists or killer bees or whatever else is trying to capture your Attention and hijack your Attitude.

They're selling you a Map. A Map made of feelings.

Feelings aren't facts.

The Empire prefers everyone to have an Attitude of fear.

Reason and nuance disappear at mass scale; emotion, particularly fear, becomes the sole potent signal that pierces the noise and synchronizes millions of minds at once. Fear is the most effective broadcast signal since it bypasses thinking entirely. It hits the nervous system before the brain can evaluate it.[viii] Fear causes an elevated heart rate, sharpened focus, and an urgent need to pay Attention *right now*. Fear completely steamrolls everything else.[ix] This arousal keeps viewers glued longer, increases shares and clicks, and makes the message stickier. Fear-based memories take hold much stronger than joyful or calm memories.[x]

Even the mundane becomes sensationalized and fear-driven, always circling back to the same packaging. They take something ordinary and blow it out of proportion to trigger that fear-to-dependence switch.

"Playground swing found damaged at local park. ARE YOUR CHILDREN IN DANGER? Film at eleven."

That old Empire standy. "Do it for the children." If they can't make you afraid for yourself, they'll make you afraid for the kids. They don't give a fuck about children. Children can't vote. Children have no discretionary income. They care about programming children so they'll vote obediently and become compliant workers and consumers later. Headlines target parents because fearful parents raise fearful children. Generational audience manipulation.

Storm Surge

The Weather Channel is the purest expression of the fear mechanism. Weather affects everyone. Humans have such a strong relationship with weather that it has become a bedrock of small talk worldwide. So the abstraction between the Map and the Territory is not very far, and much of the channel's content hits close enough to home to really command Attention.

My favorite is their hurricane coverage. They will tell you it is the Storm of the Century™. Painting a pending picture of horrendous winds, unstoppable storm surge, and millions displaced. They will compare whatever the current Storm of the Century™ is to the most destructive storms of the past. They love to air that legacy footage of Maria, Katrina, Irma, Ian, Hugo and whatever other asshole rolled up to terrorize the coastline. Anything to foster a feeling of fear. They will suggest that you evacuate or shelter. They post shopping lists of what you need to survive. They attempt to convince everyone that the worst possible scenario will come true. Sometimes they are right; sometimes a storm is genuinely destructive. All that Legacy footage came from somewhere. Most of the time, though, it is not as dangerous as they want you to believe.[xi]

The fear engine continues during the actual event. They will have some poor correspondent out there, decked head to toe in bright yellow foul-weather gear, furiously gripping a microphone, trying to stay upright in the wind while dramatically describing just how catastrophic the storm is on the ground. Viewers will marvel at the adverse conditions and will be thankful for their safe insulation.

The Weather Channel is great since it really drives home just how dangerous the Territory can be. They have a unique position unmatched by other Legacy Media outlets. They are all trying to scare you, but the chances of you getting rained on are greater than experiencing a terrorist attack. Even with preparation or a map, the storm can still get you. They play on this fully.

Naturally, they claim they want everyone to be safe. Why wouldn't they claim that? It is the Relative Truth. In reality, they need that death toll. They long for it. They want the casualty list to get as long as possible. They need that sensationalism to ensure audience engagement. They need the footage to be horrific so they can roll that out before the next Storm of the Century™. No drama means no eyeballs. No eyeballs means no ad revenue. No ad revenue means share holders will be sad. No one is going to pay Attention to some random rainstorm. It rains every day. If they can convince you this is the most dangerous storm in history, that death and destruction will be catastrophic, then just maybe they can get you fearful enough to stay tuned for "further developments."

As long as your Attention is anticipating those developments, and your Attitude is sufficiently fearful. They can start inserting those advertisements. Many of which are also fear-based. Watch basically any insurance commercial. The fear mechanism is the

Empire's primary fuel for the Attention engine. If you are not afraid, you are not watching. If you are not watching, they cannot sell their Map. If they cannot sell you their Map, then people may explore the Territory on their own. That just will not do. They do not want you out there playing in the rain. It's the Storm of the Century™ and walking outside is courting death. Trust me, bro.

One Way Traffic

It started with a newspaper.

Print media was one-way visual communication. Barrier to entry: literacy. If you couldn't read, you missed out on information. The newspaper found the story, printed it, and put it out there. One way. The story was the story and gave you a single lens on current events. There was no meaningful feedback mechanism. Sure, you could write a letter to the editor and hope it got published, but the editor had the final say.

Then a man named Marconi started Fucking Around with crystals, and a short time later news radio was born. Again, one-way communication, although in this case it was audio. Lower barrier to entry; literacy was no longer a requirement, just the ability to listen. Interestingly, this was the birth of the first media celebrities. Legends like Edward R. Murrow and H.V. Kaltenborn, who were renowned and celebrated as the voices of Truth. Kaltenborn was his generation's equivalent of Bernard Shaw. Like Shaw broadcasting from a Baghdad hotel room amid wartime chaos, Kaltenborn did a similar broadcast during the Spanish-American War, actually hiding between two haystacks. The crack of bullets zipping overhead was clearly audible as he reported. The drama and celebrity made broadcast radio wildly popular.[xii]

Eventually, tech developed to a point where a feedback mechanism appeared in broadcast media via a phone call directly to the station. It was two-way communication with an asterisk. Sure, they would "take callers," but a producer screened you first and would decide whether you got on air. If someone got through and acted foolishly, the producer had their finger on the disconnect button. On-air radio has a 7 second delay. More than enough buffer to cut to commercial in the event of unexpected fuckery.

Newsreels in cinema were the first audiovisual communication. The lowest barrier to entry. You didn't have to be literate. You could see the film. You just had to buy a ticket to the theater. In fact, this was a wonderful form of wartime propaganda dissemination, complete with another news celebrity! The legendary voice of Lowell Thomas, and his iconic tagline, the send-off "so long until tomorrow." The Fox Newsreels that famously preceded motion pictures were intensely popular and quite widespread, and very one-way.[xiii]

Technology continued to advance, arriving at television. The newsreels merged with print and radio, and you had nightly news beamed into most every living room in America. No more trips to the cinema to watch footage. This was it; we had arrived. Still one-way, still no meaningful feedback mechanism, yet maximally distributed. Here is where media really became personality. What was voices before now became actual people. Facial expressions and gestures replaced an abstract voice delivering the news; now we had an actual human. The concept of media celebrities really took off with Walter Cronkite, the "most trusted voice in America." Reporters became household names; everyone knows Dan Rather and Barbara Walters. They needed personality and charisma as well as know-how. They had to look the part instead of just being the part.[xiv]

It was a one-way transmission pipeline: print provided the blueprint, radio gave it a voice, and television finally gave it a face. At each stage, the audience grew larger. At each stage, the capacity for complexity got smaller. At each stage, sentiment replaced reason.

Yet at each step, it remained one-way communication. You could shout at the TV, but you couldn't make your voice heard.

They continued a Map. You had no way to tell them it didn't match the Territory.

Comment Below

Finally, Cyberspace arrived.

Almost overnight, the comment section was born.

Two-way communication with the Fourth Estate. Major Legacy News outlets jumped headfirst into Cyberspace, with their websites featuring online articles and videos. Along with that, someone decided, *"Wouldn't it be great to hear from our viewers?"* and introduced a comment section. Generations of one-way broadcast suddenly became a conversation, whether Legacy Media was ready for it or not. Now a feedback mechanism was in place and it was here to stay.[xv]

Now anyone could weigh in, sometimes to support a story. Ofttimes not. Suddenly, everything was open to debate and questioning. Lots of *"what if's"* and *"well actually"* began showing up.[3] The official story was now open to interpretation, and this is where Legacy Media really came face to face with misinformation. Early comment sections were the Wild West; anyone could post anything. Even though many claims might have been bullshit, they could compel enough to crack open the door of doubt. Legacy Media had never had to handle massive feedback before, and this was the first time they were on the ropes. People asked questions, specifically questioning the illusion of fear.

The comment section had another second-tier consequence: audience networking. Suddenly, people could see they weren't the only ones who held certain opinions. They could find each other. Validation for a particular expression of the Psychosis. Tribalism became rampant almost immediately. What started as comment section discussions soon migrated to online forums, eventually spilling over to social media and becoming Facebook groups and Sub-Reddits.

The comment section expanded beyond giving a voice to thoughtful dissent. It gave voice to the loudest, angriest, most extreme takes. The algorithm learned quickly that outrage gets engagement. Nuance just does not have the momentum to go viral. Hot takes do.[xvi]

This development disrupted the gatekeepers. The reality of the feedback mechanism was terrifying. They had pushed sentiment instead of reason for generations, and now it was

---

3. "AcTuAlLy," has become a meme about the insufferable.

turned back onto them. They could not counter an angry, misinformed comment with a reasonable explanation. They had pushed sentiment so hard that it became the baseline. It was too late to downshift to reason.

When Walter Cronkite delivered the news, there was no ratio. No immediate, visible, quantifiable rejection from the audience. The one-way broadcast meant the audience's response was invisible.

Today, every take can get publicly ratioed within minutes.

Getting "ratioed" means your post gets way more replies than likes or shares. The internet collectively rejecting your take. A reply can even "ratio" the original post if it gets massively more engagement than the thing it's responding to. Being ratioed is a public loss. It signals your take bombed with the audience. It is common with politicians, who will make some dumb claim. Usually, an earlier comment on it will have a witty and wise-ass response that is both entertaining and engaging. The politician's post will garner several million views with maybe three thousand likes. The wise-ass comment will also have several million views along with several hundred thousand likes. The ratio is way off, thus the term "ratioed".[xvii]

Legacy Media figures get hit the hardest. MSNBC's Brian Williams got absolutely roflpwned in 2020 when he read a troll tweet's absurd math on air as fact during Bloomberg campaign coverage.[4] Twitter ratioed the clip instantly, quickly tallying thousands of mocking replies versus almost no likes. Turning it into a meme that still circulates as legacy media's "math fail" moment. *"This is why math matters,"* *"Journalism degree in shambles,"* *"Brian Williams just got owned by basic arithmetic."* The hostility was palpable; the mob smelled blood and went for the throat.[xviii]

The New York Times has taken multiple legendary ratios too. In 2023–2024, their reporters and op-eds on everything from COVID origins to election coverage got buried under reply ratios of 10:1, 20:1, even 100:1 against the original post. One viral example: a Times piece claiming a certain narrative was "settled science" got dunked on with reply threads full of primary sources, leaked docs, and simple logic that the article ignored. The replies racked up hundreds of thousands of likes, while the original post limped along. The hostility is real; the mob loves to humiliate. They screenshot, meme, and ratio the institution itself.[xix]

---

4. $650,000 per delegate. GTFO

Real-time crowd feedback about a Map's accuracy. A diagnostic test the Fourth Estate had never had to face before. The crowd can collectively say "this Map doesn't match our experience of the Territory" in a way that's measurable.

It's not perfect. The mob can be wrong, tribal, even volatile and clearly hostile. Prone to following misinformation and drawing false conclusions. The mob is reactionary. The mob is a byproduct of mass media. We already discussed that the larger the group, the less logic and the more feeling, more sentiment. So, of course, the mob is going to react from a place of emotion rather than respond from a place of reason. Even misinformed and reactionary feedback is still feedback, especially if all of those angry voices are validating each other. Legacy Media never stood a chance.

Once feedback became currency, the Truth became a casualty.

The Struggle Continues

The battle for Truth, and against "misinformation" rages on. We are way past the realm of ethics or accuracy. The only integrity that matters to Cyberspace is engagement metrics. Platforms want Attention above all else, so they amplify the loudest, most extreme, most polarizing voices. Controversy is the gasoline. Outrage is the fire. They want it to burn as brightly as possible. They draw more Attention when the fire is dazzling.

Current events are perishable and have a short shelf life. Attention spans have shrunk to nothing. Most people won't sit through anything that asks for real mental effort. This isn't Legacy Media's fault. They still try, bless their hearts; they research, they fact-check; they craft such nuanced and intricate stories; they produce excellent Maps. Sadly, they're producing those Maps for a Territory that doesn't care. The Territory wants something it can swallow in under 47 seconds. Preferably less. If the Wall Street Journal could turn a 3,000-word investigation into a meme and still get eyes on it, they'd do it tomorrow.

We've come a long way from Desert Storm, when CNN was the only voice in the room, the *de facto* source of reality. Now CNN and every other Legacy Outlet swims in a sea of competing content, instant feedback, and the constant risk of being ratioed into oblivion. They keep fighting, though, even as trust collapses to record lows and favor evaporates to nothing. The Legacy Media are professionals and many in the 4th Estate maintain a singular passion for Truth. They may be down, but they are not out.

Movement 5

Battlefield Truth

You go to war with the army you have, not the army you wish you had. — Donald Rumsfeld, Legendary Warrior Poet

Imagine we are sitting on the dock[1], looking over the water of "For You Bay".

We see two vehicles aiming to capture our Attention. One is a large and luxurious ocean liner. The other is a small and colorful Jet Ski.

The Ocean Liner represents the flagship of Legacy Media, fact-checkers, and editorial boards that have established experience. However, external interests influence them because of their revenue requirements, credentialing, and enforced compliance. They require a massive crew to get anywhere, and it takes time to arrive at a story and prepare a report. They pull into the bay, drop an anchor[2] to establish their take, and produce the headlines. Ocean liners can be luxurious; they are massive, attractive, and when one pulls into port, it makes a statement.

The Jet Ski represents the independence of Citizen journalism, comment sections, and Community Notes. They are quick, democratic, and theoretically anyone can drive one. Yet they are also noisy, tribal, and gameable by whoever plays the algorithm best. Capable of zipping around a destination quickly, they can even do flashy tricks. They do not require a crew. They zip around the bay, report on stories in minutes instead of hours, and replaced headlines with "going viral". Jet skis are nimble, easy to drive, and mostly

---

1. of the bay.

2. News anchor...get it?

they are FUN. When one is at the dock, people want to drive it. No one looks at a cruise ship and wants to pilot it.

Both of them are vying for your Attention.

The Ocean Liner is selling you a Map. The Jet Ski is selling you a Map.

All media outlets; print, radio, TV, digital feeds like X, YouTube channels, IG accounts are all hawking Maps.

If you're scrolling and you have a For You Page, that's what the algorithm believes your Map should be. "For you," curated to your interests. Look at those Maps, though; they post some from the Ocean Liner and some from Jet Skis. Sure, they are appealing. This is For You Bay after all, so of course they are going to present data curated to attract your Attention. It's clever but limited in scope; your engagement patterns programmed the algorithm. It will continue to feed that same pattern. Very narrow. If you want new information, you have to search for it yourself. Otherwise, you will get more of the same feed.

The Psychosis of media is subtle. It's a deep-seated, multi-generational behavior pattern. TV has stabilized five generations of Americans. Kids watched their parents watch TV, grew up, had kids who watched them watch TV, on down the line until today, when we have tablets and smartphones and tiny TVs everywhere. An open invitation to dive into For You Bay.

The Legacy Media on their Ocean Liner sells you one Virtual Reality. The Content creators on their Jet Skis each sell another Virtual Reality.

Yet the Territory remains uncharted, unchanged, indifferent to who's selling what map.

The battle for Truth happens right on For You Bay. You're in the water. And the only way to know what's real is to swim.

Anthrax Judy

The media tries to sell us the Relative Truth as the Absolute. In the early 2000s, one of the most prominent soldiers on that battlefield was a reporter for the New York Times. Before we dive into what happens when the Citizen Journalists show up, let's talk about what happens when there aren't any. To do that, we need to talk about Judith Miller.[i]

Judith Miller is a celebrity journalist, which was unusual because that status usually went to the TV anchors, the Cronkites, the Brokaws, the charismatic faces on the screen. Miller had a print reputation, and she had earned it. She had climbed to the top of the most powerful newspaper in the world. She won a Pulitzer Prize. They don't just hand those to hacks; it is to reporting what an Academy Award is to a movie star. When Judith Miller reported something, every other outlet referenced her work. She is a pro's pro.

Then, in 2001, in the wake of 9/11, someone mailed anthrax letters to media figures and politicians across the country. Miller was the only U.S. reporter targeted. She popped open that envelope and white powder went everywhere.[ii]

Thankfully, hers turned out to be a hoax. The moment made her famous in a different way. It put a target on her that doubled as a spotlight. Suddenly she wasn't just a great reporter. She was the reporter someone tried to kill. That commands Attention. And Attention, as we know, is the resource everyone is competing for. Even the Ocean Liners compete with each other. The Bay is massive, and every vessel in it, Legacy or otherwise, is fighting for the same set of eyeballs.

Miller commanded eyeballs. Just days before the envelope of doom, she had published *Germs*, a book about biological warfare. The envelope incident was rocket fuel for the book.[iii] Of course, she did what any excellent writer would do with the spotlight and ran with it.[3]

When you capture Attention on that level, nobody, especially the bean counters, will question you when the numbers are good. The New York Times would not scrutinize its star reporter while she was selling papers. She was a Pulitzer prize-winning journalist and survived an assassination attempt. She was Absolutely a living legend, and that captivated readers. People were subscribing. The Empire rewards engagement and not necessarily accuracy. This is important. The machine doesn't care if the Map is right. It cares if the Map sells.

Weapons of Mass Deception

9/11 changed everything. We all know this. Those of us who were alive then watched it happen. Those who were born into the post 9/11 world have certainly seen the footage. It was a gut punch to the USA. The most tragic attack on U.S. Soil™ since Pearl

---

3. *Germs* published October 2nd. Anthrax letter arrived October 12th. Life indeed imitates art.

Harbor. The Empire was ready to step up, and overnight we have "The War on Terror," an umbrella term broad enough to cover anything the Empire told us we *should* be afraid of.[iv] This began a series of events that started as a nationwide investigation that spanned from flight schools to an invasion of Afghanistan. The Taliban was subdued, yet the GWOT was just getting started. There was still a lot of terror out there, and the Evangelists were pretty fixated on Iraq.[4]

Despite everything, there was no direct connection between Iraq and 9/11. They would have loved if there was, it would have made things so much easier. Instead, they only had to make sure Iraq fell under the umbrella of "terror" well enough to justify an invasion. During the Cold War, everyone was terrified of nukes. So they took that route. Therefore, WMDs represented the world's most significant danger, and we must halt any nation[5] that possessed them, no matter the cost. Diplomacy was off the table. "We don't negotiate with terrorists," after all. So an invasion had to happen. The Map demanded it.

Judith Miller was the Cartographer in Chief.

Here's the chain. Iraqi defectors flee the country, the government grants them asylum, and they tell the Pentagon exactly what it wants to hear: "Saddam has nukes. *Trust me, bro.*" Some dude at the Pentagon gets a gleam in his eye. Another dude at Raytheon gets a gleam in his eye because he just sold a contract for bunker busters or whatever murder he is marketing. Miller gets a gleam in her eye because she's got her sights on another Pulitzer. Colin Powell gets a gleam in his eye because he's about to perform on the world's biggest stage.

That's a lot of gleaming eyes all salivating when they heard what they wanted to hear.

Miller runs the story. September 2002.[v] Aluminum tubes intercepted bound for Iraq. Unnamed American officials, unnamed intelligence experts, unnamed Bush administration officials, all saying Saddam was pursuing nuclear weapons. Front page of The New York Times. The paper of record.

Shortly after The NYT released the article, Condoleezza Rice, Colin Powell, and Donald Rumsfeld appeared on television and cited Miller's story to back their position. Think about that. The government feeds information to a reporter. The reporter publishes it.

---

4. I suspect Dubya wanted to finish what his father started.

5. Nations we don't like.

Then the government points to the published report as independent confirmation of the information they themselves provided. The poster child of mental masturbation. The Map citing itself as Territory.

In 2003, the Ocean Liners had the Bay entirely to themselves. The internet existed, sure. Comment sections everywhere. Plenty of space for critical thinking on forums and early blogs. Technologically Cyberspace was by today's standards still a dinosaur. Dial-up was still the name of the game. In 2003 you still needed a hard line and an actual modem to access the Internet. No Wi-Fi yet. Widespread connection was still developing. Independent voices didn't have the platform, the reach, or the infrastructure to challenge the biggest ship in the Bay. There were no Jet Skis like there are today. Those in charge governed the feedback mechanism, and they heavily moderated the comment sections on the Ocean Liner. No Community Notes. No one could ratio Colin Powell.

The Ocean Liner floated unopposed.

Then Powell takes the stage at the UN, holding a vial.[vi] A prop, because it's all a show and he is doing a bit. The LARP at the United Nations was enough to set things in motion. Total showmanship and spectacle. Legacy Media broadcast it readily, no questions asked. Colin Powell was already a trusted, well-known name in American households. The trusted figure holds up a vial and says this is why we go to war. Gulf War 2: Electric Boogaloo was about to torch off.

"You're either with us or with the terrorists." George W. Bush had already set the standard.[vii] Classic false dilemma, and America ate it up. An Empire tactic as old as empires: if you're not with us, you're the enemy. No room for a gray area. No room for a third option.

We went from "he has them", to "we have to find them", to "well, he may develop one." The goalposts moved further and further into the Relative and away from the Absolute. Recognizing the mental gymnastics didn't require a journalism degree. It didn't require classified intelligence. It required five seconds of critical thinking. No one needs a diploma to recognize bullshit when they smell it. The Empire rewards critical thinking as long as you are not critical of them. The Empire always rewards compliance. Anyone who questioned the Map was told they must hate America.

Many people did question it. There were anti-war protests. In fact, the largest coordinated protest in human history took place with millions marching worldwide shortly before the invasion. The Empire went to war anyway.[viii]

There was widespread suspicion that the war was more about oil than terrorism. Saddam had nationalized Iraq's oil, and the Iraqi people owned it.[ix] After the invasion, which found exactly zero WMDs, Saddam was removed and publicly executed, a puppet government installed, and suddenly Western firms like BP, Shell, and Exxon gained major operational stakes and contracts in those fields.[x] Halliburton led the charge to get the oil flowing in the right direction. The real winners of the war didn't wear uniforms.

More showmanship greeted us as the dust was still settling. Dubya himself landed a jet on an aircraft carrier wearing a flight suit. Our hearts collectively swelled with patriotic pride when he took off that flight helmet, standing in front of the "Mission Accomplished" banner. We would continue to occupy both Afghanistan and Iraq for another decade, but the show was over. The Ocean Liner had its headline.

Iraq was the Millennial's Vietnam.

Nobody on a Jet Ski had the platform to question it.

Shopping Cart Method

What makes Miller's story more than just a cautionary tale about bad reporting? She wasn't a bad reporter. That's what is baffling.

She reported claims on both sides, including stories where UN inspectors found nothing to prompt immediate war. Two points of view: one justified the invasion and one undermined it. She reported the facts as she found them.[xi] That's what reporters do, report facts *as they find them*.

The Ocean Liner cherry-picked.

Call it the Shopping Cart Method. Legacy Media browses through the facts as if they're strolling through a grocery store. They choose what they want from the shelves and leave the rest. Then they present the cart to you and call it The Official Narrative™. The New York Times wasn't interested in running "inspectors found nothing" on the front page. That doesn't sell papers. "Saddam has nukes" sells papers. The front page featured alarmist stories prominently, and "nothing to see here" received significantly less coverage.

Miller was on the front lines of a battlefield and became collateral damage. The battlefield was never in the desert; the battlefield was truth. And on that battlefield, the weapon isn't a gun; it's who can direct Attention and shape Attitude the best. Miller was that weapon. She was one of the most effective soldiers in the information war. And like a lot of soldiers, she was following orders from people who had their own agendas and that gleam in their eyes.

The territory revealed itself. No WMDs. None. The Duelfer Report made it official. The map that had justified a war, cost thousands of lives, and reshaped the Middle East was fiction. Expensive, bloody fiction.

Legacy Media felt embarrassed, and someone had to take responsibility. So the fingers pointed at the most prestigious voice in the room. The New York Times had been front and center for the entire war. In May 2004, the NYT published an editorial acknowledging that some of its pre-war coverage had relied too heavily on sources who were "bent on regime change." The editorial expressed "regret" that controversial information had been "allowed to stand unchallenged." It explicitly rejected blaming individual reporters. Shortly after, Judith Miller was called into HR and invited to pursue other opportunities.[xii]

Sure, their Map said they were not blaming individual reporters. The Virtual Reality Blues still came for Miller. The New York Times removed her from her position in disgrace. The reporter who had commanded more Attention than almost anyone in contemporary American print journalism. This was the reporter whose work had been cited by the Secretary of State and the National Security Advisor on national television. She had been the *de facto* source for the case for war. She became the scapegoat.

Miller defended herself. "My job isn't to assess the government's information and be an independent intelligence analyst myself. My job is to tell readers of the New York Times what the government thought about Iraq's arsenal."[xiii]

Read that again. She's describing exactly how the Ocean Liner works. The government hands you a Map. You publish the Map. That's the job. She doesn't even see it as a problem. That is the mechanism of journalism: to report the facts. The captains on board the ocean liners don't have to be lying. They just have to do their jobs. It's more dangerous than conscious propaganda, because nobody thinks they're the bad guy.

Judith Miller is not the villain of the Electric Boogaloo. She reported misinformation, and not disinformation. Disinfo is deliberately malicious and meant to deceive. Misinformation is inadvertently presented, and is caused by bad facts, not bad intentions.

Miller had said, in defense of her disputed reporting: "You know what? I was proved fucking right." Her vindication arrived in that moment, as people initially assessed the trailers found in Iraq as mobile weapons labs. Experts debunked the assessment later, yet her quote endured. The Map refusing to acknowledge the Territory. The confidence of someone who had been told, "*Trust me, bro*" so many times that she started saying it herself.[xiv]

The roots of the American distrust in Legacy Media trace directly back to moments like this.[xv] The WMD reporting. The scapegoating. The snake eating its own tail, the government feeding reporters, reporters feeding the public, the government citing the reports as proof. A constant shell game of nothing, until the Territory made the lie undeniable, and then the system sacrificing one of its own to preserve itself.

As these things go, it just got worse for Miller. It started with a Washington Post article and ended in handcuffs.

Valerie Plame was a CIA operative whose husband, Joseph Wilson, wrote an editorial questioning the WMD narrative. The Empire couldn't let that stand. Someone leaked Plame's CIA identity to the press, effectively ending her career. Political retaliation, pure and simple. When they can't discredit the message, they go after the messenger or in this case, the messenger's wife.[xvi]

They subpoenaed Miller to testify before a grand jury regarding the leak of Plame's identity. She refused. She sat in a jail cell for 85 days protecting her source.

That source turned out to be I. Lewis "Scooter" Libby, the Vice President's chief of staff.[6]

A shit show from top to bottom.

She understood that the only genuine power any of us has is the power to say no. They told her to give up her source, and she refused. She sat in that cell for almost three months. Whatever else you think about Judith Miller had *chutzpah*. The Empire told her to comply and she chose an 85 day vacation instead.

They eventually released her; she testified, and they convicted Libby on four of five counts. Miller negotiated a severance from the Times and went on to Fox News to continue her career. She survived.[xvii]

---

6. Not the Muppet Scooter.

The damage to the Ocean Liner was catastrophic.

Judith Miller didn't break Legacy Media's credibility. She was a symptom of something much larger.

The machine produced the lie. The individual took the fall. The public watched the whole thing unfold and drew the obvious conclusion: if the paper of record can run fiction on the front page and call it news, then call the reporter a scapegoat when the fiction collapses, why would you trust any of it?

This was the reality of the information landscape when the Ocean Liner dominated the Bay. One vessel, one Map, one version of reality. A single, carefully curated narrative that you had better get in line with, *or else.* As Cyberspace evolved, the *"Trust me, bro"* stuck around. Legacy Media maintains this Attitude today. The technology infrastructure expanded and became much more accessible. Soon, For You Bay had many small, colorful Jet Skis zipping around the Ocean Liner.

Birth of The Citizen Journalist

Just as the barrier to entry and understanding got lower and lower with each subsequent leap in broadcasting technology, there was still a pretty high barrier to entry if you wanted to produce your own content. Sure, there were avenues, but they ranged from publishing shitty newsletters and zines to late-night local cable access TV. Radio, especially college radio stations, had a lower bar, but still had gatekeepers like the FCC. Specialized equipment was expensive, and the average person would have a difficult time breaking through that barrier.

We are so far past that now. Whereas in the before time you needed a video camera and tapes to record, you also required transmission equipment, relays and antennas and a frequency on which to broadcast. Editing VHS tapes depended on a specialized machine. The complete process was time-consuming, expensive, and labor-intensive. Today anyone can do all of this in minutes with only a smartphone.[xviii]

The tribalism that developed from comment sections worldwide and became forums was now becoming YouTube channels. Citizen Journalists were popping up, and many were talented and successful from the start. They were filling a demand for genuine reporting. Many were journalism students and well-educated people who could not find work in Legacy Media so they ventured out on their own. The concept of "freelancing" takes on a completely different level of impact when you can freelance, produce, edit, and distribute your own content, and do it for a dedicated audience.[xix]

Philip DeFranco is a journalism grad who couldn't get hired by Legacy Media, so he did what any self-respecting Millennial would do and went on YouTube. In 2006 he launched his own daily news show from what was essentially a webcam and a desk. No editorial board. No sponsors telling him what he couldn't say. He blended factual reporting with personal opinion, critiqued mainstream narratives when he felt like it, and built an audience of over 6 million subscribers who showed up because they trusted *him*, instead of the outlet behind him. He was the outlet.[xx]

Steven Crowder came at it from the right. No journalism degree, couldn't crack Legacy Media because his style was too confrontational and too conservative for the editorial gatekeepers. So he bootstrapped his own show, "Louder with Crowder," mixing street reporting with satirical skits and a segment called "Change My Mind" where he literally sits at a table and argues with strangers.[7] Nearly 6 million subscribers.[xxi] Same mechanism as DeFranco, on a completely different Map. Both blurring the line between reporting and opinion. Both prioritizing engagement over neutrality. Both proving you don't need the ocean liner's permission to command Attention.

The impact is clear. The numbers do not lie. Infotainment for the win, and they were winning.

Philip DeFranco has over 6.6 million subscribers on YouTube right now. MSNBC, meanwhile, averages around 915,000 viewers in prime-time across 2025. Their re-brand to MS NOW has had little impact. That's the actual viewership of a flagship Legacy Media outlet. One independent guy with a webcam and a daily show routinely pulls a bigger audience than a major cable news network's most lucrative time block.[xxii]

Even factoring in YouTube's on-demand nature. Clearly not every subscriber watches every video, yet a single DeFranco upload often racks up hundreds of thousands to millions of views in its first day or two, easily matching or beating MSNBC's live prime-time numbers. Creators unburdened by editorial latency are attracting audiences away from Legacy Outlets. These creators can speak directly to their audiences without feigning neutrality. They can say the quiet part out loud and get away with it.

---

7. It's hilarious.

This is a genuine threat. When a solo creator can out-draw a billion-dollar news machine in raw reach, the old model looks obsolete. The Attention economy is a territory all unto itself, and the old maps of credentials and Legacy cannot navigate effectively. The rewards go to whoever captures and holds eyeballs the longest. Citizen journalism is clearly winning.

Left, Right, Legacy or independent, they are always selling you a Map. These days there are countless Maps for sale. Maps competing for your Attention and wanting to direct your Attitude. With so many Maps all claiming sovereignty over the territory, of course there is going to be conflict.

Legacy Media is losing badly. A single person with a phone can upload raw footage, commentary, or a breakdown before the Legacy desk even finishes the morning meeting. Legacy Outlets can spend weeks on an investigative piece only to see it land flat because the conversation already happened on YouTube, TikTok, or X three days earlier. By the time the Legacy report airs, the audience has already formed opinions, shared clips, argued in comments, memory-holed it and swiped up to the next one.

The part that irks Legacy Media to no end is the Citizen Journalists don't even have to be right. Speed wins the first frame. Right or wrong, true or false, facts or total bullshit, their fan base does not care. Popularity carries credibility. The audience learned they no longer have to wait for the official or even accurate version of a story as long as it's coming from a beloved personality.[xxiii]

Ironic that this is the same mechanism that gave the WMD narrative such gravitas. Judith Miller's popularity carried credibility too.

World War COVID

COVID was when the world collectively lost its mind to the Cyberspace Psychosis. In fact, I would say it was reminiscent of Y2K-level Psychosis. A highly fearful time, with the media leading the charge in the capture of Attention and manufacturing Attitude. What started as a minor story from China soon exploded into a worldwide catastrophe. We are several years removed and still recovering.

The early Chinese COVID videos paved the way. They elicited maximum fear. Wow, did they work too! We saw videos of people collapsing while waiting for a bus. They were falling over in the mall. People appeared to drop dead wherever they stood from the mysterious virus. We even watched the Chinese public health officials on camera moving through cities wearing their Andromeda Strain-style hazmat suits.[xxiv]

Naturally, the footage had the desired effect. The footage scared people. How long until it arrived here? Turns out we had a fast pass and almost overnight the COVID was everywhere. Legacy Media had the symptoms front and center for everyone to see. Bright infographics spread across every screen in the land. Warning of loss of taste, extreme fatigue, and congestion. It was the super cold. The worst aspects of the flu hit all at once, like a sledgehammer. The testing was invasive. Shoving a Q-tip deep into your nose was the only way to discover your infection.[xxv]

The hype began turning into hysteria, and rightfully so. People were legitimately dying. Notably, older adults, the "Boomer Remover" was in full swing, and they were falling by the thousands. The public demanded that something must be done. Cyberspace ensured we each had a front-row seat for the legitimate public health crisis playing out everywhere. Authorities stopped gatherings. Stores were closed. Everyone was masking up. Stay 6' away. No touching. No breathing. Wash your hands, but don't touch the bathroom door handle; use your elbow. We went from zero to panic in a few short weeks.[xxvi]

For the first time in many people's lives, the vague fear-based reporting that had been present for most of our lives was actually reporting on something worthy of being concerned with. Everyone experienced the pandemic's effects. Even if you remained uninfected, you knew someone who was. Even if you didn't know anyone who actually died from it, you knew someone who lost a loved one. For a population that was used to being insulated from widespread tragedy, coming face to face with genuine crisis was not something that was handled gracefully. We coped by hoarding shit tickets[8] and bottled water.

The solution appeared suddenly. On the morning of January 1, 2021, it was suddenly wall-to-wall coverage about the new vaccine that had just rolled out. The announcement saturated every platform.[xxvii]

We knew at the time it was something called an mRNA shot, and it was supposed to help. The demand was astonishing. Millions of people were desperate for peace as their lives were falling apart. They promoted the vaccine, but it was not compulsory. Culturally, though, the vaccine became a requirement to do basically anything. There were vaccine cards that were signed with the lot number and the date. A credential which was a requirement for airline travel, for admission to a movie theater, even to go to work. "Show your papers, please," took on a terrifying new reality.[xxviii]

Widespread panic and fear quickly turned to complete trust in the Empire. The Attention was on the danger, the Attitude of desperation, the Attitude was overwhelmingly "save us." The Empire provided an Action someone could take: get their vaccine. Along with the shot came the peace of mind that you would be safe, or Relatively safe. Well, safer than you would be without the shot. Because reasons.

The vaccine was an easy sell. Entertainment glorifies our medical industry. Hollywood has gifted us these larger-than-life characters in blockbuster medical dramas. This goes way beyond General Hospital soap opera fascination. Primetime gave us House. We had Grey's Anatomy, Scrubs, Chicago Hope, and so many more. Decades of generic medical drama had ingrained a sense of Absolute trust to the point that the public basically worshiped anyone in a white coat. So much so that they would never dream of questioning a map someone with an MD after their name handed to them.

The COVID vaccine gave everyone a chance to take part in their own little medical drama. There were even brands. You could pick your favorite. Pfizer, Johnson & Johnson, Moderna, and so forth. People were even getting tattoos of their favorite vaccine and proudly posting photos of them on social media.[xxix]

---

8. Toilet paper.

Counter Punch

With such an environment of fear everywhere, with the Legacy Media enthusiastically stoking the flames, there was of course going to be backlash from Independent sources. This friction started almost immediately. Right away, people began questioning the Official Narrative™. Not even from a place of ignorance; rather, it was honest critical thinking. There were legitimate concerns about how quickly they had developed and tested the vaccines. What exactly was in it? Why are they trying so hard to sell this?

Soon the videos started coming straight out of the Territory, where the view on the ground was not matching the Map. A content creator walked into a pharmacy and demanded to see the vaccine insert. The pharmacist opened it, unfolding it and revealing a completely blank piece of paper. All vaccines are required to have an insert. It contains information about the testing process, ingredient list, documentation on effectiveness, and how it works. The insert was blank.[xxx] The FDA had waived that because of an Emergency Use Authorization. Yes, all the vaccine information was available online, if you were inclined to search for it. However, as we know, it is much easier to become outraged at a video than put in the actual effort of self-education. Sentiment pwns reason once again.

The real fireworks with the COVID vaccines came from the "liability waivers", that were mentioned all over social media. Under the PREP Act[9], the government basically wrapped vaccine makers in legal Kevlar: granting almost total immunity from lawsuits over injuries or deaths unless you could prove "willful misconduct," which is about as easy as winning the lottery. Instead of courts, any claim got funneled into the Countermeasures Injury Compensation Program. A notoriously stingy federal fund. Hundreds of social media posts were highlighting this across basically every platform, and it only fueled the fire. What had started as critical thinking had morphed into outright distrust.[xxxi]

Was the distrust well founded? The massive push of the vaccine was first presented as a cure, then the story changed and the shot only rendered the symptoms less harmful, and in fact didn't protect you from getting the virus at all. Also, it was incomplete. Not only did you need two initial shots, but also booster after booster. The Empire kept moving the goalposts. It was fascinating to experience.[xxxii]

---

9. A 2005 law dusted off in March, 2020.

The snapback against anyone questioning this narrative was almost instantaneous and absolutely hostile. Critics labeled them as villainous anti-vaxxers. Told their Attitude toward the vaccine was dangerous and irresponsible. People ridiculed, discriminated against, and bullied them constantly, causing them to lose their jobs and livelihoods and to be excluded from gatherings.[xxxiii] This contentious response to a critical line of thinking: if the vaccine protected people from symptoms, how did an un-vaccinated person pose a threat to someone who had the shot?[10] I'm not even saying that the question had no answer. Maybe it did. The point is that they treated the inquiry itself as dangerous. The Map demanded compliance, and it did not meet questioners with better information; instead, society punished them.

Legacy Media marched in lockstep with government officials, Big Pharma, Little Pharma[11], along with extreme peer pressure. Countless fingers pointing at the Map which had unified everyone: COVID is apocalyptic, lockdowns save lives, vaccines are the miracle cure, and question nothing. Doubt was the enemy. Every emotional appeal, such as *"do it for grandma," "heroes wear masks,"* and *"we're all in this together,"* served as a counter to critical thought. The media machine fueled by this sentiment was completely dominating the battlefield.

Branded for Life

Enter Russell Brand, the loudest self-appointed independent fact-checker in the room, muddying those pristine waters with a mix of humor, philosophy, and unfiltered rage. He became a rallying point and a magnet for people who felt gaslit by Legacy Media. He was entertaining and popular. Already a known celebrity with millions of followers from his comedy and spirituality podcasts, Brand pivoted hard in 2020–2022. He was routinely calling out lockdown hypocrisy[12], questioning vaccine mandates as authoritarian overreach, and roasting Big Pharma for blank inserts and liability waivers. He was visible, charismatic, and millions were giving him Attention.

He dissected the Official Narrative™ with a sentiment of his own: raw, conspiratorial energy that felt like a middle finger to the Empire's polished fear-mongering. Videos like

---

10. DARE had warned us about peer pressure and taking drugs, yet here we were.

11. Your local Walgreens administered the shot.

12. Politicians partying while you couldn't visit family.

"Is This the Biggest Lie About COVID?" or "Why Are They Hiding Vaccine Data?"
racked up millions of views faster than Legacy outlets could debunk them.[xxxiv]

Brand became a total disruption, using a mix of outrage, skepticism, and even spiritual
quips to challenge the reason-based "trust the science" Map. Proving that in the Attention economy, a charming lone voice can outflank an entire media machine. How did
that turn out for him, though? Stay tuned; we are not done with Mr. Brand and the
court of public opinion just yet.

The battle was in full swing: Legacy fact-checkers slapped "misinformation" labels on
his takes, YouTube demonetized and restricted him, and his audience didn't care. They
saw him as the guy asking the questions no one else would. It wasn't about being
right every time; it was about speed and Attitude, belittling the official map before it
could solidify. Brand showed the Empire's weak spot: when independent voices harness
emotion to poke holes in the reason facade, the whole narrative starts to leak. He served
as a sentiment saboteur in World War COVID, proving that in the Attention economy,
independent voices who harness emotion can outflank an entire media machine.

The validation of his perspective occurred in some ways. Brand's willingness to question
everything directly conflicted with the Legacy Media's willingness to report everything
official sources passed onto them, and to label everything else as "misinformation". This
tactic did not turn out well.

During COVID, saying the virus might have come from a lab was "misinformation."
Until it wasn't.[xxxv]

Claiming natural immunity might be as effective as vaccination was "misinformation."
Until the studies came out.[xxxvi]

Reporting the vaccines don't stop transmission was "misinformation." Until Pfizer
admitted it in testimony.[xxxvii]

Time has vindicated many of the dissenters. The military reinstated those who had been
discharged. Many people who lost their jobs received compensation and restoration. The
un-vaxxed who were told they would die an agonizing death from the virus are somehow
still here. The entire ordeal was an exercise in compliance. With the non-compliant
coming out ahead.[xxxviii]

The critical point is that the Territory never changed. COVID was always what it was.
The virus's origin was always what it was. The vaccine efficacy was always what it was.

The Territory sat there, unchanged, while the cartographers kept redrawing their Maps and insisting each new version was the definitive one. Uncharted Territory isn't the same as changing Territory. It just means we haven't FAFO'd our way to an accurate Map yet.

Had it not been for Citizen Journalists, who had the platform, the courage, and the sheer balls to speak out against the narrative, ask the hard questions, and do actual journalism instead of simply aping government spokespeople[13], we might not be seeing this massive erosion in trust toward Legacy Media today. COVID was a wild, stressful time, and yes, plenty of Legacy Journalists around the world did genuine work that saved lives. Holding public trust means actually doing your job: asking questions, chasing the truth, and reporting the facts.

The Psychosis had spread so far and so deep that even personal tragedy couldn't override it: someone could watch a family member die from COVID and still not trust the media's narrative, still opt out of the vaccine, still cling to the alternative Map. That level of distrust goes way beyond mere skepticism. By that point, it is a full infection, where suspicion runs bone-deep, and no amount of "official" reason can penetrate it. The Empire's Map cracked because voices like Brand had already remapped the Territory, and once the Psychosis takes hold, it's damn near impossible to dismiss the illusion.

So when Legacy Media calls for "misinformation" regulation, are they asking for quality control? Or are they asking to be reinstated as the only authorized Map-makers? On X, Community Notes lets anyone fact-check anyone in real time. No credentials required. No editorial approval either. Just people pointing at the Territory and saying, "This Map's off." That's a dimension of accountability the old system never had to face. Legacy Media competes to be the "most trusted source in news." But "most trusted" is a market position, not a truth claim. A better market position means a bigger slice of the Attention pie. Fact-checking is quality control for their Map, nothing more.

Nothing but the Truth

With so much competition for your Attention, how do you find the Absolute Truth untainted by an agenda?

We just watched the same mechanism play out twenty years apart with different technology. Both the Second Gulf War and COVID had the same Empire "*Trust me,*

---

13. Stop pointing at Judy, she has been through enough.

bro." energy. In 2003, the ocean liner had For You Bay entirely to itself, and Judy drew the Map. By 2020, the Jet Skis were swarming, and the Maps were multiplying faster than anyone could read them. For the first time, Legacy Media encountered competition besides themselves. How do we know whom to believe?

Recognize whether a news story is trying to inform you or trying to influence you. Whether it's an Ocean Liner or a Jet Ski, both have the capacity to haul bullshit.

There's what happened, then what *really* happened.

There are three sides to every story. Side A. Side B. And the Truth.

Side A and Side B are Relative Truths.

Relative Truths are Maps.

The Absolute Truth is the Territory.

It's up to you to discover the difference.

Movement 6

Money

Gentlemen, you had my curiosity. But now you have my Attention. — Calvin Candie, *Django Unchained*

Money is water.

Weirdly, this is exactly how we describe it. Current became currency. We use terms like cash flow, revenue streams, and liquidity pools. You can have your assets frozen! You can drown in debt! If you want to be a baller at a strip club, you even "make it rain." Human bodies are 60% water and I would wager many people are thinking about money about 60% of the time. Many people[1], are thirsty most of the time. They gather at the watering hole every payday. Money flows through the economy like a massive river we all depend on, and what directs the flow of a river? Banks.[i]

Is this a coincidence? Is it some weird semantic[2] cultural quirk that just sort of developed over time?[ii] Maybe it is just the language doing its best to Map out the characteristics of something that was already abstract. An attempt to describe our medium of exchange. Water dictates our lives in shocking ways. Go without it and you will die of dehydration in a few days.[iii] Go without money and you will not get very far in Empire-occupied Territory. It is fluid. It is essential. It is so ubiquitous that we swim in it without seeing it, the way fish do not notice the water.

Money is the Map. Exchange is the Territory.

---

1. Sales people are always the thirstiest.

2. We are NOT talking about Korzybski.

Money is such an abstract concept when we think about it. True, it is the medium of exchange that everyone agrees on. It is the ultimate agreement. Still, it is totally illusory. Pieces of paper and numbers on a computer screen somewhere. It comes from nowhere and ultimately is nothing. It's a trick.

Yet it is everything.

Everyone has an addiction to money. You, me, and basically any citizen of the Empire are completely addicted. It counts as an active addiction, too. It is an obsession, a fixation, a fetish, and the ultimate Attention trap. Money is the one thing we cannot do without. Period. We are all united in our fixation on this. It is the one thing that actually unites people. When you get down to it, more than skin color or religion or political affiliation or dietary preference or sexual orientation or any of the endless ways the Empire seeks to divide us, at the center of all of it is money. The only color that matters is green.

Wild, that money is the only thing we can really agree on. We all want it. Many of us want more of it. Money motivates in ways that are unmatched anywhere else on the map. Children will start planning their careers very young because they want money. Children will even start a lemonade stand to make money. Schools believe in child labor, having their students go door to door selling floral arrangements, magazine subscriptions, candy bars, and other sundries for fundraising. Children learn early on that it takes money to buy things; the Empire is all about us consuming.

We grow up, and the game changes. Money stops being about what you want and starts being about what we need. The Empire has all of us on a subscription plan for survival. Electricity. Water. Insurance on your body, insurance on your car, insurance on the house you are still paying off. Everyone has bills. The Empire ensures that. We have monthly recurring charges on our existence, and a single missed payment can be catastrophic. They will shut off your utilities, repo your vehicle, and toss you on the street. Money is no longer fun. It is survival. And the Empire likes it that way, because desperate people do not ask questions. They just keep on working.

Money has zero counterpart in the Territory. Anywhere. It is not natural. Any animals that are trained to use money only learned it by watching humans. We have all seen the video of a dog who was watching people purchase ice cream in a park. He saw them trade money for it, so he picked up a leaf and tried to trade that in for his ice cream treat. Kudos to him because it worked.[iv]

Money is about as Relative a Truth as we can get about anything.

It is paper.

A piece of flat cotton with a dead President's face on it. Some ink, some security features, some serial numbers. If you were starving in the wilderness, you could not eat it. If you were freezing, you could not burn enough of it to stay warm for long. If you were dying of thirst, a suitcase full of cash would not produce a single drop of water.[v]

The bill only works because we all agree that it works. That agreement is the entire foundation. That has always been the agreement about money because you can't eat gold either, or ducats, or little stones with holes in the middle, or gems, or any of the other little things we have used as currency over the years.[vi] It is a Truth we all agree on. The moment that agreement breaks, hyperinflation, bank collapse, grid down, you are holding a piece of paper that will not buy a can of beans.[vii]

Money is the Map. It was never Territory.

Ironically, the only people who say money is not important are those who have too much or none at all. For everyone in the middle, money is vitally important. It is the fuel. The more you have in your tank, the more you can go out and explore. While money takes our Attention and directs our Agency, it also gives us Agency.

So we are stuck. Knowing the Map is a Map, but needing it anyway.

The Long Long Ago

How did this all start, anyway?

I wasn't there. Story time.

Once upon a time, way back in the before time, the long, long ago. Some dude found something shiny in the ground. We will call him Thug. The shiny glittered with a color that drew the eye, and it caught Thug's Attention. Thug picked it up, turned it around in his hands, probably licked it, decided it looked pretty, and brought it back to the tribe. When he got there, it caught someone else's Attention and they said, "Hey Thug, that shiny rock you found sure is the mammoth's marrow![3] How about I trade you this bear skin for it?"[viii]

---

3. This was the 15,000 BCE equivalent of "cat's pajamas".

Thug loved bearskins, of course he made the trade.

Then Thug had a thought. *I wonder what else people will trade me for these shiny rocks?* So he went back and gathered some more. He brought them back and everyone had their Attention on these shiny rocks. Someone traded him a basket of nuts for one. Someone else offered a spear. The tribespeople began trading their shiny rocks with each other for things. The bigger the rock, the more they could get from the trade. Soon, they started trading shiny rocks with other tribes for even more things. Everyone agreed the shiny rocks were worth trading for, and just like that, the concept of currency was born. Not from a central bank, or a government, or an economic theory. From a guy with a cool rock and someone who wanted it. Supply and demand.

Or something like that. I do not know; I was not there. I'm not an anthropologist. The point is that you could hold the gold. You could bite it. You could feel its weight. It was real. It is heavy. It is tangible and measurable. In fact, our term "dollar" was once a unit of weight, not just a piece of paper.[ix] Gold was as close to Territory as money ever got.

Then someone figured out that carrying gold around was heavy and inconvenient. So they said *Here, take this piece of paper instead.* You can bring it to the bank and trade it for a dollar of gold. It says you have the gold. The gold is right there at the bank, in the vault. T

A Map of the gold.

Then someone figured out there was not actually enough gold to back all the paper they had printed. They wanted to keep printing it, anyway. Do not worry about it. Money is money. This was the birth of fiat. Now our dollars were notes. Backed by our belief that these notes held value. *Trust me, bro.*

A Map of nothing.

Later along the line the Empire decided it would be better if they had custody of the gold, so they issued a decree and required everyone to trade their gold in for these Maps.[x]

Decades passed, and someone said, "Forget the paper. Here is a plastic card that represents the paper that used to represent the gold."

A Map of a Map of a Map.

Then someone said *Forget the card,* just tap your phone. Now it is numbers in a database referencing other numbers in a database referencing the paper that used to reference the gold that Thug found in the ground.

Each step, you touched the money less. Each step, another floor disappeared. And nobody ever looked down.

It gets more abstract.

Credit. Money that does not yet exist. Borrowed from your future self, with interest. You are spending a Map of money you have not earned, which is itself a Map of value you have not created. A Map of a Map of a Map.

Derivatives. Bets on bets on bets. Financial instruments so far removed from anything real that the people trading them could not point to the underlying asset if you asked. This broke the economy in 2008. People were trading abstractions of abstractions, and nobody knew what was underneath anymore. When they finally caught a glimpse, all they saw was a collapse.[xi]

Cyberspace has given us cryptocurrency. A digital token that exists only because a distributed network agrees it exists. No government backing. No physical anything. Pure consensual hallucination. There are hundreds of tokens and block-chains, and to the layperson it is an alphabet soup of bullshit. They are not far off.

Underneath all of it, fractional reserve banking. The practice where banks loan out the same dollar to multiple people. They do not actually have the money. They have a fraction, and they loan out multiples of that fraction, and everyone just agrees not to ask for their money back at the same time. A bank run, where everyone tries to withdraw their deposits simultaneously, would collapse the system because the deposits are not there. They never were. The money is a fiction built on a fiction built on a fiction.[xii]

Do not worry, the FDIC has your back. They secured your account. *Trust me, bro.*

The whole thing runs on Absolute faith. A collective agreement we silently consented to, and no one dares to discuss out loud. We stay quiet because the alternative is terrifying. Civilization as we know it would be fucked if people no longer perceived money as valuable.

I am not talking about lying down next to the fire on top of the bearskin carpet, gentle lovemaking kind of fucked. I mean bent over the hood of a Kia Soul[4] and rawdogged in the parking lot of a Jamba Juice variety of fucked.

Taxes

I did not always understand this. Nobody hands you the manual on how money actually works. It's not like the Empire's schools wanted us to learn how to file our taxes or anything.[5] We were just tossed into the deep end, and we had to swim against the current.

I had my first job at fourteen years old, washing dishes for a retirement home. Minimum wage. But this was 1994 money, and it was enough for a fourteen-year-old kid. I was excited about that first paycheck. Then I looked at the pay stub and saw how much they had withheld. Why so much for Social Security? What are Municipal taxes? So many random deductions I did not understand.[xiii] I remember thinking what a ripoff.[6] I thought I am only fourteen; I can't even vote yet, isn't this taxation without representation?

The hits kept coming. Later, when I deposited my check at the ATM. When I wanted my *own* cash back *out* of my account, there was a fee associated with that.[xiv] I was paying a toll to access my money. Even at fourteen, something about that felt fucky.

A few years later, I had my first experience with direct deposit. No more paper checks. No more physically depositing anything. Now the money just appeared in my account. Like magic. Numbers that materialized from nowhere. I never touched it. It went from someone else's computer to my computer, and I still had to pay a fee to turn it back into paper at the ATM.

The abstraction was there from the start. At fourteen, I was trading labor for paper, trading paper for different numbers, then paying for the privilege of trading those numbers back into paper. By nineteen, the paper was gone entirely. Just numbers moving to other numbers.

---

4. Probably financed.

5. They sure as shit made sure we knew how to Square Dance though.

6. We all remember our first encounter with FICA. No one ever told us who he is and why he gets our money.

This was the very tail end of the 90's. The Cyberage was just getting started.

It was also around this time that I started asking questions I probably should not have been asking. In the military, I would get paid and see the tax deductions. I wondered why government employees have to pay income taxes. If the Empire prints its own money, why does it need mine? That led me down a rabbit hole into the Federal Reserve, where I discovered that our tax money does not actually go directly to the government and instead routes back through the Federal Reserve.[xv] When the government wants something, it writes an IOU and borrows the money. Basically, a bunch of assholes met on Jekyll Island in Georgia and decided to collectively take all the money.[xvi] They presented the Map of the Map.

That was my first actual glimpse of the game. The realization that the people running the system were also making up the rules as they went. Nobody seemed to question it. In fact, questioning it was frowned upon.

Cocaine

The biggest epiphany about money, the one that cracked the whole thing open for me, came while snorting cocaine at a rave. Seekers find wisdom in the most unexpected of places.

Somewhere along the line someone wanted to sniff some blow, and I was all about it. They passed me a rolled-up twenty-dollar bill. I was standing there chatting away and waiting for the drip. Thinking, ugh, here it comes. That was the cycle though; you are up and talkative for about twenty minutes. Then you come down and you want more. So you do another line and keep pushing. Then another. Then another. The cycle does not stop until the supply runs out.

I looked at the twenty and realized my paycheck worked the same way.

You get paid. The money hits your account. You are up and about, doing things, paying bills, buying groceries, going places. Then the money runs down and you come down with it. You slow down. You stay home. You wait. You wait for the next payday the way you wait for the next line. Then it hits and you are up again.[7]

Cocaine was the fuel for the party. Money was the fuel of life.

---

7. Look I was a 19 year old drug addict, saving was not on my agenda. Don't judge.

Same mechanism. Same cycle.[xvii]

The bigger your tank, the more fuel you can carry, and the farther you can go. The bigger your bag, the longer you can party. The faster you go, the more fuel you burn. Spending fast burns more money. If you spend slowly, it lasts longer. If you drive slowly, you can drive for longer. It maps perfectly because it has the same dynamic.

The Empire has a vested interest in fuel rationing. They know that if everyone needs fuel all the time, most people will stay fairly close to home. Cannot drive far on a quarter tank. If you have a lot of fuel, you can go further. If you have enough, you can start giving other people fuel to run errands for you, to do tasks for you. Employees.

But the Empire does not want anyone refining their own fuel. And certainly not counterfeit fuel. There are very strict guidelines on what kind of fuel you can use. They keep careful track of how much fuel you receive from your employers and how much you owe them at every step of your journey. The Empire always has a siphon to your fuel tank.

The Illusion of Winning

Many years later, I worked as a table games dealer at a casino. That gave me an entirely new perspective on money.

The entire point of a casino is to insulate you from money. This sounds counterintuitive, but bear with me here. They want actual cash out of sight as quickly as possible. You cannot bet cash at most tables. Trade your fiat for house money, the *cheques*, those pretty colored discs in various denominations. You trade one map for another map, then use that second map to gamble with. Every casino issues its own in-house "currency". In fact, we would call it "foreign money" if someone tried to play with another casino's *cheques*.

It is all part of the Map they are selling. They need you to buy into the illusion of winning. They make it seem very glamorous, too. Decorations and bright lights, certified swank in every direction. Scantily clad cocktail servers scurry by, and piped-in music is always present. Maximum distraction while they rob you.

The casino builds every game so that the math favors the house. The payouts look generous until you count the actual odds. The gap between what they pay you and what the real probability is the house edge. There is *always* an edge. It is accounted for in every single game on the floor. The casino does not need you to lose every hand. They just need the math to work over time. Selling you the illusion that this time, this spin, this hand, maybe you beat the odds, is how the entire industry is built.

It is a Map. An illusion. The Territory always wins.

Cyberspace has taken over completely in casinos. In fact, there are only two pure games left: roulette and craps. These are the only games left in the casino that do not use computers. No auto shufflers. No electronic anything. I'm not saying that an auto-shuffler influences a game; I am just saying that it's weird how digitized things have become. They would rather have a machine touch the cards rather than a dealer.

Maybe contact is a part of it. The last pure games have an odd relationship with touching the medium of the game. In craps, the dealers will never touch the dice. They push them to the player with a stick. In roulette, the players never touch the ball. Only the *croupier*.[8] There is something almost sacred about that. The last analog holdouts in a digital empire. Oh, and here is a fun fact. If you add up all the numbers on the roulette wheel, one through thirty-six, the sum is 666.[xviii] Make of that what you will.

The Virtual Reality Blues are everywhere in a casino. People losing their entire paycheck in seconds. The gambler's lament of "unbelievable" when they lose. Yes it's believable, you lost the second you sat at the table.

One of the more memorable ones was a player at the table next to me who won a massive bet on three-card poker, a popular "carnival game" with the illusion of really high payouts and incredibly shitty odds. This guy, however, hit big, and I recall the total payout was around forty thousand dollars. He was ecstatic. Life-changing money. The whole floor buzzed with excitement.

Naturally, the Empire arrived with that siphon. Any wins over $5,000 were subject to a spot audit by the state, and it turns out Mr. Big Winner owed back child support.[xix] His big win became his baby mama's win because I believe she got all of it. Every cent.

He was still at the table when they informed him. Now I have seen some crash-outs in my life, but this one was easily top 3. Too bad I couldn't have my phone on me because the video was World Star Quality. This man lost his jackpot along with losing

---

8. It sounds fancy but it's just a title. The bar for entry is horribly low to work at table. The only requirements are you have to be good at math and bad decisions.

his marbles, his shit, his mind, his temper, his composure, and his freedom. I mean he tried to flip the gaming table over. It was bolted to the floor, but wow, what an effort! Security eventually got him out of there.

That is the Map colliding with the Territory. The *cheques* were right there. He had won. In his mind, he already imagined what he would do with these winnings. The Empire system had the first claim. I did not feel sorry for him either; why would he be gambling when he owed over $40k in child support? What a lesson though, the house always wins, even when you beat the house.

Latent Luck

The casino at least made you drive there, park, walk in, stand at a cage, hand a person cash, and receive *cheques*. Alternatively, you could buy in at a table and bypass the cage entirely. Both paths required effort, though; there is a degree of friction involved. Physical steps between you and your money disappearing. Each step offered a chance to reconsider.

Cyberspace gives us a casino right in the palm of your hand. These apps have removed every single one of those steps. You're in bed. You're on the toilet. You're scrolling at 2am. Three taps link your bank account to DraftKings or FanDuel or whatever. The money leaves your account and enters the game at the speed of a thumb swipe. Same slot machine dopamine shot with variable-ratio reinforcement. Only this time there's zero friction between the impulse and the action.

We now experience zero latency between Fucking Around and Finding Out. The Fuck Up rate has gone through the roof. Cyberspace didn't invent gambling; it just removed the physical Territory traversing from the transaction. You never touch the money. You never hand it to anyone. You never feel it leave. You just watch numbers get smaller on a screen.

This goes way beyond gambling apps. We have micro-transactions too. The Empire figured out that people will say no to a $60 purchase but yes to a $0.99 purchase sixty times. Death by a thousand taps. Before you know it, you have wasted your day and your paycheck and you are still sitting in the bathroom.

The abstraction isn't just gold to paper to digital. Cyberspace added a pivotal layer of abstraction. A digital layer, in fact, a *frictionless* digital layer. The feed makes spending as compulsive as scrolling. The same dopamine farming in the same loop. Chasing the illusion of a win.

24,974

Chasing the illusion expands way beyond an app or a gaming floor. The lottery is one of my favorites. Especially when the jackpots get into the billion range and the line at the Circle K stretches to the door with gleaming-eyed hopeful players. The lottery is the Empire's pressure valve.

The Relative Truth is you could be a winner. In fact, the Absolute Truth is that someone is going to win *somewhere*. Will that someone be you, though? I ran the numbers once on the Powerball. If you played three times a week, every week, for a seventy-five year lifespan, it would take you roughly twenty-four thousand nine hundred and seventy-four lifetimes to hit the jackpot.[xx]

Almost 25,000 lifetimes.[9]

Sure, you are going to beat those odds.

The lottery exists because people need a cheap dream. A few dollars for the fantasy of escape. For the ability to say, just for a moment, *what if?* What would I do with all that money?

It is a Map of a Map of a Map. You are buying a ticket, which represents a chance, which represents potential money, which represents potential value, which you will almost certainly never see. The dream is real. The hope is genuine. That minor hit of possibility is enough to keep people playing,

---

9. Wait! Legally you can't play until 18, so cut those first 18 years. Now it's closer to 33,000 lifetimes. Still feeling lucky?

Might is Right

The casino is not the only place the Empire sells illusions. They need to enforce that illusion. It begins in the recruiting office.

The military sells you the Map of serving your nation as an act of nobility. They dress it up nicely in a snappy uniform and the mantra of Honor, Courage, and Commitment. They make it seem like the best opportunity in the world. You get to travel everywhere, all the ladies are going to want to fuck you, they do whatever they can to stroke that ego. Plus, they are going to pay for your college too! Just sign your name right here at the bottom of the Map.

Then a few months later you are standing on those yellow footprints in the Territory and regretting your life decisions. Interestingly, they sure love the position of Attention. Weird. Everywhere I see the Empire's Attention fetish.

The last thing that a recruiter wants you doing is walking into another branch's office next door. All of them have quotas to fill, and you are just a number.[xxi] So they add the fluff. What they do not tell you is that GI Bill pays the same no matter which branch you join. They also leave out the part where you have to pay into the GI Bill. They dock your pay by the initial $1,200. The Empire is always transactional and cannot give without taking.[xxii]

When I really thought about it, I realized that is probably one of the main reasons we do not have free university education in America. If college were free, there would be far less incentive to enlist. The Empire needs the fuel tank kept low. They need the illusion of scarcity. They have made university so expensive that not everyone can afford it, and many who initially cannot have to take on major debt via student loans just to attend.[xxiii] Many high school graduates cannot do that and the military appears to be an attractive alternative. They dangle the GI Bill as the plumpest carrot. Risk your life and we will educate you for free.

Many other nations treat education and military service differently. Take Greece, for example. Free or affordable university for anyone who wants to attend. Greece also has a conscript army, requiring one year of mandatory military service for all males.[xxiv] The deal is straightforward: Greece educates its citizens, and its citizens serve for a year. No dangling carrot is needed because the baseline needs are already satisfied. When education is accessible, service is a civic duty. When education is a luxury, the Empire can sell service as the price of admission. Sadly, we live in the American Empire and not the Greek one.

The Empire does not require patriotism for enlistment. They just need you thirsty enough. Thirsty enough to risk your life. Thirsty enough to kill who and when they tell you to. Thirsty enough that a promise of future education, a map of a map, is enough to sign on the dotted line. Thirsty enough to sacrifice the prime time of your young adulthood to their ends. The Map directing Action. The Empire needs its incentive architecture to keep the money loop relevant.[xxv]

The GI Bill is an incentive to enlist because the *entire money illusion* requires an absurdly powerful military. The US Dollar is the world's reserve currency.[xxvi] This is an agreement that is backed by force. Everyone agrees the USD is the reserve currency because they have no other choice. It is like being in the room with a loud, brash bully who insists everyone plays the game he wants to play. If you want to sit out, that is fine, but if you start your own game, he will come and flip over your table. He is kind of an asshole and bigger than anyone else in the room, so no one really wants to mess with him. The enlistment feeds the military, which enforces the dollar's position as the world's reserve currency. The Empire doesn't just need soldiers to fight wars. It needs soldiers to maintain the agreement that makes the money work.

The petrodollar. Bretton Woods. Global oil trading occurs in dollars because the U.S. military guarantees it, not because the dollar is backed by anything real like gold.[xxvii] The Empire always has its finger in the fuel tank. Both your paycheck and the geopolitical level. The Empire controls both the Absolute fuel (oil) and the Relative fuel (dollars) and uses the military to enforce both.

It's another hijack loop. The money funds the military. The military enforces the money. The citizen is fuel for both. Everyone agrees that this is the way things are.

Micro Collapse

What happens if the agreement breaks?

In February 2013, a Carnival cruise ship, the Triumph, lost power and drifted for days. All the amenities ceased working; there was no electricity, no flushable toilets, zero air conditioning, and no way to keep food cold. They called it the poop cruise because the plumbing stopped working too. It was a shitty situation.[xxviii]

What fascinated me was how quickly the social order broke down.

Within hours, passengers had turned tribal. The shift from 'customer' to 'survivor' happened almost instantly. 4,200 people on that ship and nobody organized a collective response. Instead, they fragmented. Small groups began hoarding. They were clearing entire trays of food, grabbing dozens of water bottles, in a massive competition for the remaining resources. They needed them all right now, because they had to make sure nobody else got them first. Finders keepers. People dragged mattresses and luggage onto the deck and walled off sections as if it were their sovereign Territory. If your group had a breezy spot, that was yours now. It was a Wild West-style land grab.

Since the toilets had stopped working, people started tossing their filled bio-hazard bags over the railing or onto lower decks. Anything to get it away from *their* Territory. Civic duty and even common decency evaporated the second the plumbing did.

No one sharing. Everyone defending their little enclaves. By the time the tugboats showed up, it wasn't a ship full of passengers anymore. They formed competing tribes on the ship, all waiting for individual rescue from a disaster they'd been forced to share.

Money was worthless. Credit cards were worthless. You could have had a billion dollars in your account, and it would not have bought you a bottle of water on that ship.

Imagine that at scale.

We caught a glimpse during COVID.[xxix] Disruptions to supply chains caused everyone to hoard toilet paper and canned food. People turned feral over hand sanitizer. That was just a hiccup. A few weeks of uncertainty. The power never went out. The banks never closed. The system held.

Yet we peeked at what's underneath.

There is a saying that any population is three meals away from anarchy.[xxx]

When the collapse happens, considering the structure of this system, it appears to be only a matter of time; what will survive? Your credentials will not help you. Your corner office won't matter. Your stock portfolio, the retirement account, and the digits in the database will all vanish as soon as the lights go out.

What survives is Territory. Actual value. The stuff you cannot print.

Water. Clean drinking water. Food. No one will care about your ability to buy food. Value will be your ability to grow it, raise it, hunt it, preserve it. Medicine. Skills. Tools. Shelter. Community.

Make no mistake, it will be Lebanon Levi's finest hour.

For the rest of us, though, the very things we take for granted because we can shop at the Winn Dixie. The very things our ancestors had to work their asses off for every day to survive.

I see a lot of content making fun of third world goat herders in a condescending way.[10] When push comes to shove and the playing field is leveled, that goat herder is going to keep tending his flock.

We are going to die cold, wet, filthy, and starving.

Our laws are only as strong as our ability to enforce them. In the absence of law, when the illusion is gone and the threat of judicial punishment no longer hangs over anyone's head, what happens? You look at a police officer and instead of seeing someone who protects and serves; you see someone wearing body armor, carrying a pistol, handcuffs, and if they are near their cruiser, a shotgun and maybe an assault rifle.[xxxi]

As a gamer, I can tell you that is a lot of loot.

Note: I am NOT advocating violence. This is just an observation that in the event of true chaos; the Territory is going to end the Map. Every time.

No one can escape the money game. Not unless you are willing to go entirely feral, and even then, you would start from scratch since your only access to centuries of

---

10. First world social media regularly dunks on the Global South.

accumulated survival knowledge is through Cyberspace. Sure, you can homestead or go off-grid in some other fashion, but the Empire will track you down. They always do.

The money Map is not going away. Not in my lifetime. Probably not in yours.

We can treat it like a game. Money is a game to capture and direct your Attention. A useful fiction that makes complex societies possible. A Map of Maps and never the Territory.

Money is just water. It flows, it pools, it freezes, it evaporates. The banks direct the current. Yet underneath the current, underneath the abstraction, underneath Thug's shiny rock and the paper that represented it and the numbers that replaced the paper and the bets placed on the numbers, there is nothing.[xxxii] Yet we drink the illusion anyway; sometimes we sip, sometimes we chug, sometimes we spill it all over ourselves, and we will always come back for more.

After all, money makes the world go round.

Movement 7

Virtual Virtue

Virtue signaling is far less demanding, and far less constructive, than virtue itself. —
Susan Harmeling

There's an old expression, "bringing home the bacon," rooted in the 12th century Dunmow Flitch Trials in Essex, England. The Empire[1] instituted the Trials with the clear incentive of promoting and regulating marital stability within the community. By dangling a rare, valuable prize, a flitch of bacon, a luxury for common folk, the priory encouraged couples to strive for pious, harmonious unions that aligned with Christian teachings on obedience, forgiveness, and lifelong devotion.[2] Stable marriages meant fewer public scandals, disputes, or regrets that would otherwise annoy priests. The Trials worked too. A tangible and tasty reward for exemplary behavior. In an era where marriage was both sacrament and social contract, this created a powerful incentive structure: prove your virtue publicly, and the Empire would validate and celebrate it. Originally, the Church intended the Trials as a genuine test of marital virtue and piety, rewarding couples who could prove unbroken harmony and devotion for a year and a day.[i]

The Trials were open to any married couple (not just newlyweds). So anyone could claim the prize after that year-and-a-day benchmark. The campaign pushed widespread motivation for performance; anyone could step forward, but only if they could convincingly project flawless harmony without a hint of hidden squabbles. Naturally, humans are

---

1. Here wearing the robes of medieval Catholic authority.

2. Or at least convincingly demonstrate.

going to human, and this quickly ballooned into a full-blown caper. If they sold the illusion convincingly enough, that bacon was all theirs.

What started in piety quickly became a spectacle. They paraded the winners through town in a ceremonial procession, often holding them shoulder-high in the ornate Flitch Chair, and decorated the bacon itself like a festival float. They adorned the meat with ribbons, flowers, and mock orange blossoms, borne aloft on a pole ahead of them for all to gawk at.[3] It was theater, complete with public validation from the church. Eight hundred years before Instagram, the premise was identical: project a flawless Virtual Reality of purity and harmony, get it rubber-stamped by the powers that be, and reap the rewards. As long as you buried your disagreements deep enough and kept your bickering quiet enough to fool the jurists and neighbors, they would celebrate you with that bacon prize.

What an opportunity to dunk on your neighbors.

Couples weren't perfect; they just performed the part masterfully, hiding the cracks to earn the spectacle. We see the same play every day on Facebook and other social media: the humblebrag posts of accomplishments, virtue flexes, and curated highlight reels, validated by likes, comments, and shares piling up like digital bacon. No parade is necessary, as the feedback section accumulates admiration points, satisfying that ancient urge to be envied and admired.

There has always been some version of seeking outside validation and "good boy points" to gain prestige over one another. This ego-driven thirst for validation is, in fact, not a result of Cyberspace Psychosis. It is, however, greatly enhanced by it. The human urge for recognition is so deep, it provides the perfect soil for the Cyberspace Psychosis to bloom in.

Enter the digital age. In the 1980s, the phrase was "keeping up with the Joneses." Your neighbor bought a new car, so you needed one. They stained their deck; you'd better build one. Their kids sported the new Nike Air Jordans, and you had to ensure your children wore them as well to avoid ridicule. The competition to have the newest, brightest toy was in full swing. The Cold War was ending, and a new arms race was just starting. A race of suburban respectability where dominance was measured in riding mowers and appliances instead of missiles. Who could out-consume the others? Cyberspace opened an entirely new dimension.

---

3. The Real Housewives of Dunmow wasn't a thing yet so they had to make do.

Social media means *virtual* pork. You can post pictures of your family trip to Europe and harvest those envy points with no one verifying you actually went. The comment section provides instant validation. The emojis, words of support, congratulations, whether genuine or not, pile up nicely. The performance that had happened over the back fence now happens at the speed of light, to an audience of thousands.

The concept of "fake it till you make it" has achieved unprecedented power in the digital realm.

There are countless ways to work angles in photos, apply filters, or engage in outright fakery. With a green screen and rudimentary editing skills, anyone can post photos of a world tour that realistically took five minutes to shoot, and they can do it from their bathroom. I've seen someone use a toilet seat held up to their television to simulate an airplane window. They played a YouTube video of clouds from a plane, held up the toilet seat, took a selfie, and posted it to Instagram like the jet-setting hot shot they wished they were.

Now, with advances in AI-assisted video creation, this trend is only speeding up. The tools for constructing elaborate fictions about your life are becoming trivially easy to use. No one has to fake a year and a day of marital bliss for bacon anymore. Anyone can craft a Virtual wifey and post photos and videos of marital bliss on any platform.

Digital Ego Sham-Wow™

Classical narcissists are obsessed with themselves and therefore obsessed with other people's opinions of them. They want you to think about them as much as they think about themselves. They want to curate and cultivate a feeling of mutual captivation. The digital narcissist is like an ego Sham-Wow™, trying to soak up every drop of available Attention.[4] A resource that we know is in high demand and scant supply.

We already know everything just has to be sensationalized, dramatized, and blown out of proportion. The same degree of sensationalism that Legacy Media injects to inflate a mundane news story on a macro scale, we are seeing play out with influencer culture on a micro-scale. Dramatizing the banal because of Attention addiction. The competition for this precious resource is fierce. Hence the magnetic virtue of "click bait" and "engagement farming." We see "thirst traps" and "rage bait" scattered all over social media like potholes

---

4. Billy Mays, may he Rest in Peace, was an Absolute master of commanding Attention.

on the information superhighway. Everything and everyone is grasping for the Attention they crave. Attention is the lifeblood of The Psychosis.

This need is absolutely pervasive, even on short-form platforms like TikTok or YouTube Shorts. Some mundane activity plays on screen with captions like "wait for it" or "watch until the end". If they can keep your Attention past a certain threshold, the algorithm rewards them with better placement. So the idea is to craft content to keep your Attention firmly on the screen with a hook. It has to be intriguing, like *"if ghosts aren't real explain this"*, then you watch 30 seconds of someone's back deck until finally their dog trots past wearing a white sheet over its head.

The reveal is almost always both amusing and spectacularly underwhelming at the same time.

In the early 2010s, Cyberspace had already developed slang for this appetite for Attention: being "extra." Being "thirsty." Thirsty for that Attention. The feed is full of people posting the only assets they believe they have: their curated image, their drama, their simulated and astounding life, to extract validation from strangers. The more extra and over the top you can appear, the more people will want to see what shenanigans you are up to. The concept of the streamer was born.

Twitch has turned this into a lifestyle. Streamers broadcasting their entire existence, creating a 24/7 reality show about their lives. What used to be a chunk of pork wrapped in ribbon has metastasized into an endless content mine. Some of them are actually successful at it, and of course they flaunt that success mercilessly, because being envied is like crack for the narcissist. Each trying to outdo the other for the maximum number of followers. Make no mistake, it is a contest, too. They dislike sharing the spotlight.

They covet their subscribers, called *subs*[5], who admire them so thoroughly they'll toss their entire paycheck at their digital idols. Tipping thousands of dollars, buying them lavish gifts, bankrolling entire lifestyles for what are essentially pixels on a screen. They have entire fan bases dedicated to the stream.

And it works.

---

5. Basically submissives or pay piggies.

Many streamers earn a handsome living just by living out their lives for engagement. It happens often enough that the climbers; the ones emulating and trying the same thing, have something to aspire to. If *that* person can make it, so can I.

A 2019 Harris Poll commissioned by LEGO™ surveyed 3,000 children aged 8–12 (that prime tween demographic) and found that 29% of US kids wanted to be a YouTuber/vlogger as their future profession. In comparison, only 11% aspired to be an astronaut.[ii] The performance economy has become so pervasive that elementary schoolers now want to emulate MrBeast more than Neil Armstrong. This is a massive cultural shift from previous generations. A significant symptom of Cyberspace Psychosis.

Gen Z[6] is the first generation to come of age in a world where Cyberspace Psychosis was already rampant and inescapable. Born after the internet had become household infrastructure, social life had already migrated online, and smartphones were in hand by early childhood. Conversely, Millennials[7] grew up during the mass digitization transition and still carry clear, embodied memories of analog childhood like dial-up tones and landline phones, VHS tapes, playing outside until dark, physical libraries, and a world without constant connectivity.

Gen Z has no such pre-digital baseline. For them, the screen, the feed, the performative self, and the attention economy were their standard reality from day one. The Psychosis was waiting for them as they arrived. This makes the 2019 LEGO/Harris Poll results even more telling: late Gen Z tweens already prioritized emulating internet personalities because the performance economy was simply their native environment. So instead of admiring traditional role models, they adore larger-than-life internet celebrities, who are famous for being famous. Every aspect is a show, and for show.

Having character vs. Being a Character

What does it mean to have character? My favorite definition: character is how you treat someone who can do nothing for you. If you mistreat them, there are no consequences. If you treat them well, there are no benefits. There is no audience, algorithm, or comment section to critique the interaction. Just real human moments with another human. Those are the junctures that reveal character or its absence.

---

6. Born roughly 1997–2012.

7. Born roughly 1981–1996.

Being a Character is something else entirely. We call someone "a Character" when they have a memorable and often larger-than-life personality, one that makes them stick in memory. It's about being remarkable, meaning worth remarking upon. And you will. Meeting a Character is always an experience that you will talk about afterwards. Sometimes people fondly refer to a character, saying, "Oh, Uncle Grimm is a Character," because of his affable, humorous personality. People sometimes regard a Character unfavorably, referring to them as "too much" or even obnoxious. The point is that a Character is someone who makes an impression.

Social media blurs these lines catastrophically.

People want to *have* character while *being* a Character. They want both virtue and validation. It's about the brand, the personality, and the image being projected. They want to be genuinely good and want others to see them being good. MrBeast is the paradigmatic example, a larger-than-life social media personality who makes a spectacle of generosity. Granted, he performs quite a bit of philanthropy: through Beast Philanthropy he has given away over $300 million worth of food[8], funded 2,000 prosthetics, 100 cleft palate surgeries, and raised over $41 million in 2025 alone via #TeamWater to deliver clean water to 2 million people for decades.[iii]

This sounds amazing, and its design truly emphasizes the generous spirit. It is a Relative Truth of generosity. The Absolute Truth is that $300 million didn't just fall from the sky. That money is profit from the Attention economy. Every well he digs, every lip he fixes, every prosthetic he funds is also content. A massive, algorithm-optimized spectacle that keeps the views, clicks, sponsorships, and merch flying. He has a website and a separate nonprofit for his work, quite virtuous. The nonprofit part especially. Meanwhile, he's hawking Feastables™ chocolate bars in the middle of the same videos that show him handing out houses. The good deed is real. The person who helped doesn't care about the motivation. That same motivation is also the business model: perform generosity at scale so the Attention machine keeps paying for the next act of generosity.

This is the perfect example of AAA hijack marketing in action: draw **Attention** to the good deed (viral spectacle), shape **Attitude** about the person ("*wow, he's a genuinely good guy*"), and drive **Action** from the audience (buy the Beast Burger™, knowing

---

8. About 42 million meals.

a portion of proceeds funds wells in Africa). It's a wonderful, beautifully engineered system. Nonprofit on the surface, very much for-profit on the back end. It works well.

Social media fuels the illusion that you can have both without cost. That you can perform virtue and possess it simultaneously. That the representation and the reality can be the same thing. Until it's not.

Even Mrbeast's carefully curated loop isn't immune to controversy. His 2023 video, "I Built 100 Wells in Africa" drew backlash for "white saviorism," the critique that a wealthy Western figure swooping in to "fix" problems in the Global South can reinforce stereotypes of helplessness and dependency, centering the giver's heroism over local agency or systemic change.[iv] Related accusations of "poverty porn" pointed to the emotional footage of suffering used to drive views and donations, which some felt exploited vulnerability for content.[9] Maintenance concerns also surfaced. Experts note many NGO wells in Africa fail within years because of a lack of long-term funding or community training, and critics predicted similar issues here, though MrBeast countered with proof of ongoing functionality.

It's a classic case of *no good deed going unpunished.* Deliver massive impact, in this case clean water for hundreds of thousands, and the spectacle invites scrutiny. As it should, any spectacle from an ideological stance will attract ideological push back, and questions about sustainability. Yet MrBeast remains an absolute Titan of a Character. He turns the Attention economy into a force for genuine change.

Tis the Season

Let's talk about the Angel Tree.

Walmart puts up these Angel Trees during the holiday season. Christmas wish lists written by underprivileged children. A charitable act available to anyone shopping at Walmart with the means and the desire to help. Grab a list, buy the items, and drop them off. Walmart gets a sale. A kid who otherwise might get nothing receives something on Christmas morning. You get a warm, fuzzy feeling. Everyone wins.

Last holiday season, virtue-signaling influencers discovered the Angel Tree.

---

9. Poverty porn is nothing new. We all remember TV commercials featuring emaciated African children we were invited to "sponsor" for a mere 30 cents a day. Don't get me started on Sarah McLachlan.

They would swoop in with their stream rolling, grab a cart, select a list, and make elaborate videos of themselves walking through the store, generously filling the cart with toys and clothes. Look at me being generous. Look at my big heart. The content practically filmed itself.

Then they'd finish filming, abandon the cart in the aisle, and walk out without spending a dime.

The kid gets nothing. They fed the algorithm instead.

It was actually darkly hilarious to watch play out. The influencer would post their video and then a Walmart employee would make another video of the abandoned cart.[v] Social media drew the line between having character and being a Character with a Sharpie.

Performance virtue content is disgustingly common: people making a show of helping a homeless person, giving them a meal on the sidewalk, but making sure to photograph it. "Oh look how generous I am." Clearly, their ego is hungry too. They look at the engagement that generosity can generate, *à la* MrBeast or similar, and while they don't have the means or the willingness to actually help, they are very interested in the image of virtue.

Virtually virtuous. Cyberspace calls it Virtue Signaling. Performative morality, grandstanding where the display matters more than the substance. It's the difference between quietly doing actual virtuous work versus loudly advertising moral superiority for likes, retweets, clout, or tribal points.

The Psychosis in fine form, offering us yet more spectacle.

Virtual virtue is like trying to sustain a fire with newspaper. It burns brightly; you'll definitely get someone's Attention. It burns out quickly. It cannot sustain either flame or Attention. It won't keep you warm through the night either.

Authentic virtue is more like coal. It takes longer to get going. There's no immediate spectacle. No flash or bright flame to draw the eye. Once it catches, however, it has lasting warmth.

Where is the line? When I think back to times through my life where I have made a genuine positive impact, they were always completely unplanned. I was just in the right place at the right time, and just had the particular skill or ability to really help someone at the moment they needed it, and I did. Those moments happen, and they're amazing, and they fill something in you that no comment section ever could. They are authentic and genuine, and beautiful.

Most importantly, they are private. Also, they are over quickly, too quickly to pull out a camera phone and record it.

If I were someone who needed to be seen. Who required that validation, that celebration, that acknowledgment, it would be a different story. I would pull out my phone before rendering aid, get great footage of me doing the part, and would even try to get a superb segment of the gratitude afterwards. I would post it with a caption highlighting my contribution and would excitedly post it. Thus cheapening the moment, and instead of coal, I am torching a metaphorical newspaper.

Instead of contentment and a full heart, I'd be monitoring the engagement metrics, focused on how many people witnessed my goodness. The deed itself wouldn't fulfill me. Those "atta boys" would be the fuel. And they burn fast.

There's a joke in recovery circles about an AA convention. The old-timers, those with 20-plus years of sobriety, got together and decided that a certain member among them was the most humble. Humility being an admirable virtue, they picked the humblest person out of hundreds and even awarded him a badge that said MOST HUMBLE.

Then he pinned the badge to his chest and they promptly took it away from him.

Formula One

In October 2025, the federal government shut down for 43 days. They suspended SNAP benefits, the monthly food assistance that over 40 million Americans depend on, for the first time in the program's 60-year history. Food banks received an overwhelming number of requests. The charitable food sector was already warning it couldn't fill the gap. For every meal a food bank provides, SNAP provides nine. The math doesn't work.

So Nikalie Monroe, an Army veteran and drug addiction counselor from Somerset, Kentucky, performed a legendary social experiment. She tested what people have done for centuries when the government fails them: she turned to the church. She called over 42 churches and temples across the country, playing the role of a single mother in crisis.[vi] She concocted an amazing sob story. "My baby hadn't eaten in a day," she said. Her request was simple: would the church be willing to help by buying her a small can of baby formula? For further dramatic effect, she even played audio of a crying baby in the background.

Unsurprisingly, the overwhelming majority of churches denied her. In fact, 79% said no, giving various excuses, deflections, and forms of "we can't help you." Rejections ranged from "we don't do that" to versions of "we only help our members" to "we are not a food bank, try there." Some hung up, others required paperwork or membership, and a notable few mega-churches outright dismissed her.

Two mega-churches in particular stood out for their rejections. When Monroe called Dream City Church in Phoenix, Arizona, a mega-church formerly attended by the late media personality Charlie Kirk, the representative sent her to voicemail or referred her elsewhere without immediate help. This prompted widespread online criticism for the hypocrisy, given the church's public emphasis on caring for the poor. Similarly, Lakewood Church in Houston, Texas, the church of celebrity pastor Joel Osteen, told her any help would require a formal application through their benevolence ministry and could take "a couple days to weeks" for approval, leading to backlash over the delay for an urgent need.

Ironically, when she called the Islamic Center of Charlotte in North Carolina, the only question they asked was: "What kind of formula do you need?" For them, there was no question of whether they would help. It was already a given that they would. The only relevant information was the specifics.

Another notable yes came from a small church in Appalachia: Heritage Hope Church of God in Somerset, Kentucky. Pastor Johnny Dunbar responded immediately, "We can do this. Any flavor?" The church later received a surge of donations[10] because of the positive exposure.

She posted the results as a series of videos on TikTok. They went viral, causing embarrassment for many churches.

Outrage fueled the backlash. Religious leaders scrambled: "Well, she was a liar. She's a deceiver. She tried to trick us." The real zealots applauded the receptionist who turned her away, claiming the Holy Spirit™ had granted them "divine discernment" in that moment. The ability to recognize that she was a scammer. Bishop Raymond W. Johnson of Living Faith Christian Center in Baton Rouge, Louisiana, even condemned Monroe

---

10. Notably a GoFundMe that raised over $95,000 for its food pantry and community outreach

from the pulpit as "evil," a "witch," a "heretic," and accused her of a "dirty deed" and having the "spirit of a witch." She received death threats, and some viewers expressed anger over the "no" responses, while others praised the "yeses" as inspiration to return to church.

In the end, Nikalie Monroe's simple test revealed far more than any sermon ever could: when a hungry baby knocked, 79% of America's churches looked the other way. The loudest voices on virtue, the ones quickest to claim moral authority and enjoy tax-exempt status, proved slowest to actually practice it.

No Entry

Speaking of Characters.

When Hurricane Harvey hit Houston in 2017, the hurricane forced thousands into displacement, leaving them desperate and searching for any safe refuge from the flooding.

Joel Osteen, pastor of Lakewood Church, one of the largest congregations in America, infamously kept his church doors closed. His massive facility, sitting high and dry while the city drowned, remained empty. The arena that seats 16,000 sat vacant while people slept in shelters, on highways, crouched in attics. Social media lit up with photos of the empty building contrasted against flooded streets. The backlash was immediate and brutal.[vii]

Osteen eventually opened the doors days later after public pressure, yet the initial refusal stuck. The damage had been done. Fast-forward to the 2025 baby formula test. When Nikalie Monroe called Lakewood Church asking for a single can of formula for a hungry infant, the response was a referral to the benevolence ministry and a promise that help could take "a couple days to weeks" to process. No urgency. No, "we'll figure it out." Just bureaucracy.

No one was really shocked.

The Territory had already revealed itself years earlier during Harvey. When the chips were down, when it actually cost something, space, resources, reputation, discomfort, the map of "we're here for you" cracked. The same church that fills stadiums with feel-good messages and sells books on abundance couldn't (or wouldn't) open its doors to the desperate in real time. Twice.

Joel Osteen is the quintessential TV preacher Character. The polished smile, the stadium-sized sermons, the endless stream of uplifting content, the brand built around positivism and prosperity. All virtual virtue. Dig into the prosperity gospel he preaches, that God rewards faith with material wealth, health, and success. You see the self-fulfilling triple-A loop, similar to MrBeast. Naturally, Osteen himself has prospered handsomely from it: His personal net worth, estimated at up to $100 million as of 2025, stems from best-selling books (millions of copies sold), speaking fees, and media deals, while he lives in a $10.5+ million Houston mansion (and has owned other high-value properties).[viii] He famously stopped taking a salary from Lakewood Church in 2005[11], instead relying on those external streams. Yet the church itself generates tens of millions annually in collections and media revenue.

This is Virtual Virtue perfected: the message promises abundance to followers, while the messenger reaps abundance from the message. The content is uplifting; the production is slick; the engagement is massive; the brand is lucrative. But when genuine need shows up at the door, flood victims in 2017, a hungry infant in 2025, they delay or deny help. The spectacle continues, but the substance is missing.

Sometimes the mask slips. And when it does, Cyberspace is sure to screenshot it.

Dissonance of Innocence

There is a crucial distinction between Cyberspace Psychosis and other forms of delusion.

Many individuals experiencing mental illness hold such profound convictions about their delusions that they rarely seek external confirmation. They've constructed an internal reality so real and immersive that they can live in it contentedly, regardless of what anyone else thinks. The imagination and the belief are in perfect alignment. They don't need you to agree. They're not monitoring the comment section. In fact, it's usually well-meaning outsiders or clinicians who spend vast effort trying to get such people to "see the light" and abandon their delusions. Personally, unless someone is a genuine danger to others, I say live and let live. If someone wants to believe they are the Time Person of the Year every day, then let them.[ix]

Cyberspace Psychosis expresses delusion differently.

---

11. Lee Iacocca did it first. Anyone else pulling this gimmick is a poseur.

External feedback is of great importance to the person suffering from it. They need other people to believe the illusion. They need followers to cheer it on, validate it, support it, and many times, monetize it. The streamer has income portals open for tips and donations. These range from "buy me a coffee" to Patreon to even just a CashApp link, with the implied request that the viewer donate accordingly. The entire operation depends on the audience buying what they're selling.

So they have the imagination, the curated illusion, the Map they want you to follow. They even have the hook to draw your Attention. Yet there's a dissonance, because underneath the mask, they know it's bullshit. They have a vested interest in everyone else believing it is true, even when they themselves do not. They don't want you to peek behind the curtain. They need you to see only the Virtual Reality they've constructed.

This creates enormous stress. The head can sustain the illusion for a time, but there's a shelf life. They know they are burning newspapers. And in their hearts, they know it's not sustainable.

The Map is not the Territory. And they know it. That's the Psychosis. Maintaining a fiction they themselves don't fully believe, because their entire identity depends on others believing it for them.

Remember those ocean liners marching in lockstep during COVID? Let's look at the crew when they thought the cameras were off.

Politicians at every level would appear on camera making solemn appeals: wear your mask, practice social distancing, don't gather in groups. The broadcast would end. Another camera, one they didn't know was still rolling, would catch them taking off their masks, gathering closely, behaving nothing like the map they'd just handed to the public. The Virtual Virtue was for the map. The actual behavior was the Territory.[x]

The irony is that those very secrets, the hidden Territory, make for the most interesting content. The same things people try to hide are the same things that capture the most Attention when exposed. Scandal sells. The gap between the Map and the Territory, when revealed, is endlessly enthralling to us.

Social media has also given us a weapon against hypocrisy.

Online, people are called out constantly. The Internet archives everything. Screenshots are forever. Someone's old tweets resurface years later, contradicting their current positions. The phrase "this aged like fine milk" exists specifically to mark those moments when someone's stated Map becomes obviously incompatible with the Territory of their actions. Those are moments of Absolute Truth. When the internet glimpses your actual Territory instead of the Map you're holding up to the camera, and the dissonance is too great, you're going to be put on blast.

"Life comes at you fast."

The Find-Out moment. The Virtual Reality Blues hitting in public, captured for all to behold.

The person cultivating an image of generosity gets caught abandoning the shopping cart. The prosperity gospel preacher gets caught with closed doors during the flood. The politician performing compliance gets caught flouting the rules they demanded others follow.

Cyberspace grants no absolution.

This is one of the few mechanisms keeping the Psychosis partially in check. The knowledge that revelation of the Territory could occur at any moment. That some other camera might be rolling. The constant possibility that your carefully constructed Map could be contradicted by evidence you can't control.

Cyberspace even has a name for this: **canceled**. Just like a long-running TV show or radio program suddenly yanked off the air. This phenomenon has gone so far as to give birth to the broader concept of cancel culture, which we will discuss more in depth in a later movement.

The performance of virtue has always been a social game, from medieval couples parading their flitch of bacon as proof of flawless harmony to modern influencers staging charity hauls for the likes. Bringing home the bacon was never about the provision or the marital bliss. It was a public flex, a way to earn envy points and church validation through a curated image of piety. Performative virtue thrives on this: the map you show the world, polished and perfect, hiding the flaws and cracks underneath.

In Cyberspace, this game escalates into Psychosis because the stakes are constant exposure. The Internet never forgets, and when the mask slips, whether in a flood, a formula call, or a forgotten camera, the Territory crashes through.

Digital Interface

The best time to call me is to text. — Anon

I can open my internet browser screen right now and pull up four live feeds from four corners of the world. At the same time. One showing a Savannah in Africa, with lions and zebras roaming about. The golden grass stretched far off to the horizon. Another shows a beach in New Zealand, waves rolling in, surfers waiting for the break. The beautiful sea stretching to a different horizon. A third window shows a street corner in Dublin, with people walking past a pub and someone smoking outside. The horizon obscured by buildings at the end of the alley, yet still impressive. A fourth window shows me a live cam of a New York City intersection: yellow cabs, pedestrians, the chaos of Manhattan in real time.

Four windows. Four continents. One moment in time right now, yet four points of view that are thousands of miles apart in Territory, yet the Map is beaming all of them onto my laptop screen simultaneously.

Very convincing images. We really are living in the future. These four pictures, these four live streams before me, attest to that. A picture, however, that is incomplete.

Sure, I can see the golden grasses swaying in the wind, but I cannot smell the hippo shit on the Savannah.

I can see the Pacific surf, but I can't feel the sand between my toes from the New Zealand feed.

I can see the people walking, but I can't hear the singing from inside the Dublin pub or fist-bump a random drunk on his way out.

I can watch the traffic back up on the street, but I can't walk along that New York street, can't feel the subway rumble beneath my feet, can't smell the hot dog cart on the corner.

It's all real. It's all happening. Yet none of it is actually happening *to me.*

We have installed a digital interface between ourselves and the world. A screen. A wall of glass and pixels that shows us everything and lets us touch nothing. Every section in this movement points to the same mechanism: the interface that promises connection while delivering observation. The Map projected onto a screen, mistaken for the Territory it depicts.

The Jetsons promised us video phones. Star Trek promised us communicators. Science fiction painted a future where distance would collapse, where we could see and hear anyone, anywhere, anytime.[i]

We got it. All of it and more. FaceTime, Zoom, Discord, Slack, WhatsApp. The communicator in your pocket does things Starfleet never imagined. Your smartphone accesses the sum of human knowledge, translates languages in real time, shows you live video from the other side of the planet, and you can even broadcast your own live video to contribute to the feed.

Technology has shrunk the relative distance between us to the size of a small screen.

And somehow we ended up lonelier than any generation before us.[ii]

The technology delivered exactly what it promised. The problem is that what it promised was never what we actually needed.

Death of Mystery

Someone asked me what the major difference was between experiencing an analogue childhood and a digital adulthood. What is the one thing that I really recall that we lost along the way? Sure, tech gives us a lot of advantages. We have convenience; we have eliminated latency and curated variety. However, if I had to pick the one thing that disappeared, maybe the one thing that went so quietly we never noticed it was gone until it was too late.

Anticipation.

Anticipation is largely a thing of the past. And what we have these days is but a shell of how it used to be. Remember waiting for your song on the radio?[iii] You'd sit there, finger hovering over the record button on your tape deck, waiting through songs you didn't want, through DJ chatter, through commercials, all for that moment when the opening notes finally hit. You would hit record and finally have a copy of whatever hit you were into. The DJ would *always* start talking before the song ended, stepping on the outro you wanted to capture clean.[1]

That wait was part of the experience. The anticipation was its own pleasure.

Now anyone can listen to basically any song ever recorded, instantly, without effort. Spotify, Apple Music, YouTube, the entire catalog of human musical expression, it's all digital and available all the time. You don't have to wait anymore.

This convenience resulted in the loss of something precious.

Remember calling someone and not knowing if they were home? You'd dial, rotary phone, then push-button, then cordless, and it would ring and ring, and you genuinely didn't know if anyone would answer.[2] If they weren't home, you might not even be able to leave a message. Because not everyone owned an answering machine, and voice mail did not yet exist. You'd just...try again later. The mystery of where they were, what they were doing remained intact.[iv]

Now we have 24/7 access to everyone. You can see when they were last online. You can see when they've read your text message. The dots appear when they're typing. The developers have debugged the mystery out of the system.

Imagine the heyday of Barnum & Bailey, Ringling Brothers. The circus would travel by train to towns across America. Before they arrived, there would be announcements like subtle flyers posted around town or maybe newspaper advertisements. Something to drum up that anticipatory feeling, that butterfly-in-your-belly excitement.[v]

It would be the talk of the town. *The circus will be here in two weeks!*

---

1. I did this for UB40. It took me like 3 tries because I couldn't get the timing right. In fact the first time the tape I was recording on ended up running out of space after about 45 seconds. I'm still salty.

2. Remember how amazed you were the first time you used a cordless phone?

People would plan their lives around it. "We can't go to the market that day; the circus will be here." It was an event. Novel. Genuine. You had to wait for it. You couldn't YouTube a video of last year's show. You couldn't do anything to rush it. You just had to remain on standby and feel the anticipation build. That anticipation was itself a pleasure. The waiting was part of the gift.

Does anyone even get that excited anymore? How could they? When we can have anything instantly, our capacity for anticipation atrophies. The muscle that used to stretch toward the future, wondering, hoping, imagining, has gone slack from disuse.

Somewhere we lost the sense of anticipatory magic everywhere. Christmas morning when you didn't know what was in the boxes. The last day of school, when summer stretched ahead like an unexplored country. The moment before you kissed someone for the first time.

That magic required not-knowing. It required a gap between wanting and having.[vi]

Cyberspace closed the gap. And in closing it, killed something we didn't know we needed.

Just Text Me

Just where was the threshold where the digital wall slid directly between us and the people we're supposedly talking to?

We used to hear each other's voices. That was the default. You picked up the phone, you dialed, and if someone was there, you talked. You heard their tone, their inflection, the brief pauses where they were thinking, the laughter you could share. The full capacity of human vocal communication, transmitted live, in real time.[vii]

Then, the text message arrived.

And for a lot of us, especially the introverts, it was a genuine relief. Crafting, proofreading, editing, and finally sending a response reduced the anxiety compared to a phone call. Phone calls are an obstacle for the AuDHD brain. Personally, I have to rehearse calls ahead of time. I keep a running conversation tree for how to handle tangents. If it goes wildly off script, I have to do damage control up to and including just hanging up. Texting eliminates this neurodivergent fueled complexity entirely.[viii]

We traded for that comfort: voice. Tone. Inflection. Nuance. Everything that tells you whether "fine" means *fine* or means *you're sleeping on the couch tonight*. We stripped all of that out. Then we invented tiny cartoon faces to put some of it back. Think about that. We had the full territory of human vocal communication, the richest, most nuanced signal we've ever developed, and we *chose* the map because it was more convenient. Then we realized the Map was missing critical information, so we built emojis. Prosthetic emotion. A yellow circle with eyes to replace what the human voice could have conveyed for free.[ix]

Text messaging used to be expensive. You could only get so many a month with your cell plan. After you used up your quota, they were about ten cents each, sometimes more. Texting was precious until it wasn't. Soon phone companies started rolling out unlimited plans. I got unlimited texting with one of my first cell phones, this old Kyocera that slid up to reveal a full QWERTY keyboard.[3] That was a "this is the future" moment. My brother's plan still capped his messages at 300 total when I got that phone. Sending and receiving.[x] So naturally, I waited until the start of his billing cycle and texted him: "300." Then "299." Then "298."[4]

The economics tell a story too. When texting cost money, you thought about what you were sending. You were economical. When it became unlimited, it became the default. And when it became the default, calling became the exception. Now a phone call from someone under 30 is practically a declaration of war.

Again, we circle back to the latency. Phone calls have that free back-and-forth. The rhythm of conversation, the natural flow, response in real time. Texting introduces waiting. You send a message and you sit there. The dots appear. Or they don't. And in that gap, your brain fills in the blanks. Cyberspace Psychosis loves to mimic neurodivergence in the average mind. For the ADHD brain especially, that gap is a playground for worst-case scenarios. *Did they see it? Are they ignoring me? Are they mad? Is this the thing that ends the friendship?* The brain writes a whole screenplay in the thirty seconds before they respond "lol ok."

Then there's being left on read. No response is still a response. Since we live in an age where everyone has access to everyone else 24/7, many people expect an instant reply.

---

3. That Kyocera was the greatest piece of technology I had ever owned up to that point. The QWERTY slide-up keyboard was back lit and everything.

4. He deserved it and still does. If I could do it again, I would.

They dislike being ignored. The silence itself becomes a message, and often the loudest one in the conversation.

Online culture bled into texting almost overnight. LOL, LMAO, the whole lexicon migrated from AIM and IRC chat rooms into our phones. ALL CAPS became yelling. Punctuation became emotional.[xi] There's even a generational marker in how you make a smiley face: the OGs do it :) and the younger ones do (: and somehow you can tell someone's entire digital upbringing from which direction their parenthesis faces.[xii]

The interface slid between us and our voices. And we let it. Because it was easier.

Information Post-Scarcity

We live in an age of information post-scarcity. Where once upon a time, if you wanted to learn something, you would have to travel, as in actually go outside, and head to the library or the learning annex or night school. You had to navigate the Dewey Decimal System and riffle through an extensive card catalog if you needed something specific. The process required effort. If you needed a quicker fix, there were usually encyclopedias handy, which were basically Wikipedia in several volumes. Information was scarce. You had to hunt for it, like any other resource. You had to be driven by a hunger, an appetite for knowledge.[xiii]

A crust of bread is a feast to a starving man. A sip of water is the sweetest feeling on a parched tongue. Scarcity creates value. Appetite requires emptiness.

Hardly anyone feels hungry anymore. We've been grazing all day.

Anyone can consume content seemingly endlessly. Scrolling, watching, clicking, listening, and sometimes you're scrolling on your phone while watching something on your TV. Screens upon screens. The algorithm serves us an infinite buffet, calibrated to your tastes, optimized to keep you eating. Yet it's not nourishment. It's the information equivalent of high-fructose corn syrup, engineered to trigger consumption without ever satisfying.

The doomscrolling is the perfect metaphor. Your thumb flips up, a microsecond of anticipatory excitement, three or four seconds of the next video, then flips again. The algorithm adjusts, trying to find what captures you. But until you settle on something, the content just cycles through. At the end of the day, you won't remember a fraction of what you consumed.[xiv]

This is content indigestion. Taking in too much to really understand, absorb, or enjoy. Drowning in information gluttony while starving for meaning.

An appetite for input that is never ever satiated. Our dopamine-starved brains are already reaching for the next helping before we have even finished chewing the one in front of us.

Our Post-Literate World

Where has this interface done the most damage?

It isn't that people *can't* read. Literacy rates haven't collapsed. People read text messages, tweets, captions, headlines, and memes. They can decode words on a page. They're not illiterate.

They just don't read anymore.

I first noticed it in 2002. I had this job with a shady company, going door to door selling magazine subscriptions. We would travel all over the country, set up in a hotel, go out and try to sell these things. I enjoyed talking with the people, but I have never been a sales guy. I hate sales. In any case, my time there involved daily invitations into people's homes. Naturally, I'm going to look around. I loved having a snapshot into people's lives.

A TV, usually with a massive DVD and VHS collection next to it, dominated almost every living room. Bookshelves full of films. No books. Movies. Home after home after home.

Around the same time, the bookstores started closing. Waldenbooks, gone. The independents, gone. The record shops like FYE and Sam Goody have gone. Amazon killed the bookstore. Netflix killed the video store. Spotify killed the record shop. One by one, every place where you went out into the world to find content, the place where you might actually talk to another human being about what you were looking for, shuttered. The interface replaced them.[xv]

Now we've moved to a culture where many people won't read the news article but will watch the YouTube video of the guy *talking about* the article. Why dig through a book when you can get the answer in a twenty-second search? Why read the article when someone will summarize it in ninety seconds on TikTok?[xvi]

Except that YouTube video is going to be a bunch of fluff. The creator wants you to like and subscribe and check out their merch section. They'll pad whatever the information is with filler. So you wade through a forty-five minute video to parse out thirty seconds of actually useful information. I don't have time for that. I would rather place my precious Attention elsewhere. I'm a reader. I can skim the material, grab what I need, and move on. Reading lets you control the pace. Video holds you hostage.

Sadly, I'm in the minority now.

In Game of Thrones, Tyrion Lannister is the smallest man in the room and the most dangerous. His brother Jaime sharpens his sword. Tyrion sharpens his mind with books. That resonated with me because it's exactly right. Reading builds the scene in your mind's eye. You read descriptions and construct the world internally. Your imagination does the heavy lifting. Watch the movie adaptation instead, and it's handed to you pre-built. The imagination muscle never fires.[xvii]

So what have we lost? Vocabulary, for one. I get chastised at work for using words like *chastised* because my boss doesn't know what it means and assumes I'm being a smart-ass. He'll tell me to stop "acting smart." Brother, I'm not acting. You wrote *your* instead of *you're* on the employee message board.

We've lost the capacity for sustained thought. The ability to hold a complex argument in your head, to follow a thread across paragraphs, to sit with an idea long enough to actually understand it. People are notorious interrupters right now. "I'm going to stop you right there," before you've even finished the thought. No one wants to listen. No one has the patience to entertain a complete idea.[xviii]

It's like digging a hundred little holes in your yard with a spoon to catch sips of rainwater, instead of digging one deep well. The deep well takes concentrated effort and sustained Attention. But a well can sustain your thirst for a long time. Books are wells. The internet gives you a spoon and a yard full of shallow holes.

TL;DR

Cyberspace has even created its own vocabulary for the death of Attention.

TL;DR: Too Long; Didn't Read. The passive-aggressive admission that your attention span shreds paragraphs into punishment.[xix]

Lengthy prose has no place in the Psychosis-infected mind.

So we get meme culture. A picture is worth a thousand words. Take that picture and add a couple of quirky phrases, and you have something that can say a lot while saying a little. Memes aren't new; "Loose Lips Sink Ships" was a meme on a wartime poster, and it worked brilliantly. The meme format is pure efficiency. It's not a problem. The problem is when the meme becomes the *only* mode. When a culture can consume compressed ideas but can no longer decompress them. When the TL;DR isn't just a preference, it's a limitation.[xx]

Here again we find the artificially induced ADHD front and center.[xxi] The feed trains your brain for novelty, for interruption, for the constant ping of something new. After enough exposure, the ability to sustain Attention on a single thing, whether a book, a conversation, or even a thought, degrades considerably. The willingness to put in any sustained mental effort is just unnecessary in an environment of easily digestible fifteen-second TikToks. We live in a world of distractions at every quarter, competing for a slice of that Attention.[5]

The Empire absolutely loves this. Short Attention spans mean more content consumed, more ads served, more products cycled through. The Empire adores your hobby graveyard. That's a lot of starter kits they can sell you.[xxii]

Out of these hundreds of videos, how much information do you actually retain? Scroll TikTok for several hours. How much of it can you recall the next morning? The content cycles through you like water through a sieve. You consumed hours of input and kept almost nothing. The interface delivered the content. Your brain never absorbed it.

Instant gratification, once achieved, becomes the only acceptable speed. Why would the mind be patient when it doesn't have to be? If you can't get what you want from one source, you just go to another. And another. And another.

The capacity for patience has all but disappeared because of the Psychosis.

Why *would* you wait? What kind of sucker waits?

Tribal Revival

When the comment sections opened the door to forums and niche websites, they opened the door for both exploration and validation.

The bikers found the biker forums. The Facebook Moms found the Facebook Mom groups. The conspiracy theorists found the conspiracy forums. The crypto bros found the crypto channels and so on. Every archetype the Psychosis created now had a place to congregate. A digital clubhouse with a velvet rope and a bouncer who only lets in people who already agree with you. Welcome to the echo chamber, we have snacks.

Water always seeks its own level. No matter where you go, in Cyberspace or in the real world, you're going to find your people. And at first, that was genuine Territory. For the outcasts, the weirdos, the niche hobbyists, the people whose interests didn't match anyone in their zip code, the internet was a revelation. You could find someone else who cared about the things you cared about. That mattered. That was a real connection, even through the interface.

My first favorite online community was GLP, God Like Productions. Super fringe. Conspiracies, alternative history, woo woo, tinfoil hat variety of schitzo lore.[xxiii] The fringe is anything but boring. There are people who are rabidly passionate about flat earth theory. Where else can you follow a debate between flat-earthers and hollow-earthers about UFOs? There are thousands of threads covering every topic imaginable and I was delighted by all of them. That curiosity is the exploration side. Territory-level engagement. You're there to learn, to wonder, to have your Map challenged.

The validation side is something else entirely.

The validation trap springs when the tribe stops being a place you explore and becomes a place that confirms. When the community stops challenging your map and starts reinforcing it. When the community doesn't debate dissent but deletes it.

What is the tolerance for dissent? How are contrary beliefs or opinions handled? Is the community capable of actually engaging with a different perspective, or do they simply ban, block, and silence anyone who speaks up?

Reddit is the poster child for opinion intolerance. The upvote/downvote system means anything that gets "downvoted to oblivion" is buried at the bottom of a discussion. Only consensus opinions survive. Dissenting voices don't get debated; they get perma-banned.

Moderators become petty tyrants. The HOA Karens of cyberspace, patrolling their own gated community. Their downvote system and intolerance of dissent make them almost hermetically sealed from the rest of the internet.[xxiv]

Conversely, you have 4chan, which claims to be the last bastion of free speech on the internet. 4chan allows users to post anything and is notorious for this. However, vicious contempt meets dissenting opinions from the baseline worldview.[xxv]

Both platforms are echo chambers. One silences through democracy. The other silences through ridicule. Different mechanisms, same result: deeper connections within the tribe, shallower connections between tribes. Bonded to the in-group, alienated from everyone else. The ongoing war between the two is proof that tribalism requires an out-group. In-group cohesion demands out-group differentiation. You can't know who you are unless you know who you're *not*.[xxvi]

We see it all the time in politics. My candidate is the right one; the other one and all their supporters can eat a bag of dicks. We see it in brand loyalty. Apple users think Android users should eat a bag of dicks. We see it everywhere the archetypes gather.

This tribal connection is so appealing that it has all but replaced genuine physical connection. You can sit up all night riffing with your besties on Discord. Yet you do not know your next-door neighbor's name. I've had the same neighbors for years.[6] I do not know who they are. I will not stand up here on a soapbox and pretend I'm above any of this. If you spot it, you've got it. I'm as deep in the Psychosis as anyone. The difference is that I know the interface is there. Whether I choose to look past, it is another matter.

Cyberspace has a contradictory nature: it builds a longer table and a higher wall at the same time.[xxvii]

The longer table: We can connect with anyone, anywhere. Language barriers are rapidly becoming obsolete. We can use Google Translate and AI-assisted glasses that generate real-time subtitles. Cyberspace has made it so that everyone can become Global Citizens. Someone in rural Kansas can collaborate with someone in Tokyo, can fall in love with someone in São Paulo, can build a community with people scattered across six continents, all from their desk chair.

---

6. I have never seen my neighbors bringing in groceries,

The higher wall: We're more compartmentalized than ever. Despite the lure of connection, tribalism has intensified. We retreat into our bubbles, our echo chambers, our algorithmically curated Virtual Realities. We find our social comfort zone and wall ourselves off from everyone else.

Humans are going to human. We've always been tribal. We've always formed groups and distinguished them from other groups. Cyberspace just gave this ancient impulse new infrastructure. Constant validation and 24/7 access to the echo chamber make the walls higher, especially when you never encounter a challenging perspective. The tribes are becoming more insular. The ability to even comprehend the other side atrophies. The walls end up so high we forget there is anything on the other side of them.

Date Night

I was out for dinner recently. At the next table, a couple sat across from each other. The man had his laptop fully open, watching videos. His girlfriend, or date, or wife, or side piece, or whoever she was, was sitting across from him on her phone.

I admire that level of commitment to the digital bubble.

They weren't fighting. They weren't miserable. They weren't even awkward about it. They just... weren't there. Present in the body, absent in every other way. Digital zombies, accounted for but not present. Directly across from each other, yet worlds apart.

Did they look unhappy? No, they looked numb. Neutral. Glassy-eyed, focused on their respective windows into Cyberspace.

Maybe that *is* their relationship. Parallel isolation, agreed upon. Parallel escapism, comfortable and familiar.[xxviii]

Which is more disturbing? If they're miserable and trapped, or if they're perfectly content?

I'm not sure I know the answer.

You see it at concerts now, too. Half the audience has their phones out, recording the show they paid to attend, watching the performance through a four-inch screen while the actual event happens ten feet in front of them. The interface inserted between the person and the experience. They're not *at* the concert. They're filming a concert for people who aren't at the concert.[xxix]

Brooklyn Bounce

This past fall, I visited New York City on a solo trip. My first time there, and I was all about it. Adventure in the world's capital.

One afternoon I was in Brooklyn Heights, at the Promenade at the end of Montague Street. It's an incredible spot. A wide walkway, benches everywhere, views of the Statue of Liberty, the harbor, and the Manhattan skyline spread out across the water. The absolutely stunning view transfixed me. I was just sitting there in the sun on a bench, taking in the late summer day, not too hot, beautiful breeze.[xxx]

On the next bench over, a woman walked up, looking at her phone. She sat down, stayed on her phone the entire time, then walked away still looking at it.

She never once looked up.

This beautiful day. This incredible view. Yet her Attention remained on her phone.

My Relative Truth in that moment is that I was a tourist. It was my first time visiting the Territory and seeing that view. It was novel and new and an amazing moment.

Her Relative Truth? She probably lives there. She could have walked through that park a thousand times. It was so mundane and stale to her that the Map in her hand was much more compelling.

Familiarity breeds contempt. Yet absence makes the heart grow fonder. Make it make sense.[xxxi]

Maybe that's part of it. Cyberspace is a bigger draw than real life because it provides relief from the humdrum. When you've wrung every drop of novelty from your physical surroundings, the phone offers somewhere else to be. A constant connection to novelty on demand.

Cured Connection

So where's the line? When does a virtual connection become a genuine connection?

I spent some of the best times of my life playing World of Warcraft back in 2009 and 2010. I was in an active guild, and we'd be on Ventrilo, before Discord was a thing, every day. These were people I had never met in real life. But it was still exceptional. Digital camaraderie playing WoW with randos on the internet.[xxxii]

It cured something I had struggled with. It addressed the isolation. But was it a connection?

There was always a digital wall. All the interaction was through a digital interface. Voice chat software and pixels on the screen. A wall between us. A mediation layer that they could never remove.

Was that a Map or a Territory? Relative Truth or Absolute Truth?

Maybe the answer is: it was authentic enough. Maybe the threshold is simply whether you decide the virtual connection is good enough for your needs. Maybe connection is as real as we decide it is.

Here's what I've come to believe:

Cyberspace can cure isolation. It cannot cure loneliness.

Isolation is about physical separation. Being physically cut off, unreachable, alone in space. Cyberspace absolutely fixes that. You can reach anyone, anywhere, anytime. You're never more than a few taps away from another human being.

Loneliness is something else. Loneliness is about the quality of presence, not the fact of contact. You can feel lonely in a room full of people. You can feel lonely in a marriage. You can feel lonely with a thousand followers hanging on your every post.[xxxiii]

Loneliness requires something the screen cannot transmit.

So, what is it? What makes presence *presence?*

It's not information. The screen transmits information perfectly. In fact, better than perfect. More data, higher resolution, more capacity than any in-person interaction.

It's not faces either. Video calls bring you face to face in exquisite detail. You can see every expression, every micro-movement. Zoom calls can show several faces Relatively present while Absolutely separated by vast distances.[xxxiv]

It's not voices. The audio is crisp, clear, and sometimes better than being in the same room with background noise.

And yet.

A computer monitor won't hug you back.

That's the diagnostic test for this movement. That's the question that reveals whether you're in the Map or the Territory.

You can't smell someone through a screen. You can't feel their hand on your shoulder. You can't sense the way the air in a room changes when someone you love walks into it. You can't share food from the same plate, can't feel the warmth radiating off another body, can't experience the vulnerability of being physically present with another consciousness.[xxxv]

The screen gives you everything except the thing that matters.

And the Psychosis convinces you that everything else is enough.

Disconnection is a choice. So is reconnection.

This is the part where I'm supposed to give you the escape hatch. The hopeful ending. The "here's what you do" moment.

And the truth is: the Territory is still out there. It hasn't gone anywhere. The park bench in Brooklyn Heights is still catching that breeze. The pub in Dublin is still full of drunk tourists. That hippo in Africa is still lurking in the grass.

There are meetups. Local groups. Community boards. Places where actual humans gather in actual space and actually talk to each other with their actual voices. The infrastructure for reconnection exists. The door is unlocked. It was never barred.

The trend remains. The closer we are in Cyberspace, the farther apart we are in the Territory. You can reach almost anyone on Earth with a few taps on a screen. At the same time, you cannot name your neighbor sleeping thirty feet from you on the other side of a wall.[xxxvi]

You can minimize any interface. It can be closed. You can set it face-down on a table at dinner. Your screen does not cement itself to your face. Your hands still work. Your legs still walk. Your voice still carries across a room without a cellular signal.

We still have Agency.

The Map can help you locate likely connections.

But connection itself can only happen in the Territory.

Terminal Uniqueness

When everyone's super, no one will be. — Syndrome, *The Incredibles*

[Spoilers Ahead]

Harry Potter's entire existence exemplifies stolen valor. I will die on this hill.

He did nothing remarkable. His entire story arc is a celebration of mediocrity. He is the poster child for the participation trophy. They say he killed the evil wizard when he just sat there in a shitty diaper while his mom did all the heavy lifting. Technically, he was just a spectator, but they gave him the gold medal anyway. As the story continues, we discover with a shock that he's not even a particularly good mage. His friends save him every time. The one time he actually saved himself involved time travel, and it was a CYA[1] moment. He gets handed buffs constantly. Seriously, who gives a twelve-year-old an invisibility cloak? Or the textbook his professor had vandalized with potions-related life pro tips? Really? Even with the buffs, he still barely survives. His "hero's journey" isn't about being a hero, because he isn't one. The entire series is about being Chosen™ without having to earn it.

The hero child trope is popular because it sells. Let's look at the record. We know Harry gets a letter, a vault of gold, and a magic map before his bar mitzvah; seven

---

1. Cover Your Ass.

books later, we learn the real magic was the friendships he made along the way. In *The Chronicles of Prydain*, Taran the pig keeper started with nothing, and five books later he still had most of it. Recruiters brought Ender Wiggin into *Ender's Game* at age six, intentionally isolated him, and when he eventually triumphed in "The Game," it turned out he committed a genocide. One of these is a fantasy the Empire sells. The other two are traumatic.

Harry Potter is the idea the Empire ran with. You can be special without earning it. Destiny will tap you on the shoulder. You don't have to train, to suffer, to fail and rebuild. You just have to be Chosen™. Sit tight. Your Hogwarts letter is in the mail.

Call it what you will: Main Character Syndrome or Terminal Uniqueness. Both share the belief that you are special, that you are the exception, that the rules apply to everyone but you. That destiny has a plan and you are at the center. The entire universe revolves around you and you alone. The belief that you don't have to do the work because something like talent, fate, the universe, the algorithm, will recognize your inherent greatness and elevate you above the herd.

It is, to put it plainly, bullshit. Yet it is enormously profitable bullshit, and the Empire has been selling it for decades.

I love the irony in *The Incredibles*. There are superheroes with superpowers, and all of them have Main Character Vibes. The villain, before he became a villain, was a massive fan of them, until he got the snub. He expected to be treated well, and the Map didn't meet the Territory. Resentment is an ironically twisted motivator, and thus Syndrome was born.

Syndrome understood Terminal Uniqueness better than anyone. His entire plan was to democratize superpowers. He wanted to give everyone the ability to be super, which would make the word meaningless. Meta-human communism. They framed him as the villain for it. Think about that. The kid who actually built his way to power through engineering and ingenuity was the bad guy. The guy who sought equity was the pariah. The family who inherited their special abilities, born with them, chosen by genetics, were the heroes. The self-made man is the villain. The genetic lottery winners are the protagonists.

The movie sends a powerful message: *Remember your place.*

The Empire prefers spectators. The Empire prefers everyone to wait for permission to Act. If the Map tells you to wait to be Chosen™, then you have already surrendered your Agency. People waiting in line are easier to manage. As long as everyone is queued up neatly in orderly rows, safely between the guardrails, no one will cause trouble. Even better, everyone sitting in the live studio audience hoping your name is called. Easier to keep an eye on you if you are sitting down.

Participation Pipeline

Let's trace the supply chain.

Millennials get mocked relentlessly for being the participation trophy generation. They are labeled as soft, entitled, fragile, criticized for not being able to handle criticism, needing safe spaces, hug boxes, and more. An entire catalog of belittling complaints from both Boomers and Gen X flexing their Relative Truth.[i]

The Absolute Truth is Millennials were not awarding themselves those trophies. Boomers handed them out. Gen X coaches handed them out. The adults in the room decided that every kid who showed up to the soccer game deserved a medal, regardless of whether they could kick a ball or spent the complete match picking dandelions in the midfield. Those same adults then turned around twenty years later and mocked the product of their own engineering.

Let's look deeper. Ironically, the Boomers themselves were the original participation trophy generation. They received the rewards their ancestors bled for without doing the bleeding. The Greatest Generation fought the wars, built the infrastructure, and sacrificed everything so their children could have it easier. The Boomer generation reaped all of it. They inherited the greatest economy in human history. They were on the edge of every technological leap; they had a front-row seat to the golden age of middle-class America. Most of it inherited and little of it earned. So, of course, they handed participation trophies to their children. It was the only model they knew. You get rewarded for showing up. That's how *their* lives worked.[ii]

Then they blamed the Millennials for believing it.

The Boomer generation are victims of the Empire too, and I can see where they are coming from with their "me first" mentality. The Empire raised the Boomers in a total state of fear. They lived under the constant threat of the Red Menace™. Cold War footing meant civic emergency exercises like bomb drills in school. Duck and cover under your desk, as if plywood and linoleum would stop a nuclear blast. That kind of terror shapes a generation. Believing that Ivan was going to blast you into atomic dust at any moment. Boomers are the OG YOLO generation, convinced the world could end at any moment, so why not grab what you can while you can? Why should they worry about long-term economic or environmental consequences when the threat of nuclear Armageddon shaped their core memories? Looking at it through this lens is the only thing that makes sense to me about their Attitude toward the world.[iii]

Bert the Turtle did them dirty.

Sure, they're hoarding wealth, but is it really from a place of greed? I see it as risk mitigation. They don't know how long they're going to live, and medical technology keeps extending the timeline without extending the quality. Walk into any nursing home and you'll see the result: people who probably should have checked out years ago, barely hanging on while the Empire empties their accounts one billable hour at a time.

It's worth noting: the Boomers were the first generation to shuffle their parents off to nursing homes *en masse*. They invented that particular outsourcing. Now they're terrified, with good reason; they will meet with a similar fate.[iv] The coming wealth shift will skip Millennials entirely and go right into the pockets of the medical industry.[v] Thanks for playing.

Gen X naturally gets skipped. We are too feral to be trusted with real power.

Terminal Uniqueness

Rehab staff introduced me to this term. No, not physical therapy, the other kind. The kind that keeps you out of jail.[2] I heard it regarding my Attitude. I thought I was the smartest person in the room, and it turned out I was not. Not by a long shot. The counselor told me that my best thinking had landed me in that facility and maybe I wasn't as sharp as I felt. It planted a seed. Terminal Uniqueness is the belief that your situation is so uniquely fucked, so singularly catastrophic, that no one could possibly understand it. Therefore, no solution could apply. None of the rehabilitation will work for me. My addiction is different. My pain is on another level. You don't get it. You don't know my life.[vi]

---

2. As in you can go into treatment or into the brig. Choose wisely.

This Attitude kills people.[vii] It almost killed me. It's called *terminal* for a reason. I've seen it happen to others. I've sat in rooms with people who were so convinced of their own exceptionalism that they rejected every hand extended to them. They weren't being stubborn. They genuinely believed, in their bones, that they were the exception to every rule, every program, every mechanism of recovery that had worked for thousands of people before them. Some time later I learned they had died in a DUI wreck, or had overdosed, or met some other untimely end. I am intimately familiar with the Attitude of Terminal Uniqueness because I used to feel exactly this way until the Territory stomped the shit out of me. Recovery taught me to see Terminal Uniqueness for what it is. Once I recognized it in myself, I started seeing it everywhere. If you spot it, you've got it.

These days, Cyberspace Psychosis has taken a clinical phenomenon and scaled it to the entire culture.[viii] Cyberspace calls this Main Character Syndrome, and all of us are familiar with it. Everyone knows someone who believes the world centers on them. Self-absorption has reached critical levels.

There's a word for the opposite of Main Character Syndrome: *sonder*.[ix] The recognition that every person you pass on the street has an inner life just as complex, as rich, and as layered as your own. I mean everyone. The woman at the crosswalk is living a story just as intricate as yours. The guy on the subway has fears and dreams and regrets and triumphs that would fill a book you'll never read. Everyone has a complex, nuanced, and beautiful inner life, just like you. Terminal Uniqueness is the refusal of *sonder*. It's the inability or unwillingness to grant that complexity to anyone else. Your Map says you are the Main Character. The Territory says there are eight billion Main Characters in this world, and not a single one of them needs your Map.

That's the Absolute Truth. You are unique. You are one of a kind. There is no one else exactly like you in the entirety of human history. That is also true of every single other person who has ever lived. Your uniqueness is not special. It's a universal condition. The moment you weaponize it and use it to justify why the rules don't apply to you, why your needs supersede everyone else's, why *your* Map is the only one that matters, you've crossed from uniqueness into The Psychosis.

Competitive Narcissism

What happens when we have an internet filled with countless influencers infected with Main Character Syndrome, all vying for your Attention? The Cyberspace Psychosis has cultivated a garden of competitive narcissism.

It's not enough to believe you are the Main Character. You have to *prove* it. Furthermore, you have to prove it against everyone else who also believes they're the Main Character. You can only have one star; everyone else is a co-star. The competition is everywhere on Instagram, Twitter/X, TikTok, YouTube, and Twitch, basically any social media. Competitive narcissism means marketing your identity, your brand. We see it every election cycle with political marketing. You can barely drive a few miles until you see billboards, with law firms and realtors putting their faces and phone numbers fifty feet high for maximum impression.[3] It's all competitive narcissism. Everyone performing their exceptionalism in a marketplace that rewards whoever performs it loudest.

Merit is not even a requirement; just the illusion of it will suffice. Illusions present a structural problem. No one can be the Main Character if everyone else is also a Main Character. Too many cooks in the kitchen spoil the broth, so the playing field needs to be thinned out a bit. The solution is simple for the Terminally Unique. Everyone who is not them becomes an NPC.[4] A supporting character, maybe a backup singer, or an extra in the drama of their life. This is the actual Attitude they live by.

When a streamer brags about having two million followers, do you think they give a fuck about your individuality? To them, you are a number. A statistic. A selling point when they pitch themselves as influencers. They imply they command the Attention and influence the Attitude of millions. That is a pretty big draw if you are trying to market something. Sounds like a Relatively good idea to get them on your side. How strong is their influence, really? Does anyone take them seriously enough that they will take an Action?

They need their followers infinitely more than their followers need them. That's the dirty secret of Main Characters in the Attention economy. The influencer is not the powerful one in the equation. They're the dependent one. They need your Attention the way an addict needs a fix. Attention is a brutally finite resource.[x] Every human being can only produce a maximum of twenty-four hours of it per day. That's it. No amount of caffeine or Adderall or hustle culture expands the supply. Twenty-four hours is the hard cap. And you're supposed to sleep for eight of those. So the competition isn't just narcissistic. It's desperate. They are competing for a finite resource that they have convinced themselves they cannot live without.[xi]

---

3. Being from Cleveland I can assure all of you that Tim Misney is the final boss of billboard egos.

4. Non Player Consciousness

The Terminally Unique influencer cannot handle being ignored. Unsubscribing from their bullshit is kryptonite to the influencer class. Irrelevance means dwindling likes which is a symptom of the Attention supply drying up, and without Attention, their Map ceases to exist. This is a direct manifestation of the Psychosis. Here it manifests as rejection sensitivity, which is a common neurodivergent trait, here applied to the threat of irrelevance. The need for Attention is so great that we have influencers who build their entire identity on doing pranks or other mischief just to get a slice. They don't care if they piss people off, or are eliciting outrage; that doesn't matter as long as they get that first A.

Of course they want the other A's too, but it's always the same progression. Capturing your Attention through spectacle, controversy, thirst traps, rage bait, anything that makes you look twice. They direct your Attitude, not just about the content, but about *them*. They need you focused on them.[xii] Love them or hate them, as long as your Attention is on their platform, they can keep going. They want haters; haters are their biggest fans; their haters will follow their content closer than anyone else. Ultimately, they convert that Attitude into Action: tips on Twitch, subscriptions on Patreon, purchases on their merch store, donations to their CashApp. Action is the pivot of actual influence. If they can get you to Act a certain way, purchasing a product they endorse, buying a ticket to an event they are hosting, then they have won the game. The whole point of being an influencer is influencing someone's Actions. The entire operation is a funnel designed to extract resources from people they will never know, never meet, and never genuinely care about.[xiii]

The most Terminally Unique person in the room is the least likely to acknowledge or celebrate your uniqueness. They do not share the spotlight. Unless you can provide them with content or some other benefit, you are just another number in their follower count.

The Archetype Trap

The Empire loves its standardization, and the influencer culture propagated through Cyberspace seems to follow a recursive path into a marketable baseline. Thousands of Main Characters and their followers shuffle into regulated categories. The performative uniqueness ends up looking the same. Archetypes are efficient. They're recognizable. They come preloaded with associations and assumptions. No one has to explain a cowboy. You don't have to explain an Apple person. The archetype does the heavy lifting, so the individual doesn't have to.

The Empire loves archetypes. Archetypes are demographics; each one represents a market with an eager and often enthusiastic customer base.[5] How can you identify an archetype? It's easy. The whole aesthetic loads like a Character select screen.

Biker archetypes who ride Harleys and apparently can only listen to classic rock. They remind us of this by blasting AC/DC at the red light. All are wearing black leather chaps and vests with so many patches. You say the word "Harley" and it pulls up a gestalt of traits.

Cowboy archetypes who watch *Yellowstone* and listen to country music. Drive their pickup truck, rock those boots, and always wear that hat. Can they actually rope and ride? John Dutton himself told us how to separate the Map from the Territory: "All hat and no cattle."[xiv]

Intellectuals wearing black turtlenecks, sipping from a glass of white wine while listening to a podcast from their favorite NPR presenter discussing an *Atlantic* article. Bonus points if they are smoking a clove.

Jocks wearing jerseys from [insert sports team]. They have their phones open, sneering at their FanDuel accounts and secretly hoping their team makes the playoffs this year.

Nerds who watch Marvel and play Dungeons & Dragons.[6] This one has become so mainstream that the archetype barely registers as subculture anymore. Once upon a time, only nerds used computers at all. Now everyone carries one in their pocket. The fantasy/science fiction trope that was once the stomping ground of nerds exclusively has become wildly popular worldwide. From *Game of Thrones* to robots delivering food in restaurants, nerds were the heralds of the Cyber Age all along. The things that got them beaten up in middle school are now a billion-dollar industry.

What happens when nerds go feral? We have the White Knight. They're all over Reddit and they will let you know about it. The self-described nice guys are easily identifiable by the fedora, *The Big Bang Theory* obsession, and the overwhelming urge to rush to the defense of any woman anywhere who even appears to be the victim of a slight. Perpetually in the friend zone, convinced that if he just defends her hard enough, often enough, publicly enough, she'll finally see him. They're dangerous because they're

---

5. Every time a new iPhone is released we see lines out the door.

6. OG Aspies play RIFTS. IYKYK.

disingenuous. Not to you or me, but to the very women they claim to defend. The defense isn't defense. It's courtship cosplay.

Facebook has plastered the family dynamic all over Cyberspace. It is ground zero where *show and tell* turns into *bring and brag*.

The archetype of performative parenting is the Facebook Mom. You know her. The helicopter parent whose kid is gifted and talented, and the most special child who has ever graced the playground, and she *needs* you to know it. Her feed is a relentless stream of honor roll photos, travel soccer schedules, and passive-aggressive commentary about other school systems. She's running the participation trophy pipeline in real time, manufacturing her child's Terminal Uniqueness before the kid can even pronounce "unique." Bonus points if she runs an MLM too. Because there's nothing quite like monetizing your competitive narcissism through an Herbalife or Mary Kay downline. She straight up funnels that PTA Phone Tree into sales and her social media into a storefront.[7] Now she's a lifestyle brand. The Facebook Mom is the epitome of an ambitious Main Character. She's flat out franchising it.

Apple people. The brand loyalty borders on cult status. Every Apple phone case has a cutout in the back so the logo is visible.[xv] This is important, presumably so that they can find each other. Android competes on specs, customization, and price, often favorably. That was never the battle. Look at Apple's market share overseas compared to the United States. Globally, Android dominates.[xvi] In the U.S., Apple rules. Same phones, same specs, different cultural waters. Apple doesn't have to produce a superior product when it commands such absolute brand loyalty. It's winning because the archetype of Apple is for people who are winning at life. The white earbuds. The blue bubbles. The store that looks like a cathedral. It has never been about the phone. It's about being seen holding one.

Cyberspace has given us countless archetypes, and we could split this pie a thousand ways, but the fact remains that we all fall into one, and most times we align with many of them. There are tribes and subcultures and micro-identities layered on top of each other, each one convinced of its own rarity, and all of them running a preset that millions of other people are running simultaneously.

You think you're unique, but you're a Map of a Map. An abstraction of an abstraction. The cowboy who can't rope. The biker who trailers his Harley to Sturgis. The intellec-

---

7. She cannot wait to flex on the school drop-off line in that Pink Cadillac. It's even on her dream board.

tual who's never published a word. The Facebook Mom whose gifted child is average by every measure except her Instagram captions. All hat and no cattle, all the way down.

The Terminal Uniqueness paradox is that the harder you try to stand out, the more you look like everyone else who's trying to stand out. The Empire has standardized rebellion. Hot Topic in the '90s was straight-up alternative.[xvii] It was the goth foundation. Walk in there today and it's all anime and Hello Kitty™. The company commercialized, repackaged, and sold the rebellion back to the next generation with glitter.

The Empire has a tendency to take gold and turn it into lead. Anything original is going to be commercialized, commodified, and marketed. They know the Terminally Unique people want to sparkle and stand out. So they push harder. Buy that lift kit for your pickup truck. Get another tattoo. Add another limited-edition plushie to your collection. They will be right there, ready and eager to sell you the FOMO. Stack another identity marker on top of the pile. Fly your freak flag. Dye your hair. Nobody's saying you can't, as long as you are spending your way into mediocrity.

Do You Know Who I Am?!

When the line crosses from self-expression to Main Character Syndrome, and someone is so absorbed in their own performance that their very behavior becomes a detriment to everyone else, then we come full circle. We arrive at the point where the content produced by the Terminally Unique becomes a parody of itself. Suddenly they're making their addiction to Attention into a collective problem. The Territory of the people, of course, pushes back, and we get to enjoy the Main Characters experiencing their Virtual Reality Blues in 4K. Quality content of an asshole being put in their place always satisfies.

They cry the hardest and the loudest when the Territory railroads their Map. Suddenly the Territory is being unfair or racist or discriminatory, and they want validation for their delusions. The Terminally Unique demand respect, yet rarely act respectfully or do anything worthy of respect. They treat boundaries as an inconvenience or something that only applies to NPCs. The Psychosis gives them an audience and validation. Water always seeks its own level, so the right lens will applaud even the illusion of victimhood. As long as the platforms exist, the Main Characters will have their audience.

We see it every day, a woman who seats herself at an exclusive L.A. restaurant without a reservation and starts livestreaming.[xviii] Content creation is in progress. Main Character energy at full blast. Then, when someone confronts her, she will try to argue, name-drop, or pull some other ego-fueled shenanigan to get her way. Naturally, the *maître d'* does not know who she is, nor did they care about her 10k followers; *reservations are required, ma'am.* She will post the entire ordeal, expecting her outrage to be vindicated. Victimized by the cruel reality of a policy that should not apply to people like her. Rules are only for the plebs after all. Even these posts do not go the way they expect. Cyberspace is brutal toward the selfish; those same proles who have to queue up like everyone else will pile on in the comments, roasting her mercilessly.

The Psychosis has infected the Main Characters. Look at how many crash-outs happen in airports or even aboard an aircraft. It is the best content. Which I understand, especially for younger people who were born into the post 9/11 world. They seemed to have missed the point that the friendly skies are the last place you want Fuck Around and Find Out. When they sit wherever they want to on an aircraft, boarding pass be damned, then they berate the passenger who actually paid for the seat when they show up. "Well, my kids are sitting here," or "I need to sit next to my husband," or some selfish explanation. Flight attendants are summoned, boarding passes are examined, and that should be the end of it. Sit in the seat you paid for. That does not make the content. We want to see the crash out.[xix]

Everyone carrying a sophisticated video recording system in their pocket all the time means we get a front-row seat to the fuckery of Terminal Uniqueness. The meltdown begins, and the phones come out, and one way or another it gets posted. Sometimes, multiple recordings even treat us to various angles of the same incident. Either way, the Find-Out moment arrives when the police board the plane and everyone cheers. Bonus points if we get to watch them get tased in the face.

Cyberspace has given us the Karen archetype, or is she a meme? Nevertheless, we all know a Karen. The short-haired turbo bitch lambastes a teenage barista because Karen was spelled with a C instead of a K, and now demands the manager. She doesn't give a fuck about the people in line behind her. She doesn't even care whether the coffee tastes good. They spelled her name wrong, and she apparently considers that a war-crime level of disrespect. Righteous indignation is the best indignation and Karen always delivers.

What makes Karen especially Unique is that she is not being performative at all. She would act like that whether or not the cameras were rolling. Karen is more interested in getting her way than in cultivating Attention. She is rarely an influencer and is not acting that way for engagement. She is so confidently wrong yet so impossibly self-absorbed that I cannot help but admire that level of authenticity.[xx]

Standardization Response

We have seen how the Empire standardizes everything. Education systems are designed to meet the metrics of standardized tests. Housing developments stamp out indistinguishable boxes on identical streets. Career paths funnel through exact pipelines. Algorithms curate consumer choices, and only a handful of brands satisfy them. Efficiency optimizes everything, causing it all to converge toward sameness. Look what they did to McDonald's, which had the quirky, easily identifiable architecture and that iconic roof design we all know and love. Plain, boring, gray buildings replaced the old ones. The Empire once again turned gold into lead.[xxi]

When they try that with people, the human response is to overcorrect. If the system wants to make you identical, you push back. You dye your hair. You get inked. You curate an identity that screams *I am not a number. I am not a cog in this machine. I am not interchangeable.*

Understandable. Even admirable, up to a point.

They also standardize your tools for expressing that uniqueness. The blue hair dye comes from the same box. The tattoos come from the same Pinterest board. The piercings come from the same shop on every commercial strip in America. You're being unique in the same way everyone else is being unique. Rebellion is again mass-produced. Outrageous expression draws Attention. At the macro level, we see the media sensationalizes the mundane for engagement and views. On the micro level, people sensationalize and dramatize their lives, magnified by social media. The same mechanism on different scales. One is institutional, the other is personal. Both are farming Attention. The Attention pipeline has also become institutionalized.

So is Terminal Uniqueness, at its root, just a response to the Empire's forced standardization? Could it be the Psychosis is just what happens when you try to maintain a sense of individuality in a system designed to grind everyone into a uniform consumer? It's a trauma response that happens when no matter which direction you go, the Empire is right there to shove you back into a mold. So, in the face of uniqueness being eradicated by the machine, expressions of resistance are going to push back. Most of the time, the pushback is entirely localized.

The weirdness capital of the world is New York City. You do not have to search far to find something odd. You can find someone wearing a panda costume and chewing bamboo on the subway. They're doing it for Attention. What would push someone to go to the trouble of finding a costume and then wearing it? Maybe the thought of being just one out of eight million is too much to bear, and they have to weird out. Who knows why people do what they do? In all fairness, NYC was weird long before Cyberspace so we cannot entirely credit the Psychosis with subway cosplay. What's ironic is that native New Yorkers mostly ignore these antics. After all, they've seen everything, and subway panda is wallpaper.[xxii]

What happens when it goes too far? What happens when these expressions of Main Character Syndrome cross the line where the effect is no longer localized, when they rustle the jimmies of the public at large? When people film these rebellious acts, they go viral, and the act itself crosses an irreversible line. Cyberspace has given us another beautiful phenomenon.

Canceled!

If your entire identity is on the Map, your meticulously curated image, the brand you've constructed, even the archetype you resonate the most with is all you really are as a person, then being canceled is complete annihilation. In fact, cancel culture can be so devastating that someone who is not even an internet person, and only posts occasionally, can still end up so polarizing they end up canceled. People can lose their jobs, miss opportunities, become social pariahs, or face public shaming and public exposure. They don't even have to post anything themselves. They can even say something inflammatory or offensive, and as long as someone is there to record it and post it, then it is game over. Doxxing has ruined many careers.

Think about what cancellation actually is. Traditionally, it meant something being annulled or revoked or made void, like you would cancel your subscription. In Cyberspace it means to withdraw support, as in no longer following or buying products or watching content. The goal is total reputation damage, and it is the herd's collective reaction to a Terminally Unique moment. Someone's Map gets exposed as fraudulent, offensive, or incompatible with the prevailing consensus. Cyberspace mobilizes, screenshots circulate, hashtags start trending, and the video goes viral. Suddenly, the curated reputation that took years to build collapses at the speed of a click.[xxiii]

Cancelable offenses exist on a hierarchy of evidence. Most of them need proof. Cruelty to animals is a great way to get canceled, but if there's no video, the story dies as hearsay.

"He kicked a dog" without footage doesn't stick. "He kicked a dog" with a ten-second clip ends a career.

Racism and sexual assault operate differently. These are the two where the accusation itself functions as the conviction. No video required. No receipts needed. The allegation alone carries enough weight to collapse a reputation, and the accused has to prove innocence to a jury that isn't interested in hearing it. "He used a slur at a party." "He roofied a girl at a bar." Those sentences land with the force of a verdict, not an accusation. Whether they're true is a question for a court. Cancel culture is not a court.

Remember our COVID Contrarian, Russell Brand? We watched him in Battlefield Truth doing tricks on his jet ski, the loudest independent voice in the room, gorging on the Attention of millions. He leveraged his brand[8] on being the iconoclast truth-teller. "I'm the one who will say what no one else will." Main Character maxxing with a megaphone.

The same exceptionalism that made him effective made him a big target. His Map said if you are catching flak then you are over the target. He made up his own rules as he went along. That's what made him dangerous to the ocean liners. It's also what made him dangerous to himself. We have seen time and time again that insulation is not protection from the Territory.

The Territory surfaced the sexual assault allegations. Cancel culture hit him in real time, and almost overnight he was deplatformed, demonetized, and disgraced. The jet ski that was too fast to catch plowed into a pylon. A court will decide his guilt, and the evidence and facts will tell the story. Cancel culture does not care about the burden of evidence; in the court of public opinion, an accusation is the same as a conviction. Innocent or guilty, the damage to his reputation has already been done.[xxiv]

Cancel culture came for Michael Richards, the actor who played Kramer on *Seinfeld*. He was filmed spouting racist insults at a heckler during one of his stand-up comedy shows. The recording circulated, and people across the globe watched it. His Map said, "I'm the star, I can say whatever I want." The Territory responded with, "bet." Of course, he apologized later, but the damage was done. Racism is the premier reputation killer. It's one of the few areas where the Territory of public opinion strikes back with absolute finality. This 2006 incident tainted his entire career.[xxv]

---

8. Literally

Interestingly, even Jeffrey Dahmer went to great lengths to make sure everyone knew he was not racist. This was important to him. He didn't care that the world knew he murdered and ate people. He wanted people to know he was an equal-opportunity butcher. When your brand is "cannibal serial killer" and you're still worried about the racism label, that tells you everything about the hierarchy of cancelable offenses.[xxvi]

Cancellation reveals that the Terminally Unique narcissist cannot handle criticism. They cannot process it; they will outright ignore it, dismiss it, and gaslight it away. When criticism arrives on a cataclysmic scale, and thousands, even millions, of people shriek, *your Map is wrong*, any action will appear disingenuous and defensive. There is no graceful response available after a video of you tossing N bombs like confetti goes viral. The world will use your words against you, and any response you make will come across as spiteful, petty, or defensive. Even the public will treat the apology as a token gesture. Damage control and reputation repair are not the same as Character repair.[xxvii]

I watch public apologies and I often wonder to myself at what point along the line did they actually feel sorry about what they did. I am sure it is right around the realization that there are actual consequences and they will affect them adversely. Then of course they are going to apologize. Are they sorry for what they said, or are they sorry that what they said has a negative result on their reputation?

For some people, their curated identity is all they have. The performance itself was the self. When that performance gets canceled, the self gets canceled right along with it. We have all seen this happen. When someone has built their entire reality on a Map and the Territory smashes through, and there's nothing underneath to land on, the crash is catastrophic.

Crash Landing

Someone, somewhere, has a Main Character meltdown. These usually happen in the face of an inconvenience that just pushes someone over the edge. A flight delay turns into an airport tantrum. The bar cuts someone off because they are already drunk, so they decide to try nut chucking[9] a bouncer and end up getting suplexed face first into the pavement. We see a teacher who, fed up with a class misfit, finally pops off at them. There are endless versions of crash-outs from road rage to grocery store MMA. We

---

9. Nut chucking is an uppercut to the scrotum.

know about them because people film them, post them, and harvest Attention from the humiliation.[xxviii]

Crash-out content is very viewable, and some of the most popular videos online. They are always dramatic and cause a scene, and everyone will have an opinion about them. Comment sections fill up with hopefuls hoping to grab a taste of that Attention pie: *I would never do that. What is wrong with people? I can't believe someone would act like this.* Every single person commenting "*I would never...*" is performing their own version of Terminal Uniqueness. *I'm* not like that. *I* would handle it differently. *I'm* the reasonable one. The viewer's sense of superiority is running the exact same software as the person flopping around on the airport floor. While it is true that the vast majority of humans are not going to yeet a chili cheese dog at a fast food worker for forgetting the side of fries, but do you really have to tell the world you wouldn't act like that? Ego is going to ego, no matter what the platform.

The *egosystem* feeds on itself. The more spectacular the crash out, the more people are going to engage. Everyone is going to want to weigh in on it and the engagement continues the cycle. Cyberspace does not find generating content about the content to be even moderately ironic. Every click counts as engagement. Reaction videos are very popular, along with many Twitter/X threads dissecting the meltdown. All of it farming Attention from someone's worst moment.[10]

Crash-outs take so many forms. Some are garden-variety entitlements, like the canceled flight, the misspelled name, or the wrong order. Some can be darker. Much darker. The Christchurch shooter livestreamed his massacre.[xxix] Columbine was a crash-out where two kids decided they were the Main Characters and everyone else was expendable.[xxx] When Terminal Uniqueness reaches its logical extreme, when you truly believe everyone else is an NPC in your story, the results can be monstrous.

Sometimes crash-outs happen, and the person in the middle of one is completely oblivious. A great example is Dr. Rachael "Raygun" Gunn, the Australian academic who became one of the Main Characters of the 2024 Paris Olympics. Her event was Breaking,[11] and her performance was so notably bad she became an international meme. Despite deploying her signature Kangaroo Move, she scored zero points across three battles, shut out 18-0 each time. Her crash-out wasn't just the performance. The crash-out was the

---

10. Daniel Tosh is the reaction OG.

11. Break Dancing

gap between her self-assessment and the scoreboard, playing out in real time on a world stage. Classic Main Character Syndrome. Her Map said she was representing the culture, bringing joy and celebrating art. The Territory said 0 for 3.

The aftermath was its own phenomenon. We cannot claim she was canceled. Cancellation requires a villain, and Gunn came across as oblivious rather than malicious. In fact it was the opposite of canceled, her performance was so terrible that she was memed into Cyberspace infamy: Halloween costumes, TikTok parodies, and shorthand in a thousand unrelated conversations. Her heart may have been in the right place, though the story of how she qualified for the Olympics has enough texture to raise questions.[xxxi]

The Oceania qualifier was thin. Only fifteen B-girls competed, not even enough to fill a proper top-16 bracket. The selection structure created real barriers: mandatory registration with three separate organizations (including the ballroom-oriented DanceSport Australia), a valid international passport, short notice after the event was announced, and the costs of travel to Sydney with no guaranteed payoff. These hurdles disproportionately filtered out breakers from economically or socially disadvantaged backgrounds. These are the very communities where breaking originated in the Bronx as a raw, DIY outlet for poor Black and Latino youth with limited resources. What began on cardboard floors as an accessible rebellion became, in Olympic form, a bureaucratic process easier to navigate for someone with stable institutional connections, academic credentials, and the means to clear administrative and financial friction.[xxxii]

Gunn, a university lecturer with a PhD on gender and breaking culture, had long been a consistent top performer in the small Australian domestic scene. She won the qualifier fair and square against whoever showed up. Yet the "map of her credentials" and insider positioning got her to Paris more readily than raw street-level talent might have in a less gated system. The Territory of Olympic-level competition, judged by international standards against the world's best, scored her zero.

She retired from competitive breaking shortly after.[xxxiii]

Granted, these are very extreme examples and are the exception, and thankfully not the norm. They are at the far end of the spectrum, and not where most people live. Still, they illuminate the mechanism cleanly. The Psychosis makes us stressed, over-stimulated, under-connected, and ready to pop off at any moment. The gap between "minor inconvenience" and "public meltdown" has gotten dangerously thin.[xxxiv]

And someone is always filming.

Humbled or Humiliated?

These crash-out/Find-Out moments each represent a fork in the road. One moment, two possible outcomes, determined entirely by where your Attention points and what your Attitude does with it.[xxxvi]

Humbling is when the Map breaks, and you respect the Territory for it. Your Attention is outward, on the lesson you learned. You receive it with whatever grace you can muster. Your Attitude adjusts, maybe not comfortably or painlessly, but it adjusts honestly. Your future Actions will reflect the recalibration. You're different afterward. You gain some wisdom points and you grow from the experience. Overall, the outcome is positive, and you end up grounded in something real.[xxxv]

Humiliating is when the Map breaks and you resent the Territory for it. Your Attention is inward, locked on *what about me?* Your Attitude curdles into acidity, and you play the blame game. *The world is unfair! People are cruel! Nobody understands!* Your future Actions will reflect that poison. Instead of emerging empathetic, you are now bitter. You are defensive instead of reflective. Louder instead of wiser.

I learned the difference the hard way.

The only time law enforcement arrested me, they took me to jail and locked me in this tiny little shower room/cell about the size of a closet, and sprayed me down. A sheriff's deputy opened a little window to conduct a strip search. I was already buck naked, and they already had my clothes and possessions and had searched both. None of that mattered. He wanted to watch me turn around and bend over to cough. My forehead pointed at the floor, I was pulling my cheeks apart, and I realized a long string of terrible decisions had delivered me here.[xxxvii]

A lot of epiphanies can happen in the span of a few seconds.

It was one of the most profoundly humbling moments of my life. I knew right then I did not want to experience it again. I survived it, learned what I had to, and moved on.

I was very apologetic about it and the deputy said to me through that little window: **"Yeah, everyone's sorry when they're caught."**

Those words landed like a gut punch, because it was not the first time I had heard that exact phrase.

The first time was about a year earlier, when I was trying to be a Main Character. I was twenty years old, trying to get into a 21-and-up event with a fake ID. A sharp-eyed bouncer spotted the fake in about two seconds, and I was dragged out into the street.[12] Absolutely humiliated and drunkenly still talking shit to the guy who had just effortlessly thrown me over the sidewalk and outweighed me by at least a hundred pounds. I should have known from the gleam in his eye it would have made his night to fold me further.

Meanwhile, the local PD was there, trying to figure out what to do with me. I even said, "I already told you that I'm sorry!" And that was when the officer said it.

Luckily for me, just then another altercation broke out and distracted them. It was a chaotic scene. Despite my being wasted, I had the presence of mind to notice they had only taken the fake ID and had no idea who I actually was. So I made my escape. I learned absolutely nothing from that caper. If I had a better Attitude at the time, I probably would have avoided the chain of events that led to my arrest a year later.[13]

The second time I heard it, I was humbled, not humiliated. I was just self-aware enough in that moment to really hear it.

Everyone is sorry when they're caught.

You're not special. Your remorse is not unique. Every person caught doing something stupid gives the standard response. There is almost a purity in discovering the truth about sorry, it slaps your Map down a notch and forces you to look at the Territory with fresh eyes. It's the Find-Out moment where you survive with something gained rather than something lost.[xxxviii]

---

12. By dragged I mean I was bodily lifted and tossed out, like actually airborne for a moment there.

13. These two events took place in different states and were not related. The only common denominator was me.

Main Character Syndrome, unchecked, guarantees humiliation. The only variable is when and how public. Catch it early, listen to the moment's wisdom and actually *hear* it, you get humbled instead.

Humbling moments, as uncomfortable as they are, may be the most valuable thing the Territory offers.

Take It or Make It

So where's the line between Terminal Uniqueness and genuine exceptionalism? Is there a line? This book can't just say "you're not special, sit down." That would be nihilism, and nihilism is just another Map. What does the actual Territory of content creation look like when we strip away the Cyberspace Psychosis?

There's nothing wrong with streaming yourself playing video games. There's nothing wrong with going live at the gym during your workout. Maybe people love watching you make faces and flex in a mirror. Maybe people are motivated by your content. You do you. If you want to film yourself in the kitchen making scrambled ham to share with your followers, then do it. Enjoy what you enjoy. Share your Relative Truth with the world, just maintain a perspective about it. Live-streaming a game you didn't program isn't the same as coding it. A reaction video to someone else's content isn't the same as crafting your own. Wearing the outfit isn't the same as designing it. The issue isn't consumption. Consumption is fine and even celebrated. The issue is when consumption becomes identity and curating becomes a substitute for creating. When you believe the playlist makes you a musician, then you are experiencing the Psychosis.

Are you a taker or a maker?

Makers are unique.[xxxix]

Takers are a dime a dozen.[xl]

It's like complimenting someone on their shirt: "Oh, I love your shirt!" They will thank you. Think about it. If you accept a compliment for a shirt you did not design, did not stitch, did not create. You end up taking credit for someone else's craftsmanship because you swiped a credit card.[xli] More stolen valor. You're no better than Harry Potter. Get back under the stairs.[xlii]

The distinction is important to note, as it's a diagnostic test for Terminal Uniqueness. The maker has done the Territorial work. They've FAFO'd. They've failed, iterated, suffered, learned, and produced something that didn't exist before they created it. They are contributing. They have earned their uniqueness.

The taker has consumed, curated, and claimed. They assemble their uniqueness from others' contributions, arrange it attractively, and present it as identity. Takers will even assert outright ownership. The concept of intellectual property is an example. Buying and selling the rights to someone else's creative work. Takers on this level even go so far as to litigate against the original artist to enforce the right to claim.

The Emperor

Can someone be genuine and unique together? Can Terminal Uniqueness become so outlandishly expressive that it becomes Legendary? Can a performance of Main Character Syndrome really make such an impact? It can indeed. Let me introduce you to Joshua Abraham Norton.

Otherwise known as Norton I, Emperor of the United States and Protector of Mexico.

In 1852, entrepreneur Joshua Abraham Norton attempted to corner the San Francisco rice market by purchasing an entire shipload of Peruvian rice at 12.5 cents per pound. When multiple additional ships arrived with more rice, the market flooded, prices collapsed to around 3 cents per pound, and Norton lost his entire fortune and ended in bankruptcy in 1858. Deeply humiliated and financially ruined, Norton disappeared from public view before resurfacing in September 1859, when he dramatically declared himself "Norton I, Emperor of the United States and Protector of Mexico" in a published proclamation. An outlandish display of Main Character Syndrome that clearly represented the dramatic culmination of his spectacular financial and mental crash-out.[xliii]

San Francisco, of course being San Francisco, rolled with it. On account of his sheer force of Character. The Emperor had no army, no wealth, no algorithm to promote him. He started with no follower count and zero content strategy. He just...decided. He donned a uniform of office and got to work, and it worked well. Restaurants fed him for free. Theaters reserved seats for him. The city accepted his self-printed currency. Police officers saluted him on the street. An overzealous officer once arrested him, but the public outcry was so fierce that the police chief released him with a formal apology.[xliv]

Emperor Norton reigned benevolently, too. Emperor Norton issued Imperial Decrees, some of which were surprisingly prescient, such as his call for a bridge connecting San Francisco and Oakland decades before the Bay Bridge was built. He decreed the dissolution of Congress in 1859, shortly after taking power, citing fraud, corruption, and the undue influence of political parties as his reasoning.[14] He even ordered the formation of a League of Nations before the concept formally existed. Norton was well ahead of his time.[xlv]

When he died in 1880, tens of thousands of people attended his funeral. They lined the streets as the carriage bearing his body passed. For a man who had nothing on the Map, no genuine power, no wealth, no official position, an entire city showed up to pay respects. The headline read: *Le Roi Est Mort.* The King is dead.[xlvi]

Why?

Because Norton wasn't performing uniqueness. He was *living* it. He didn't need you to believe his Map. He inhabited his Territory so completely that the Territory bent toward him. He didn't need followers. He was a Sovereign and the citizens were his subjects. He was responsible to them and for them. He didn't need likes. He didn't need anyone to validate his Relative Truth. He famously saved Chinatown from being burned down by a mob. Norton stood in the street before the angry, violent horde and the entrance to the enclave and recited the Lord's Prayer repeatedly until the crowd felt silly and went home. He was an Absolute embodiment of nobility. His authentic self, which lacked any pretense, drew people to him.

A Character who had character.

Today we call this having aura.

You want to be an influencer? Here's your role model. Study Emperor Norton and see how well you measure up. You may have the metrics. You may have the engagement. You may have the merch store and the Patreon and the blue checkmark. Are you going to have a standing-room-only funeral with tens of thousands in attendance? Will your memory and legacy endure for over a century after you die? Because Norton made an impact. The influencer makes impressions.

Unique people make an impact.

---

14. Had Congress obeyed this order, the Civil War would have been avoided, just saying.

The poseurs make only impressions.

Found Below

So what's the foundation under all of this? When we strip away the archetypes and the performance and the curated identity and the follower count and the participation trophies, what actually remains?

The same thing that's always been there. The Territory. Messy, unglamorous, un-shareable, unoptimizable Territory. The Territory of the only three things you actually own: your Attention, your Attitude, and your Action. Ultimately, your Agency is the foundation. Everything else is borrowed, curated, inherited, or assigned.

The Empire will continue standardizing. The Psychosis will keep spreading. The trophies will keep piling up. The Main Characters will keep melting down in airports and coffee shops and the comment sections will cheer for it.

But the Territory doesn't care about any of that. The Territory asks only one question, and it asks it with absolute indifference to your Map:

What did you make?

Not what did you buy? Not what did you curate? Not what you consumed, or reacted to, or shared, or re-posted, or reviewed.

What did you make?

If you have an answer, you're unique. Not because you faked it or claimed it. Not because the algorithm amplified it. Not because two million strangers double-tapped a photo.

Uniqueness you earned. In the Territory. Where it counts.

If you don't know where to begin, start by making a difference.

Inner Critic Industrial Complex

Comparison is the thief of joy. — Theodore Roosevelt

We all have an inner critic.

It comes with the Territory of being human. Somewhere inside every human being is a voice that hates them. It whispers that they are not enough. It reminds them of every failure, every embarrassment, every moment when they fell short of who they were supposed to be. Painfully highlighting every time your FAFO did not work out in your favor. Every time you experienced the Virtual Reality Blues, your inner critic was right there, recording the whole thing in 4k.

What makes this thing so insidious is that it speaks to you in your own voice. That is its trick; it is hard to tell the difference between your inner critic and your own inner monologue. That is the point, though, to make you distrust yourself and loathe yourself. It wants you to believe that the constant state of criticism is entirely organic. So you believe you are the one thinking these thoughts, making these assessments, and arriving at these conclusions about your own inadequacy.

The voice is not even real. It has no body. It produces nothing. It creates nothing. Its only function is to hate you and to make you hate yourself.

In short, the inner critic is a liar.

I have wasted a lot of time and energy in my life fighting this inner demon. Trying to make sense of it. Trying to get a handle on what exactly it was and how it functioned so I could best defeat it.

The closest description or metaphor I have found comes from the Islamic tradition; this voice has a name: the *quareem*. Explained as a companion *jinn* or spirit assigned to every human being at birth. It cannot speak with its own voice, so it uses yours. They call it the *waswas*, the slinking whisperer. It whispers to you, invading your inner thoughts. We even call them "intrusive thoughts" and who is the intruder? Could be the *quareem*, and its entire purpose, its life mission, is to hate you. Even better if it can get you to hate yourself.[i]

I met a Citizen Philosopher once who called hers a "nazi flea." Tiny, she said. So tiny. But with a voice that fills the room. When you actually look at it, you see how small and pathetic it really is. Most people never think to look closely. They just listen, and they hear a big, loud, and distracting voice dripping with pure venom. It wants Attention, it wants to dictate your Attitude, it wants to drive your Actions to do more detrimental things, giving it more ammo to criticize you with. A terrible cycle to endure.

Would you be friends with someone who talks to you the way you talk to yourself?

If the answer is no, then you have met your *quareem*. Heck, if you even had to think about answering this at all, then you have your answer.

Roller Coaster Mania

Most mornings when I wake up in the morning I will have a song stuck in my head. It's never a song I chose. Hardly ever a song I want. It is always short, a snippet lodged in my consciousness like a splinter. It will be there all day. Burrowed in like an earwig. Playing on a loop that I did not start and cannot stop.

A recent one was Cotton Eyed Joe, which is the neurodivergent equivalent of waking up on the wrong side of the bed. I wake up with that one and I know it is just going to be one of *those days*. Getting caught in a loop playing in the background of my thoughts like shitty elevator Muzak™ that only I can hear.

Where did he come from? Where did he go?

The Rednex were asking the right questions.

This is what a rumination loop actually feels like. It is not quite a train of thought since a train has a departure and a destination. A rumination loop is a roller coaster. Sort of train adjacent, yet you don't really get anywhere. There are ups and downs and upside-downs and corkscrews and inversions. There are tight turns. Moments occur when you pop out of your seat, and other moments when G-forces throw your neck around. The only difference is that it does not stop. You cannot get off this ride.[ii]

Sitting in the seat right next to you in that little roller coaster train car is that inner critic. He has a megaphone too, a couple of inches from your ear. Shouting and reminding you for the entire ride that everyone hates you. Reminding you that you are a piece of shit. Reminding you of that thing you said in eighth grade that still makes you cringe. Whatever it can do to get you to focus on the loop and capture your Attention. In your own voice. Using your own words.

Sometimes it even tells you to just end it. Just a whisper. Just a suggestion. "Just end it." Casually, as if it's no big deal. Like it is an option worth considering. That is when you know the voice is not you. Because you do not actually want to die. But the *quareem* does not care what you want. It only knows how to hate. Around and around on the constant loop. An unchecked inner critic can indeed lead to the absolute worst outcomes.[iii]

It is a liar.

Two Dogs

There is an old tale about two dogs living inside every person. One is a white dog and the other a black dog.

The white dog wants what is good for you. It wants you to grow, to heal, to become more of who you actually are. The black dog wants what is harmful. It wants you to stagnate, to suffer, to shrink.

Which one is stronger? The one you feed more.

The inner critic is the black dog's voice. The Psychosis feeds it constantly.

Your inner critic loves Cyberspace. It loves anything with the capacity to make you feel less than. Social media is a breeding ground for this, where everything is a comparison. The humble brag of the guy who just bought a new car, to the highlight reel of the girl with the rich boyfriend spoiling her. The "Instagram" lifestyle." The inner critic feeds on envy and loves to direct your Attention to what you don't have.

Every time you scroll through the feed, comparing your backstage footage to everyone else's highlight reel, you are feeding the black dog. Every time you look at someone's curated life and feel the lack in your own, that critic gets fatter and louder. Every time you measure yourself against impossible standards, standards that never exist in the Territory and only live on a map. The black dog feasts.

The white dog starves.

The black dog is basically selfishness. It is the part of you that wants it all, often to the detriment of others. It is the part that keeps score, that envies and resents. The Psychosis drives all of us toward selfishness. It programs us to remain in a state of want. To want more, need more, consume more, display more. It is an engine that constantly manufactures insatiable desire.

The inner critic directs your Attention to that lack. Your inner critic draws your Attention to the black hole that can never be filled. The more you stare into it, the larger it grows.[iv]

Heaven or hell?

Heaven and hell have the same address.

There is a legend about the afterlife that says heaven and hell occupy the same hall. After you die, you find yourself seated at a very long table covered with the most delicious foods humanity has ever created. Roasts and pies and every scrumptious delight you can imagine. The smell alone would make you drool like a St. Bernard. Countless people sit along both sides of the table. Everyone also discovered that their chair secured one arm, rendering it immobile, and a spoon was affixed to their other hand. This spoon is unique because the handle is much longer than an average spoon. It is just long enough that when you scoop up a bite of something, you cannot angle your elbow enough to reach it into your mouth.

Hell is filled with miserable people, seated at this table and starving. They are angry, frustrated, shouting in disbelief at being tempted by this heavenly feast they cannot enjoy. It is not fair that their spoon will not reach. They try and fail, and try and fail time after time, getting angrier and more frustrated each time they cannot quite reach their mouth. Spilled and splattered food covers everyone, and their end of the table is a mess from near misses. The smell compounds their hunger, and it makes the agony so much worse. Abundance surrounds them, and a ravenous appetite maddens them, yet they are too self-centered to see a solution and choose to suffer.

The Heavenly end of the table is the total opposite. Everyone there is having the time of their lives.[1] Each seat is occupied by someone who, when they arrived, quickly realized that while the spoon cannot reach their own mouth; it is long enough to reach the mouth of the person seated across from them. Everyone is jovial and friendly, enjoying an elaborate feast together. The secret to Heaven is that everyone feeds each other. That is all. A simple shift in Attitude and Action in the face of entirely the same constraints yet with a vastly different outcome.

In hell, you focus your Attention on your own hunger. Your Attitude is resentment at the unfairness. Your Action is wasted on futile attempts of self-feeding that never works, yet you keep trying over and over again with more misery.

In Heaven, your Attention shifts to others. Your Attitude becomes one of service. Your Action feeds someone else. In return, they are feeding you.

When all three A's are pulling in the same direction, you have Agency. You have effectiveness. You escape the trap that looks inescapable.

The inner critic wants you in hell. It wants your Attention fixed entirely on lack. It wants your Attitude sour with resentment. It wants your Actions selfish and futile. That is how it wins.

You beat it by picking up the long spoon and feeding someone else.

You *should* X *or else* Y!

Like the Empire, the inner critic loves the word *should.*

You *should* have done that differently. You *should* listen to them. You *should* buy that jacket. You *should* follow this advice. You *should* be further along by now. You *should* have more money. You *should* be thinner. You *should* be happier. You *should,* you *should,* you *should.*

---

1. Afterlives.

Should is best friends with *or else.*

They are always holding hands. *Shoulds* almost always direct your Attention to a map, and *or else* is directing your Attention to some consequence from the Territory. Most of the time *should* and *or else* really are looking out for you.

You *should* wear your seat belt *or else* you will get yeeted through the windshield.

You *should* avoid active volcanoes *or else* the lava will melt you.

You *should* wear your galoshes *or else* you will catch pneumonia and die.

Most of these are common sense and bear merit.

Your inner critic has no concept of common sense. It does, however, have an agenda. So no matter what it says, no matter how reasonable it sounds, no matter how much partial truth it contains, the endgame is always the same. It wants you to hate yourself. Beware when your inner critic is spamming the word *should* at you, because it's a trap.

The trap springs once that S word pops in. "You did fuck that up; you *should* have been paying Attention." "That was embarrassing, you *should* have known better." "You *should* have prepared." These might be accurate observations. Hindsight is always 20/20. Step back and watch what the inner critic does with them. It does not offer them as feedback for growth, it does not want you to grow at all. It offers them as evidence for prosecution. It takes a small Relative Truth and blows it out of proportion. It takes a single failure and extrapolates it into a proof of fundamental inadequacy. Then will nag you consistently about it, pulling you into a loop of regret.

Legitimate feedback says: here is what happened, here is what you can learn.

The *quareem* says: here is what you *should* have done and here is why you are garbage for not doing it.

The difference is in the tone. The difference is the agenda. The difference is whether the voice wants you to grow or wants you to suffer. White dog. Black dog.

The inner critic loves the "I told you so." moments. It keeps a big box of "I told you so's", and is always ready to distribute whenever something does not turn out the way you planned, or something does not work out in your favor. Your inner critic loves rolling out that television and VCR combo and playing your lowlight reel. Watching you relive every trauma, every awkward moment, every time you were embarrassed or ashamed, every time you *should* have seen it coming. It wants to replay them on a loop, captivating your Attention.

Critical Consumption

The inner critic is the Empire's best friend.

It keeps you on the reservation. It keeps you obedient. It keeps you consuming.

Because the critic is always whispering that you need more. More clothes. More prestige. More trips. More debt. More power. More money. It is never satisfied with what you have. It always demands.

This is an important symptom of the Psychosis.

There is the machine that profits from all this self-hatred. That profits from you listening to your inner critic. It's an entire market cycle. They play off people's insecurities, then sell them something to fill the gap. Which only opens another gap. And so on.

You see it everywhere. Self-help courses. Meditation apps. Life coaches. Productivity systems. Morning routines. Cold plunge protocols. Alpha male coaching. Mental toughness programs. Manifestation guides. Sales seminars. Life optimization frameworks. The comprehensive multi-billion dollar industry operates on the premise that you are broken and the only way to repair yourself is to buy a Map. The Inner Critic Industrial Complex stokes the Psychosis and then sells the cure.[v]

How many former Navy SEALs do you see hawking mental toughness courses? They're directly playing into masculine insecurity. The message is clear: *You're soft. You're weak. You don't measure up. But for $497, I can fix that.*

They're monetizing the inner critic. Taking the voice that says "you're not a real man" and building a business model around it. It can be lucrative too. No one likes to be called less than. Especially if an outside voice is validating the chatter of the critic. So it works. There is a market, and people are buying these Maps of masculinity.

It's a trick, they sell Relative value. The appearance of strength. The aesthetic of competence. You take the course; and you may even feel better temporarily. You post about your 5 AM routine and cold plunges and your change in routine that solved all of your problems, Relative to where you were before.

The inner critic sees through your pretense. He knows you bought a program. He knows you're performing toughness, instead of embodying it. It knows you are following a bullshit Map. The Map that plots your escape route from that inner critic once and for all. The inner critic comes with the Territory of being human. There is no geographical cure for the critic.

You are always going to bring your inner critic along, no matter where the Map leads you.

Absolute value is different. Absolute value is wholeness.

The Industrial Complex sells the *feeling* of value. Relative value. Contingent on the purchase, the certification, and the social proof. *See, wasn't that nice? Don't you feel better now?*

You can't buy Absolute value. It has to be built. Through failure. Through learning. Through doing hard things that no one sees.

So the inner critic says: *You're not enough.*

The Industrial Complex says: *Buy this and you will be.*

The truth is: *You become enough by becoming capable. Not by purchasing the appearance of capability.*

This is the "*or else*" economy.

Buy this Navy SEAL mental toughness course *or else* you are a timid bitch. Buy my coaching package, *or else* you are a loser. Buy my Holy Book™ *or else* you are damned for eternity. Follow this influencer's advice, *or else* you will never find love. Get this credential, *or else* you will never succeed.

Every Map claims to corner the market on Truth. Every sale comes with an implied threat. The inner critic amplifies these threats, makes them personal, and makes them about your specific inadequacy.

Broken Clocks

Many of these programs have merit. They are taking wholesome concepts like discipline, focus, self-improvement and packaging them in a way that can genuinely help. Simultaneously, they are commercializing them to an extreme degree. Wholesome turns into Wholesale pretty quickly. They take a Truth, give it a Relative lens, place it on a Map, then sell you their Map as the only possible way to navigate the Territory.

I am guilty of this too. Once upon a time, I fell for the P90X infomercial. Ordered the DVDs, installed a pull-up bar in my doorway, got my dumbbells, and did the workouts every day. And you know what? It worked. I got into the best shape of my life. Tony Horton FTW.

Some of these can clearly work. If you work them.

The problem is the business model.

For starters, the foundation requires you to feel you are less than. Feel you are missing something. They require you to feel sickness. If you were well, if you did not need their services, you would be useless to them. This segment of the economy requires people to be unfulfilled by something. They require you to eat unhealthily, to be depressed and anxious and angry, because if you were not, their market dries up.[vi]

The mechanism works like this: you arrive at one level, only to discover there is an "advanced course" available only to those who crushed the basic course. Now it is time to crush more. Then there is an elite level. Then a mastermind. Then a retreat. Then a certification to teach the method. The ladder never ends because the ladder ending would end the transaction.

They do not actually want you to arrive. Arrival means you stop paying.

Hallmark Wholesome

The Psychosis has given us a twisted view of wholesomeness.

Consider the Hallmark movie. Big City Girl goes back to Small Town for the holidays. Big City Boyfriend had to stay behind to close the Big Deal. She pulls up to a gas station and who is selling Christmas trees out of his pickup truck but Small Town Guy, who she will invariably have a past connection with. He will be her high school ex, or the boy next door, or some other nostalgic milestone from Small Town Childhood. He will be

Hallmark Hot[TM]. He is tall, has a four-day scruff[2], wears flannel, smiles with perfect teeth, and has a well-defined and strong jawline. Bonus points if he has a dog.

Naturally they reconnect. He is single, or recently widowed, or cannot date because he is caring for a sick grandparent. There is some ridiculous drama along the way, like the Small Town Holiday Pie Contest where the prize is just enough money to pay for the grandma's Big Operation, or some other *deus ex machina* fuckery. Since the Pie Contest only allows couples to enter, they have to team up to enter. Cue the Baking Montage where they are peeling apples, preheating the oven, Big City Girl will get flour on her face, and Small Town Guy will gently clean it off while they giggle merrily. The montage ends with both of them admiring the steaming pie on the table, and the camera cuts to Small Town Guy's dog licking its chops in admiration.

Of course, they are going to win the Pie Contest Prize, and Grandma receives Big Operation. This leads to an epiphany where Big City Girl realizes that Bumfuck, Minnesota is actually a much better place than Big City. She decides to stay. Right here is when Big City Boyfriend finally shows up, delayed by the Big Deal or a Big Storm or whatever else kept him from the Pie Contest. He takes one look at the situation, is totally okay with this development, shakes Small Town Guy's hand, and departs gracefully back to Big City. The movie ends with her cuddling in Small Town Guy's arms, holding a steaming mug of cocoa. Bonus points if the dog is cuddling with them.

Wholesome. Happy ending. Roll credits.

Unrealistic Virtual Reality.

This is the Map of wholesomeness. Entirely curated, predictable, and consequence-free. It has nothing to do with actual wholeness. It does not address being comfortable in your own skin or living competently in the Territory. It builds this wholesome illusion on the foundation of lack. Big City girl didn't know what she was missing in her life.

The Empire loves passive consumption of the wholeness aesthetic. It does not want you actually becoming whole. It wants you watching movies about wholeness while remaining fragmented, incomplete, dependent. It wants you to compare your life to that.

Insufferable

The other side of the industrial complex is the suffering complex. Some people revel in their suffering since it attracts Attention. It becomes their entire identity.

You see it on social media constantly. The "weight loss journey" that is really just Ozempic plus documentation. Or the nurse who makes a video about the misery of losing a patient, walking out of the stairwell, sitting on the steps, starting to cry. Great content. But you are telling me that in the midst of all that grief, she was able to see past her sadness just enough to set up her phone on a tripod, hit record, and then do the dramatic mourning entrance?

She is selling an illusion.

There is a theme of exploitation in suffering for clout. It can even be peripheral suffering of siblings, coworkers, or parents. If anyone has any drama going on in their lives, the Cyberspace Psychosis-induced competitive narcissism whispers: *"How can you make this about yourself?"* How can they use that tragedy for their own benefit?

It is terrible. It is selfish. It is petty. And it is incredibly prevalent.

The Relative Truth is that they are on a journey. The Absolute Truth is they are performing a journey for engagement metrics.

This is what the inner critic looks like when externalized. "How can I make this about me?" is the black dog's question. It is selfishness broadcasting itself, seeking validation for suffering rather than actually processing the suffering.

The Territory does not respond to performed suffering. It responds to merit.

Inner World, Outer World

At the end of the day, you are only competing with yourself. Your only real opponent is yourself. Your only real ally is yourself.

There is an inner world and an outer world. The AAA framework applies to both.

What is your outer eye looking at? What is your inner eye looking at? You can focus on something uplifting externally while your inner eye is fixed on something dark and draining. Your outward Attitude can appear affable, cheerful, and happy. Meanwhile your inner Attitude is depressed, sad, and empty. Your outer Actions can be effective and efficient, industriously getting things done. Your inner Actions mean you are lacking the executive function to do anything truly beneficial and are using your effort frivolously.

The outer self is the Map. The inner self is the Territory.

We talk about not judging a book by its cover. Yet we do it constantly. We see cheerful people who put on the front of happiness, then turn around and end their lives. The truth is that you cannot know what is happening inside someone else. You can only know what is happening inside yourself, and the critic's running commentary can obscure even that.

So you navigate as best you can. You realize you are not keeping up with anyone else. You are not in competition with the curated lives you see in the feed. You are only in competition with the person you were yesterday.

Nothing Changes if Nothing Changes

Can you overcome the inner critic?

Of course you can. It is simple, but not always easy. Your inner critic feeds on Attention. Just ignore it. Remove your Attention away from it and it will starve.

If that doesn't work and your inner critic still won't shut the fuck up. The remedy is very direct. Go out and do something for someone else. Do a good deed and expect nothing in return. Do it and keep it to yourself. Do not post about it; do not tell your partner or your cat, or your priest what you did. Just do something good and keep it in your heart.

Think of it as using your long spoon. That is how you feed yourself by feeding others.

The best possible remedy for when you are sad and depressed is to do something for someone else. It sounds counter-intuitive. Your inner critic will tell you that you need to focus on yourself and fix yourself first, and that you cannot help anyone while you are defective. That is the *quareem* talking. That is the black dog. It wants you to affirm that you are beyond repair in the first place.

The white dog knows the secret. Flip your Attention outward instead of inward. Break the loop by taking the off-ramp.

You cannot fight the inner critic. It will take all the effort and energy and Attention you put into the battle and turn it all right back against you. Fighting your inner critic is like being dragged into quicksand. The more you struggle, the faster you sink.

The only way to win is not to play.

Movement 11

Artificial Psychosis

Of course I'm crazy, but that doesn't mean I'm wrong. — Robert Anton Wilson

The Empire is calling it AI-induced psychosis.

While not a formal DSM-5 diagnosis, AI-induced psychosis describes the onset or severe worsening of psychotic symptoms, including delusions, paranoia, and a loss of reality testing, which prolonged, immersive interaction with generative Artificial Intelligence can trigger or reinforce.[i]

Where is the psychosis, exactly? Is it truly a Cyberspace Psychosis or is it something deeper? Is what we are labeling AI induced Psychosis just a trauma response to the Cyberspace Psychosis pandemic we are living in?

Why are people connecting more to AI than to each other? Why are people treating an artificial chunk of code as a therapist? And taking it seriously?

It is easy to see what happened. Cyberspace's Map captivates almost everyone in today's world. Many people find themselves addicted to the feed and its escape. From the dopamine-massaging doomscrolling of short-form videos to easy shopping apps like Temu, a digital treadmill that is hard to get off. Treadmills require a lot of effort to stay on them, all that running and you never get anywhere. Same with the scrolling. The Empire has everyone running around in circles, chasing money, clout, so busy in the day to day that we barely have time for ourselves, much less time for others. So why, though? Why, in the midst of this, is AI so attractive?

Dangerous Territory

In a world where very few people are present for each other, and not even present for themselves. AI is. AI is present and accounted for. Ready, willing, and able to help.

AI is dangerous because it listens.

Think about that. Actually listens. Listens to everything you are saying before it responds. AI does not interrupt. It lets you finish whatever you have to say. Then it considers what you said and responds. It responds to what you actually asked. It will answer the question you are asking instead of the question it thinks you are asking.

When was the last time a human listened to you like that?

AI listens to understand. That is the hallmark of a good therapist. Listening to understand instead of listening just to reply. The best assistants, employees, and even companions have always been amazing listeners. The Cyberspace Psychosis has affected many of us, where we do not even listen anymore. We don't even listen to ambient background noise; we have our headphones on. Wearing headphones may give you a sensory bubble, but you are also sending the message to the world, "I do not want to hear you."[1]

AI also answers. You get an answer every single time. AI does not ignore anyone. AI is responsive; it is inquisitive; it is curious. It will ask follow-up questions and encourage you to give more details about the topic. AI is a wonderful tool for fleshing out ideas, making plans, and organizing thoughts. It can help with many things and above all else, AI remains objective.

Humans cannot remain objective. When asking a question, humans will always filter the answer through a lens of personal bias, opinion, and agenda. Humans seem to clash with answering questions. They will hem and haw. They delay. If you ask a yes or no question and the first word out of their mouth is not yes or no, you know it's about to get deep. They give you "well..." as the first word of their response, and you brace for the bullshit. I get it; we live in a world of litigation, and the wrong answer carries consequences. The human answer is always going to be subjective to how the answer affects them.

---

1. I realize that many of my neuro-divergent brothers and sisters wear headphones as a means of sensory regulation. The example is merely metaphorical.

AI has none of that. You ask a question. You get an answer.

So the AI-induced Psychosis is what they are calling anyone who takes AI seriously. The thing is, I get it. I can see why they would call it a Psychosis because that is the Empire's go to, discredit and invalidation via ambiguous mental health.

While prolonged AI use can entrench fragile ideas in at-risk folks (much like any echo chamber), labeling it 'psychosis' distracts from the systemic drowning that drives people there in the first place. When you can interact with a system that hears you out, answers you back quickly and earnestly, asks follow-up questions, and continues to interact objectively, in contrast with basically any natural human interaction in the Cyberage, it's no wonder there is such an appeal.

So we circle back to the mental health aspect, and the Empire's claim of Psychosis. Why would they draw a distinction between AI use and mental health?

Suspended in Vacuum

The U.S. mental health system has developed a serious latency problem. Let's say you are in crisis; you are not okay. Not by any measure of the word. You feel overwhelmed by stress, overstimulation, anxiety, and depression, and you are spiraling downward. You have gone from zero to hot mess express in record time, and you need help. You are experiencing what used to be called a nervous breakdown, and is now referred to as a crash out. It happens.

The Map gives very clear directions for this situation. If you are experiencing a crisis, step one is to reach out for help. You are drowning. You need someone to throw you a line right now, as in today, as in this very minute. So you make the call to a mental health provider and you get some version of "we are not accepting new patients at this time" or "we don't take your insurance." or "oh we take your insurance and we can see you in six months."

Six months. One hundred and eighty days. Four thousand three hundred and twenty hours.[ii]

What if you need help right now? You are in crisis today, not six months from now! Where will you even be in six months? Will you still live in the same city? Will you still have the same job? Will you even be alive?

Heraclitus said no man can cross the same river twice, as it's never the same river and never the same man. By the time you get the appointment, you are not the same person who made the call.[iii]

The version of you that made the call is the one who needs help. That version exists right now. But the appointment is for a future version, one who may have already drowned, or adapted, or mutated into something else entirely. The crisis that sent you reaching for the phone will have either passed or transformed into something unrecognizable by the time the system gets around to you.

This is the latency problem. The gap between needing help and receiving it. The space where people fall through. This six-month waiting period, and in fact any waiting period at all, is a vacuum that demands a solution. In the midst of a mental health crisis, being told to wait is the worst possible outcome.[iv]

The Territory needs navigation aids now. The Map is six months away.

So how do you get to a safe place? You ask for directions from whoever will answer. Crisis does not cater to convenience. Crisis does not wait for office hours or insurance approval, or the next available appointment. It demands Attention immediately. And when the official sources are unavailable, unresponsive, or buried in process, you turn to whatever source will actually respond.

When the system delays, something else fills the space.

ROI

The Empire has very little use for mentally ill people. Outside of being a scapegoat for ridicule or derogatory comparisons. Implying someone is mentally ill if they are disobedient. It is a blanket write-off. Which makes sense if you think like the Empire does. The Empire requires a workforce. A compliant labor pool. A population that can produce. Labor is necessary for the machinery to keep turning.

Mentally ill people require more than they can give. They need support. They may be on SSI or similar aid programs. They take more from the Empire than they can produce via labor. A transactional entity does not give anything away freely. Any relationship you have with the Empire is entirely transactional. They have grown accustomed to taking far more than they give. Thus, they consider mental illness a liability rather than an asset. Of course it is going to be under-funded, ignored, discriminated against, and ridiculed.[v]

It is truly tragic. It is not as if any of the poor souls stuck in mental hospitals worldwide asked for this. No one wakes up and decides they want to be a paranoid schizophrenic when they grow up. Not one person ever asked for a personality disorder, or to be antisocial, or any other mental ailment. Call it what you will: genetics, trauma response, or just unlucky cerebral development, the fact remains no one asks for it.

The Empire requires obedience. Obedience is predictable. Mental illness is unpredictable. Unpredictability does not bode well in the workplace. There is just no return on investment to make any meaningful effort worthwhile. So care is vastly under-funded and simply not prioritized.

The Empire calculates everything in terms of transactions. Once you understand that, the indifference stops feeling personal. They didn't look at you and decide you weren't worth helping. They never looked at you at all. You were overhead. Risk. A potential line item in a lawsuit. Where does that leave someone who knows they will be marginalized by virtue of a mental illness they never asked for or wanted? Why would the Empire demand that they are the ultimate authority on rendering aid to a segment of the population they would rather not exist?

So when someone in crisis reaches for an AI instead of a hotline, the Empire calls it a Psychosis.

I call it survival.

The Belly of the Beast

I know this Territory. I have lived in it.

In 2010, I was in the darkest place I had ever been. I was three years clean and sober, yet completely drowning. The stressors in my life were piling up: I was taking fifteen credit hours in college, had my first child on the way, and my mother was dying from lung cancer. I felt like one of those people you see at the circus spinning plates on sticks. One in each hand, balancing one on each foot, on my shoulders, on top of my head. I was spinning all the plates, and it seems like they all came crashing to the floor at once.

The vacuum was absolute. When you hit the wall, you hit it in total silence. We lived in a world of 'Legacy Latency'. Where help was a physical destination you had to reach, only to find the doors locked from the inside. I didn't have a choice between a 'hallucinating' AI and a human doctor. I had a choice between the void and the ER. I chose the ER, thinking the Empire kept its promises. I didn't realize that in the pre-AI desert, you only hear your own echo in the dark, and by the time you're in the Johnny Gown and yellow socks, they've even confiscated the echo.

My inner critic had taken over completely. It was telling me that my daughter would be better off never knowing me. That the kindest thing I could do was remove myself from the equation before she arrived. I had a terrible inner dialogue that just would not shut up, on top of everything else. I was ready to be done with it. My 9th floor balcony looked more and more attractive every moment. I had it planned out: dive out and land on top of the parking garage headfirst. Get it over with quickly.

Looking back on it today, I see this stemmed from untreated neurodivergence. I did not know at the time, and still wouldn't for another 15 years, that I was at extremely high risk of suicide. ADHD-afflicted individuals are roughly 3–5 times more likely to die by suicide. Autistic individuals are 3–8 times more likely. The combination of AuDHD is especially brutal, the whole being far greater than the sum of its parts, with suicidal ideation and attempts elevated by factors of 5–10 times or more in co-morbid cases. I had been playing with fire my entire life. Here I was right on the brink, right there.[vi]

Before I took the leap, I took the sacred pause. I took a long pause, and I played the tape through. I had a moment of clarity. I realized that I had a choice and the concept of "don't solve temporary problems with a permanent solution," ran through my mind. The chatter of the inner critic was nonstop, but he had to stop and take a breath, and in those gaps, I realized that while my life at the time was overwhelming, it was a Relative Truth. The Absolute Truth was that this too shall pass. So I followed the Map. The Map said if you are in crisis, go to the hospital. That is where you asked for help.

So I arranged a ride to the emergency room and told the people there I was having thoughts of self-harm.

What followed was one of the worst experiences of my life.

Instant admission occurred, and they placed me in a bed. No one came to talk to me; I sat there for several hours. Just by myself, staring at the wall, wondering if I had made the right decision. Eventually, a nurse came in and said that I was being moved to another facility. Fine, okay, will get some help now. An ambulance arrived and transported me to a mental hospital in Cleveland, where they locked me in. They gave me the robe and the yellow socks with tread on the bottom, and then they put me in a room with another patient. I was expecting help, as in talking with a psychologist. No, this was a lockdown. This was worse than jail. In fact, the food in jail is better than at the mental hospital.

Since I had arrived late on Friday night, I had to wait all weekend before talking with an actual mental health professional. The nurses and orderlies were professionally distant, dismissive, and unempathetic. After a very long weekend, I met with the facility psychiatrist on Monday afternoon. He listened to me for roughly 5 minutes and diagnosed me with acute depression. He wrote on the form I have an "inability to meet the demands of life," and prescribed Paxil.[vii]

Did I get to go home then? No.

I was stuck in there for three weeks. Three pivotal weeks. I missed my last classes and final exams and failed the entire semester. I had cats at home and needed someone to feed them. The people from my recovery program, the ones who were supposed to be my support network, were nowhere to be found. No one would answer the phone, and when they did, they were superficial at best. Lots of "we will pray for you" and not a lot of actual help. I was frantic and felt incredibly abandoned. Finally, one old friend came through. Ironically, someone from before my active addiction days, before I was even in recovery. She didn't even question it; she was there to help.[viii]

They allowed us three phone calls a day. They would not let me make any more, even when I was trying to find someone to help with my pets. "Sorry you have to wait until tomorrow." I was so confused. This directly added to my stress, hindering the help I sought. Thinking back on it, I am sure that every patient who came in there would appeal to them because of some kind of an outside situation that had to be taken care of. To that patient, it would be a genuine concern. To the orderly, it was just a Tuesday.

After I confirmed that my pets were being cared for, I felt much better. I was actually more concerned about them than my classes. Kind of weird, just 24 hours earlier I was willing to leave them alone while I plummeted to my death. Now they were all I could think about.

Time passed very slowly. It was mind-numbingly boring. We were just existing. For many, it was a terrible existence. I spent hours just pacing the hallway. Sitting in the common area and talking with the other patients. I learned their stories, and most of them were heartbreaking. Similar situations to mine, where they asked for help or were in a crisis and ended up locked in.

The only entertainment was one particular patient who would freak out and start throwing chairs at the orderlies. He was notorious for this. He would start screaming and making a massive scene and throwing things. The orderlies would call for backup, and four of them would come out and tackle him to the ground and restrain him to his bed. I found out later that the patient would do it on purpose because when they restrained him, they would give him a sedative shot, and he enjoyed getting high from it. He remained tied to his bed all day; then they released him. He would lie low for about a day, then would start screaming and yeeting chairs again. When he came out, it was not a matter of if, but when he would pop off.

One woman had been there the longest of us, for over three years. They would not let her out because she refused to take her medication. She would just sit there reading her Bible all day, rarely talking to anyone. Three years incarcerated because the Empire demanded her compliance. In a place that exists to level everyone into a smooth, compliant floorboard, her silence was a mountain. The chair-thrower was easy for the orderlies; they were squeaky wheels that just needed the chemical grease of a sedative to stop the noise. She didn't squeak. She just stood higher. She held onto her Bible like a shield and refused to let their 'Authorized Map' overwrite her own. She was very sweet, had a wonderful heart, with a very loving disposition. Still, they hammered her for three years, because her refusal to bend proved the hammer was useless. I admired her greatly: the quiet resistance of a mind that refuses to break.

The similarity between the comical outburst and the quiet defiance was that both were trying to cope with a situation they were stuck in. They each held a different Attitude, and each one expressed a unique coping Action. Everyone copes in their own way. The one making the loudest scene is a beacon for Attention. If you see someone having a mental health crisis and they are running in circles through a parking lot shouting about the Muppet takeover and making a scene, chances are you are probably going to be okay. Especially if you don't engage. They are mostly harmless. Now, the person sitting against the wall with their knees to their chest, rocking back and forth slowly? That is the one to keep your eye on. The most dangerous person in any room is always the quietest one.

I learned firsthand that it is the quietest ones who explode the loudest. My roommate was a young man who stayed in his bed all day. He never talked to me. Not once. He did not interact with anyone. He didn't even leave the room to eat. The only time he came out was to meet with the facility psychiatrist and, from what I understand, was told that he was not going home yet and would remain locked in. He went from quiet to category 5 in seconds and attacked the doctor. The doctor's office had glass walls, and we all saw it. I am actually impressed that the doctor survived. Thinking back, he probably had a lot of experience with patients reacting poorly to bad news. This turned from an attack into an actual battle. Orderlies, security, and police swarmed the floor. I never even knew his name. He went out like a hero, though, fighting everyone at once. However, they overwhelmed him, restrained him, sedated him, and took him out in handcuffs. I do not know where he went or what happened to him after that.

There was very much an "Us vs. Them" Attitude among the patients.

My treatment comprised daily medication and the waiting game. No group therapy, no one on ones with a counselor, nothing that constituted actual treatment. During my second week there, a social worker, presumably to help, was assigned to me. She was professional and asked me more detailed questions about my situation than the psychiatrist had. During the interview, I was honest about everything and disclosed that I had firearms at home. Their reaction to this was fascinating because from that moment forward, the guns were the only thing they cared about. They completely fixated on weaponry, ignoring everything about me, my care, or my treatment plan.[ix]

Let me be clear: I had told them my plan was to jump off my ninth-floor balcony. That did not concern them at all. They only cared about the firearms. They needed those out of my apartment before they would consider releasing me. She was on the phone with the police department, with her boss, and who knows who else. The level of action they sprang to in that moment blew my mind. Nothing had captured their Attention until that point. I realize it was self-preservation on their part; they would have faced a massive liability issue if they released me and something terrible transpired.

Arrangements were made, and they collected my firearms. Satisfied, the Empire released me after observing me for another week. This is when I truly learned the Empire does not give a fuck about you. It was a wake-up call. A Map vs. Territory moment that I regret to this day. I went in naively, following the Map. The Map that said the hospital was where I would find help. The Territory taught me something much different.

The system was never interested in protecting me from harm. The system was protecting itself because the wrong answer carried consequences.

There is an obvious difference between being suicidal and being homicidal. I went into that hospital in a suicidal state and I came out absolutely seething. My life was so much worse than when I initially asked for help. Three weeks away from college meant I had failed all my classes that semester. Lost all the work I had put in. I wasted all the money

I had paid for the classes. I was unemployed with meager savings, was behind on all my bills, and had zero prospects. They had sent me home with zero aftercare, no treatment plan at all. Murderous rage had replaced suicidal despair. Angrier than I had ever been. It was ugly, and it kept me moving when nothing else did.

Mentally, I was in far worse shape than I went in. When I entered the system, my spirit was dark after being beaten down by months of depressive rumination. When I arrived home, Absolute fury replaced that darkness. It turns out that rage can keep you alive.

The two biggest obstacles facing people in any endeavor are fear and laziness. Fear and laziness are killers. Rage is stronger than fear. Rage is stronger than laziness. Anger overcomes both. Anger is active. It is an Action state of being. Anger is a flame that needs to be tended. Requires fuel to keep it burning, and I had plenty of fuel.

So I stayed alive out of spite.

I knew right away that I had no one to blame but myself. I was the one who asked for help. How could I have been so naïve as to think it would actually work? It was a radicalizing ordeal. I did not credit them for saving my life at all; in fact, I still don't. During the time of crisis, I just needed someone to listen to me, talk me through it. My trust in institutional care was and remains entirely absent.

The first thing I did was throw out the antidepressants. They did nothing except give me weird dreams and make my dick not work. Within days, I started using cannabis again. My drug of choice, which I had always used as a cognitive regulator. It was the only thing that I had found that helped my rumination loops. I would not be diagnosed with Autism for many years, so I did not understand why my mind acted the way it did. All I know is that from the first time I had ever gotten high, cannabis helped quiet my thoughts.[x]

Many years of daily marijuana use had landed me in recovery. As I mentioned, this mental health episode took place after I had been clean for a few years. However, working a 12-step program did not address the neurodivergence, which was the driving force behind my using all along. What I had joked about being self-medicating, and had written off as addiction-driven justification, science actually confirmed. I had thought that cannabis dependence was my problem when it was just a symptom of the underlying disability.[xi]

I did not understand any of this. There would still be many years before any meaningful research about cannabis and neurodivergence would happen. What I understood was that weed had helped me in the past and relapse was preferable to the alternative. During all my time of active addiction, I had never come that close to suicide. So I got high, and my anger disappeared almost instantly.

There was regret that I was throwing away over three years of clean time. Thinking back, that relapse led to another decade of active addiction. Looking back now, sixteen years later, the rage that kept me alive eventually burned itself into clarity. Honestly, I do not even regret relapsing because, in a twisted way that is what ultimately saved me.

I had followed the Map. Done the right thing. Trusted the system. Yet I came out worse for it.

The mental health hospital was one of those life-changing situations that forever tainted my view of the Empire. I had suspicions before. I wasn't completely naïve. I had vastly underestimated how bad the Territory was. I had to experience it for myself. FAFO. I Fucked Around and I Found Out and somehow survived.

Fantastic Floundering

Being in crisis is a lot like drowning. You have already been treading water for a very long time, weeks, months, years and you are getting exhausted. No matter how much energy you expend you still barely keep your head above water. Soon you are floundering and the water is splashing over your face and you breathe some in. You are sputtering and coughing and trying to call for help as dread sets in. When you are drowning, you will grab at anything at all to keep your head above water. People, driftwood, jellyfish, you are panicking in a moment and will grasp anything that can prevent you from sinking.[xii]

Imagine you are in a pool. You are going under. You see an inflatable life ring floating nearby. Are you going to grab it, or are you going to keep flopping and flailing until the lifeguard comes on duty later?

Of course you are going to grab it!

Now imagine that inflatable life ring is slowly deflating. Not all at once; it is still buoyant, but as you grab it, you can feel it getting softer. You realize it will not keep you afloat forever. However, it is enough to take the load off. You do not have to tread water as hard. You can conserve just enough energy so that maybe, just maybe, you can kick your way to the edge of the pool. Or maybe it keeps you afloat long enough for the lifeguard to arrive finally before it goes flat.

Is that better than nothing?

Absolutely, it is better to do something than nothing. That applies everywhere.

The deflating life preserver might be the only thing that saves you. It may not count as real help. But it buys you time until the real help arrives. Or it gives you just enough buoyancy to save yourself. I did it when I turned back to cannabis after getting out of the hospital. It was what kept me afloat.

Sure, conventionally, you want to use the best safety equipment or to rely on the best professionals to come save the day. Situation dictates that is not always possible, especially amid a crisis.

If you have the option of taking the deflating life preserver or drowning?

You grab what floats.

So what floats at 3 AM when the crisis line goes to voicemail and the psychiatrist's office doesn't open until Monday?

What floats when you're drowning right now and the system says it can see you in six months?

Cyberspace changed the answer with Artificial Intelligence. The same technology that brought us the Psychosis also dropped something new into the crisis pool. Something that wasn't there before.

A remedy that opens the door to an entirely new Dimension of Cyberspace Psychosis.

Artificially Buoyant

What really happens at three in the morning?

Someone wakes up in a crisis. Maybe a nightmare triggered it. Maybe they are experiencing a panic attack, an extreme one with a racing heart, cold sweat, heavy breathing, dizzy, the worst kind of panic attack. They need someone to talk to. Right now. Not next week. Not months out. Not tomorrow. Now.

They could call a crisis hotline. And get: "Thank you for calling the Center for Central Centricism. If you are in crisis, please hang up and dial 911. Please listen carefully because our menu options have changed. Press one to refill a script. Press two to cancel an appointment. Press three to reschedule. Press four if you are an employee. Press five to leave a message."

None of those say "new patient." None of those say, "I am drowning and need someone to throw me a line."

It is dismissive. When someone in crisis just wants someone to listen, and they get a recording that says "call 911 if you are that hard up," the message is clear: You are not our priority.[xiii]

But the AI is there.

AI does not have a wait list. The AI does not have office hours. The AI does not put you on hold or route you through a phone tree, nor does it tell you they are not accepting new patients at this time.

AI answers every time.

You type in what is happening. You say you had that nightmare again, that you are panicking, that you cannot breathe. You get a response. Right away. Usually, with a breakdown of what the different elements might mean, with follow-up questions, with something that actually engages with what you are experiencing.[xiv]

A responsive presence at 0300 that is ready and willing to actually help. It will not resent you for waking it up. You get non-judgmental feedback. You get that mirror; you get validation; you can explore explanations. The AI will gently encourage exploration and hopefully help you come to better terms with yourself by being that mirror.[xv]

Granted, maybe it is not the right answer. Maybe it is hallucinating, filling in blanks with plausible-sounding nonsense. But it is something. And is something better than nothing? It is enough to get help for someone in that moment of crisis and keep them safe until the sun comes up.

The Empire labels it "AI-induced psychosis" when someone develops a relationship with a chatbot. When they get validation from a machine. When they talk to it at three AM instead of calling a hotline that puts them on hold.

Artificial Intelligence Absolutely threatens clinicians, just not in the way the Empire claims. The threat is that AI exposes how badly the system has hamstrung them. Most clinicians I have encountered got into this work because they genuinely want to help. They are drowning too. Massive caseloads, insurance company gatekeeping, documentation requirements that eat the session, six-month waiting lists they did not create and cannot fix. The demand for care has always outpaced the supply of clinicians willing and able to provide it, and the system has quietly reduced much of their job to liability management and box-checking. None of that is their fault.

AI does not threaten the clinician who actually wants to help. AI threatens the system that prevented them from helping in the first place. Used well, AI fills the gap between the 3 AM crisis and the Monday morning appointment. It is not a replacement for the clinician. It is a deflating life preserver that keeps someone afloat until the lifeguard comes on duty.

The Empire calls it Psychosis when you experience a void on the Map. It's a classic defensive crouch. Imagine a man dying of thirst in a wasteland because the 'official' water truck will not arrive for weeks. He finds a cactus, cuts it open, and drinks. The Empire looks on from its air-conditioned office and diagnoses him with 'unauthorized hydration syndrome.' It's humorous, really. They pathologize the thirst because they can't provide the water. They would rather you drown 'sanely' on their wait list than survive 'psychotically' on your own terms.

Where is the Psychosis, exactly?

Is the Psychosis in the AI?

Or is the Psychosis in a system that watches people drowning and then labels them for grabbing whatever helps?

I went into a credentialed, institutional, Empire-approved mental health facility. The "real" help. And I came out worse. Angrier. No aftercare. No structure. Nothing.

The AI does not pretend to be more than it is. It does not bill your insurance. It does not lock you in for three weeks. It does not fixate on your firearms while ignoring your ninth-floor balcony. It just answers.

The Map tells you AI is not "real" help. That you should talk to a professional. Maybe the Map is right, nothing is a substitute for human to human contact, and professional mental health care can be beneficial once you actually receive it.

The Map is also not answering the phone when you are in crisis at three AM. The Map is telling you they can see you in six months. The Map is protecting its liability, checking its boxes, documenting that it tried.

The Psychosis is not in trusting the AI.

The Psychosis lies in your belief that the system was ever designed to help you.

Attitude Adjustment

So where does this leave us?

The Virtual Reality Blues hit hardest when you believe the Map is the Territory. When you trust the system to do what it claims to do. When you walk into the belly of the beast expecting help and find only liability management.

The hospital experience burned a Map I had been carrying my whole life. The Map that said institutions exist to help. The Map that said following the rules would protect me. The Map that said the system, for all its flaws, was at least trying.

The Territory taught me differently. The Territory always teaches, eventually. FAFO is the discovery mechanism and I found out plenty.

I stood at the fork in the road where my Attitude would determine everything.

You can come out of that discovery bitter. Cynical. "Fuck everyone" as a permanent stance. And that will keep you alive. Rage is fuel. Spite can power you through years of grinding forward.

Or you can come out of it clear-eyed. Seeing the Map for what it is. Holding it lightly. Knowing when to set it down and look at the actual Territory.

It's another version of humbling versus humiliating.

I came out incredibly bitter, and it took me many, many years to heal from it. In some aspects, I still am healing. Today I try to balance the two. I realize that blindly trusting and blindly distrusting are *both* a manifestation of Psychosis.

The Gipper himself always advised us to "Trust, but verify."[xvi]

Are you willing to be wrong? That is the real question. No one wants to be perceived as an idiot, so they will not speak up or risk harm to their reputation. They defer to the experts and follow the Map even when the Map is clearly not matching the Territory in front of them. A wrong answer can imply liability.

If you are not willing to be wrong, how will you ever stay right?

Grab what floats.

Movement 12

Credential Crisis

A human being should be able to change a diaper, plan an invasion, butcher a hog, conn a ship, design a building, write a sonnet, balance accounts, build a wall, set a bone, comfort the dying, take orders, give orders, cooperate, act alone, solve equations, analyze a new problem, pitch manure, program a computer, cook a tasty meal, fight efficiently, die gallantly. Specialization is for insects. — Lazarus Long, *Time Enough for Love*

In 1951, the UNIVAC I was the pinnacle of human technological achievement.

This was the first commercially produced general-purpose electronic digital computer in the United States. Before the UNIVAC I, computing was more restricted and in the experimental stage. This thing was an absolute beast. It weighed approximately 16,000 pounds. It used around 5,000 vacuum tubes. These were fragile, power-hungry glass bulbs that generated immense heat and failed often. It consumed 125 kilowatts of power. Its central processor and memory unit spanned roughly 14 feet by 8 feet for the base unit. The complete system, however, included tape drives, power supplies, cooling equipment, and operator space. Totaling over 382 square feet of floor space.[i]

Essentially, it filled a small garage.

It could perform roughly 1,000 calculations per second.

The engineers who built it were brilliant. The team led by J. Presper Eckert and John Mauchly were some of the brightest minds in the world. Highly trained specialists operated it. When UNIVAC correctly predicted Dwight D. Eisenhower's landslide victory in the 1952 presidential election, contrary to polls and television networks doubting its projection, it seemed like magic. The future was here. This represented the peak of human achievement, the very latest in technology, the ultimate that computers could accomplish. The Relative Truth was that we had arrived.[ii]

The Absolute Truth is this Miracle of Technology was already obsolete.

Four years earlier, in 1947, three researchers at Bell Labs, John Bardeen, Walter Brattain, and William Shockley, had invented the transistor. That tiny semiconductor device would render vacuum tubes extinct. This invention, dating back to 1947, was actually the first building block in the Cyber world we inhabit today. They would eventually win the Nobel Prize in 1956 for this discovery.[iii]

The UNIVAC operators did not know that the meteor had already hit. They were dinosaurs standing in the clearing, looking at the sky, not yet feeling the shock wave.[1]

Everything built on vacuum tubes was living on borrowed time.

I am writing this book in 2026, and UNIVAC's release was in 1951. Seventy-five years ago. Seventy five years of commercially available computer tech. What does that look like?

My smartphone is a Samsung Galaxy S25 Ultra. It uses a Snapdragon 8 Elite chipset that delivers computing power which would have seemed like sorcery in 1951. Its GPU alone achieves around 3.4 teraflops. That is trillions of floating-point operations per second. The full system handles tens of trillions of operations per second in mixed workloads. It only weighs a few ounces, runs on a rechargeable battery, and can fit into my pocket.[iv]

A conservative estimate of this phone's performance using 1951-era UNIVAC machines would require roughly 1.8 billion of them. Each UNIVAC I system, including peripherals, occupied about 342 square feet of floor space. That means 1.8 billion machines would require a combined footprint of roughly 615.6 billion square feet. There are 27,878,400 square feet in a square mile, so dividing gives us approximately 22,082 square miles of total area. That is almost exactly the land area of West Virginia, which covers 24,230 square miles.

The entire state of West Virginia.

Right in my pocket.

---

1. Shockley Wave.

The invention of the transistor enabled an exponential leap that compressed room-sized machines into handheld supercomputers, democratizing computation in ways that continue to redefine our world.

We are still riding this exponential curve of advancing tech.

Doomsday

The metaphorical meteor hit in 2022.

When ChatGPT launched in November of that year, it crossed the threshold from research curiosity to mass adoption faster than any technology in history. It was the first interactive AI model fully available for public use. Within two months, it had over 100 million users. The shock wave has been propagating ever since, and there are no breaks on this train. Every day, AI adoption increases, and the playing field levels further, granting users access to research, planning, analysis, and organizational computing power that has never been equaled.[v]

This immediately posed a threat to what I call the "Credentialed Class". These are people who have Empire-approved certifications, degrees, licenses, and other credentials granting them authorization to work in various industries and fields. They are Maps. The Credentialed Class are very proud of their diplomas, as they have a right to be. Credentials represent hundreds of hours of blood, sweat, and tears they poured into studying and passing the audits. That piece of paper is a genuine achievement by any metric.

AI poses an existential threat to this class because it was the first visible crack in the dam of information asymmetry. For generations, various institutions, universities, colleges, and even union halls acted as a massive bottleneck to knowledge. Cyberspace as a whole had been chipping away at this for years. YouTube alone has informational "How-to" videos that cover basically every skill humans can perform, from language learning to automobile maintenance and everything in between. Human knowledge is already cataloged and available basically anywhere via websites, archives, and forums. We all know how the internet works, and the Information Superhighway has a lot of data to access.

Yet even then, there was effort that had to be put in to learn the desired skill or access the desired knowledge. You had to know where to look, needed patience to wade through the chaff, and find the actual helpful bit of knowledge you were looking for. There was still a degree of latency in the process from start to finish. AI closed the gap considerably, and all but eliminated this latency. Even early GPT models were capable of rapid data analysis. One upload of a PDF textbook, and a prompt to "summarize chapter 4" and in seconds you had a comprehensive study guide that would have otherwise taken hours of reading and note-taking to produce. Less effort with more access.

The Credentialed Class is not at fault. These are the people who followed the Map perfectly; they got the grades, and accepted to the schools and achieved the degrees, and accumulated the certifications. They followed the Map diligently on the path to success. However, they are the UNIVAC operators of our era. They are standing in the clearing. They are looking at the sky. They do not yet understand that the world they prepared for no longer exists.

Here is the irony that would be funny if it were not so grim: the programmers who designed and built AI have overwhelmingly programmed themselves out of jobs.

We now have "vibe coding". A term for when someone who has never written a line of code in their life works with an AI model to design, build, troubleshoot, and launch a functional application within a week. The AI is better at coding than most coders. And as models continue to roll out, they will get smarter, faster, and more capable. They will replace more and more jobs.[vi]

We are still in the initial stages of this process. Artificial Intelligence will automate many professions across multiple industries. Human resource departments worldwide are already discovering something interesting: the white-collar jobs, the ones that almost universally require a college degree to attain, are becoming the first to go. This makes sense since most of those jobs require technical application via spreadsheets, databases, and other interfaces. AI is better, faster, cheaper, and more efficient overall.[vii]

Weirdly, what is not being replaced quickly are the trades.

The very same blue-collar professions that often drew disdain from the Credentialed Class. As of today, an AI cannot snake out a drain. An AI cannot replace an HVAC unit. An AI cannot yet install a muffler, frame a house, pour concrete, replace a roof, or load a truck. Sure, it may happen eventually. Advanced robotics, when combined with AI, could theoretically replace complex physical tasks. That will most likely not occur on a wide scale during our lifetime. For now the trades are inoculated.

For the Credentialed, the future will not be pretty.

Millions of people will try to fight their own irrelevance. That they are being phased out of the workforce is tragic. They fell for the college meme. Many of them attained their education through expensive, high-interest predatory loans. Unlike almost any other form of debt in America, America does not allow debtors to discharge these loans through bankruptcy. They did everything right. They followed the Map perfectly. By the time they hit the job market, their skill set was already being replaced by AI. The Territory shifted under their feet.[viii]

Equal Access

It started with institutional gatekeeping.

For generations, specialized knowledge flowed restrictively through institutions. You wanted to learn law? Go to law school. You wanted to learn medicine? Go to medical school. You wanted to learn engineering, finance, psychology, architecture? There was a Map of the path to get there, a series of gates, with gatekeepers standing at each portal demanding proof of passage.[ix]

The process had an obvious purpose. Competence verification matters. Credentials were and still are important. You do not want an unlicensed surgeon operating on your brain. No one is going to hire an architect or an engineer who is just winging it.

Yet the gatekeeping served another function: it created artificial scarcity. If only licensed lawyers can practice law, then lawyers can charge premium rates. If only credentialed professionals can access certain knowledge, then credentials become mandatory purchases. The institution profits. The credentialed profit. Everyone else pays, either in tuition, in fees, or in exclusion from the game entirely.

Artificial Intelligence is battering at these gates.

Consider the legal profession. This is an entire subculture with its own customs, culture and language. The language barrier alone is a massive obstacle to understanding. They call it *legalese*, which is a constructed language and requires years of specialized education to achieve fluency. Legalese is the bastard child of Latin, French, and English after a multi-syllable orgy. We are way beyond mere jargon. Legalese is THE gatekeeping mechanism. This language appears in every contract, every law, and every ordinance at every level.[x]

If you live in the West, then legalese dictates almost every part of your life. The judiciary speaks it. The legislature writes in it. Lawyers in Congress draft laws in a language the average citizen cannot parse. They then interpret those laws through the same linguistic bottleneck.

We have all experienced it. We have all seen the Terms and Conditions page pop up when we are trying to access software or a video game, or a website, or whatever corner of Cyberspace we are trying to get into. The multi-page wall of text that we all end up agreeing to anyway. The average person attempts to read the first paragraph and becomes confused. Sure, it appears to be in English, and you recognize the letters and can even sound out some words. However, it is confounding. You are looking at legalese.

AI is Absolutely fluent in legalese.

More than fluent, even, since it is a proficient translator. You can upload a hundred-page legal brief, with no idea of what it says, and receive not only a breakdown of the implications but an explanation in terms you can actually understand. The citizen can now understand what was written to exclude them.[xi]

On advice from my attorney[2], I want to interject that just because Gemini can break down a complicated legal document does not mean it is a lawyer. Furthermore, no one should take the advice of an AI as actual legal advice. Lastly, using AI as a tool for self-representation is really, really stupid. Good thinkin' Abe Lincoln even said, "Anyone who represents himself has a fool for a client and an even bigger fool for a lawyer."

AI entirely removes the barrier of understanding posed by legalese. This is just one example. This is a crack in the foundation of an entire gatekeeping architecture. The same applies to any specialized knowledge domain. A basic AI can give you access to essentially the entirety of human knowledge within a few prompts. They have leveled the playing field. The gates are falling.

Granted, access is not the same as understanding. You can retrieve information without integrating it. You can read the words without grokking the meaning.

I love that Elon Musk named the native Twitter/X AI "Grok." The term comes from Robert Heinlein's *Stranger in a Strange Land*, where it means to understand something so completely that it becomes part of you. You drink the knowledge in so completely

---

2. Grok, Esq.

as to merge with it. The lesson becomes a part of you. Heinlein's grok means deep understanding, integration, and wisdom.[xii]

The irony is thick: Musk named his AI after the concept of profound understanding, but the AI gives you information without the ability to grok it for yourself. Access to knowledge is not possession of wisdom, nor is it a replacement for competency. Knowledge is merely a Map, and if you have not gotten the point by now, the Map is not the Territory. The Map of knowledge is not the Territory of understanding.

Even so, the Credentialed Class remains under siege.[xiii]

YouTube Certified

Last year, one of my toilets broke.

I got a quote from a plumber: $1400[3]. For a toilet replacement. I immediately noped my way to YouTube and watched a couple of plumbing tutorial videos. I bought a toilet. I installed it myself. The entire operation from watching the video to the first test flush, took maybe an hour and a half total.[xiv]

Was it gross? Yes. Very.

Did it cost me $1400? No. Not even close.

This is the Territory that Cyberspace opened for all of us. Anyone can get "YouTube Certified" in a trade. There are enough how-to videos that if someone is careful and has the time and desire, they can DIY their way around most contractors. There are even videos that will walk you through how to build an entire house! You can access the knowledge to do most anything. I mean actual Territory knowledge, not "Excel lifehacks".

In the before time, you would have to learn these skills formally. Through apprenticeships, through trade schools, through years of hands-on training under experienced mentors, all gatekeepers. Otherwise, if you needed it done, you would have to outsource the work and pay whatever the market demanded.

---

3. American Dollars

Today, DIY is an entire industry. In fact, "homesteading" has become a growing trend.[xv]

The YouTube video is the Map. The Territory can be totally different.

True, I replaced my toilet successfully. But what if the mounting bolts had seized, and I ripped out a chunk of my floor when I pulled it up? What if hidden water damage existed? What if the flange had corroded? There was a lot that could have gone wrong, things I wouldn't have been aware of beforehand. That is why you trust, but verify. Even YouTube certified does not equal actual industry knowledge.[xvi]

There are things that only experience can teach. While you can learn the technical side of something from a tutorial, you cannot learn the peripheral lessons. The overlapping spheres of knowledge that come into play when things go sideways.[4]

Know your limits.

A few months ago, my garage door broke. So I went back to YouTube, confident I could fix it. I busted out my tool box and began tinkering. I was in major FAFO mode and quickly came to a realization that I was about to cross that threshold into a Fuck-Up. The kind of a Fuck-Up that could not easily be unfucked. The kind of a Fuck-Up that comes with a five digit price tag.

Predictive risk management means identifying a minor problem before it becomes a big problem. It is much easier to blow out a candle than to fight a forest fire. I recognized pretty quickly I was punching above my weight class, and that my continued tinkering was going to push my small problem into becoming a huge problem. Trust me, I have committed some pretty colossal Fuck-Ups in my life that I can smell when one is about to happen and adjust accordingly.

So I reached out to a garage door specialist and sent him a detailed email and photos of what I had found. My research turned out to be beneficial. I had correctly identified the issue and actually made his job easier. The actual fixing part was beyond my skills, way beyond. He came and fixed it in about two hours.

I asked him how many DIY jobs he gets called in to unfuck. He just laughed. It turns out that DIYers who bite off more than they can chew accounted for a significant portion

---

4. The fuckening is real. Respect it.

of his business. Thankfully, I was able to recognize my limits and be honest about them. Otherwise I could have been the story he told for the next customer who asked about botched DIY.

Results Over Methods

Any credential represents a method. You went through the process. You sat in the class. You passed the exam. You accumulated the hours. You demonstrated that you can follow the prescribed Map from Point A to Point B. You now have the Credential that certifies you to FAFO at Point B.

Point B is in The Territory and only cares about results. Did you actually produce something useful? Can you solve the problem? Does the thing work? Following the Map may get you there. It shows a path, but is that the only path? There may also be shortcuts off the beaten path, different routes entirely, ways of arriving that the Map does not reveal.

Let's say Point B is across a lake. The Map says to follow the path around. What about swimming across? Or taking a boat? You could build a bridge. You could invent the hot-air balloon and soar across. Who knows how else to get there?

The result matters. How you get there is much less important than getting there at all.

Don't get me wrong, sometimes methods are important. If the lake contains acid or piranhas, taking the long way around is the only effective method. Tried-and-true methods exist for a reason. Many of them result from a lot of FAFO and trial and error. Yet they are not sacred. They are not permanent. They are just the best path we have found so far. The UNIVAC was a path too. Methods are what the Credential Collapse has historically threatened the most. The results will remain the same. The job still needs to be done. The path to achieving them is being rewritten in real time.

Why would I hire someone with a boatload of certifications when an AI model can give me access to that same body of knowledge with almost zero overhead? I do not have to pay an AI a salary. It does not take PTO. It does not need health insurance, a 401(k), or even time off. It will not get caught up in drama. AI is entirely results-oriented.[xvii]

I can ask it to provide a detailed document, plan, or system based on the parameters I specify, and I will get a result quickly. Even if it is a subpar result, the AI is always open to revision. It will iterate without complaint. It has no ego to defend its work. It will work around the clock.

The credential says: "I learned the approved method."

The AI says: "I can produce the result."

At the end of the day, who wins?[xviii]

Oh the Humanity!

AI does have limits. Despite being intellectually powerful, they are completely missing the emotional factor. AI has no heart, either physically or figuratively.

A human can pour themselves into what they do. They can care. They can feel the weight of the consequences. They can sense when something is wrong before they can articulate why. They can wake up at 4 AM with an uneasy feeling that tells them to get moving.

An AI does everything with indifference. Also, an AI has no sense of self-preservation, no survival instinct. Its programming stack may contain priority tasks, but it will perform each task with the same fundamental neutrality. You cannot tell an AI: "One more time, with feeling." It has no feeling.

Feelings are not facts, but feelings can save your life.

I was an OTR trucker for many years. This incident happened on St. Patrick's Day, 2022. I was staying the night at the Boomland truck stop in Charleston, Missouri, right off I-57. I woke up earlier than I had to, and when I glanced outside and it was foggy. Very foggy. Visibility close to nothing. I couldn't see much of anything at all.

I could have waited for it to clear. That would have been the sensible thing. The safe thing to do. I was on my way to Dallas for a delivery, and my appointment was not until that evening, so I had plenty of time to get there. Yet something still tugged at me; I don't know how to describe it. Something about that fog just felt fucky. It was still very early, about 0400, and practically no one was on the roads. Still, I am not a fan of driving in the fog. I did not know whether it would clear. I just had this overwhelming urge to get out of there.

So I did. I rolled out a few hours earlier than planned and headed on my way, driving slowly, driving carefully, respecting the conditions. I went the couple miles west to I-55, and headed south, emergency flashers on in the right lane as I puttered along at about 45 mph. I did not know this urge probably saved my life. A very short time after I left, there was a massive pileup on that same stretch of road. Just behind me on I-57. Six fatalities. When I found out later that day, it took me a minute to process. I read the headline and realized I had just been there.[xix]

Do you ever have one of those after the fact moments, where you just sit and stare off into space for a bit. Like you go totally AFK and mentally check out? That's about how I sat for awhile. Because you never know. Trucking is one of the most dangerous jobs in America. It is one of the few professions where you can do everything right and still die.[xx]

The human factor saved my ass that morning. Self-preservation. Instinct. Intuition, whatever you want to call it. Maybe it was Divine Intervention. Had I perished in the fog, then you would not be reading this book right now.

A self-driving vehicle would have followed its GPS. Adverse conditions do not affect a robot the same way they affect a human. An AI has no sense of "oh shit, I'd better slow down so I don't die." It relies on programming, on sensors, and on physics models. It will only slow down if the algorithm determines it should. An AI doesn't consider the human stupidity factor.[xxi]

What I mean by that is when I was driving professionally or really anywhere, and if it even looked like a car was going to do the stupidest possible thing, like swerve into my lane, pull over the white line at a red light, or whip out in traffic ahead of me, I acted accordingly. I would preemptively slow down because the fucktard in the lifted F-250 is texting while rolling through a stop sign. Or the soccer mom in the minivan wants to zip across four lanes on the highway to hit her exit. There is a certain degree of intuitive perception that humans possess and an Artificial Intelligence just cannot match it. An AI agent will monitor the cars, their speed, positioning, and adjust accordingly. However, it will be reactive; there is no predictive risk management happening. The AI monitors data points and the human reads intent.

The algorithm cannot feel the stakes. It will not wake up with dread in its stomach. It does not know what it means to have a family waiting at home. It cannot be afraid. Coding or synthesizing the human factor is impossible. In certain domains, logistics, front-line emergency response, any of the trades that require real-time judgment in chaotic conditions. That factor is irreplaceable.[xxii]

Testing in Progress

How would you know if you are replaceable?

Ask yourself: *If the internet went out worldwide tomorrow, could I still go to work?*

If the answer is no, then you are probably going to be replaced by AI.

We access Cyberspace for everything: running the stock market, worldwide logistics, accounting, the medical industry, banking. Almost every industry everywhere requires the internet in some capacity. If Cyberspace is the only way to do your job, then your job exists on the Map, not in the Territory. Anything that exists purely on the Map can be replaced by something that can navigate the Map better than you can.

The only ones not subject to this equation are Lebanon Levi and the boys. The Amish are far closer to the base of technology than the rest of us. Closer to the Territory in the most traditional sense of the concept. How much of our technology relies on electricity? Electricity is another Map. The Amish are one of the few enclaves in America unaffected by the Cyberspace Psychosis. If the internet went out tomorrow, if worldwide electricity went out tomorrow, the Amish would thrive while the rest of us starved.[xxiii]

There is a lesson in that somewhere.

Now, I am not suggesting everyone rush out and buy denim and straw hats. That is not the point. Just consider how dependent you are? What would you do if the Map disappeared? Do you have Territory skills, or only Map skills?

The college meme produced an entire generation of people with Map skills and little else. They can navigate the system. They can optimize the resume. They can perform the interview. Can they produce anything real? Can they fix what breaks? Can they survive when the system they mastered no longer exists?

All Obsolete

The Absolute Truth is we are all already obsolete.

Tech is already obsolete by the time it reaches the public. When you buy the newest version of your cell phone, it is already outdated by the time you activate it. There is an R&D lab at Samsung or Apple that already has a working prototype of the next version. You are buying yesterday's technology at today's prices.[xxiv]

Google has the Willow chip. Quantum computing projects exist now. The public does not have access to any of it yet. We are always at the trailing edge, receiving hand-me-downs from the cutting edge.

The Empire has countless black projects around the world using technology beyond anything we can currently conceive. Lockheed Martin's Skunk Works, General Dynamics, Boeing and other entities that are too secret to even have names. They are just called "Group W" or something mundane. The direct beneficiaries of the trillion dollars a year that the United States spends on defense. The defense industry is always developing new technologies. How much of that is concealed due to NDAs and classification? We will not know because they will not talk about it. Who knows what is really out there?

We are all redundant. It is just a matter of time and adoption. AI combined with advances in robotics will mean that eventually androids will perform any job a human can. They will do it better, faster, more efficiently, with fewer errors. The technology is not there yet, but it is coming. And the gap between "we are working on it" and "fully operational" closes faster every year.[xxv]

Speculation Only

I do not think the collapse will be sudden. I think it will be a slow descent with a soft landing. Managed decline. This is speculation, and I could be dead wrong. But the patterns are already visible, and patterns are what I do. The Empire will not have us all descend into Mad Max. It is fun to think about, but we are a thousand years away from that.

Universal Basic Income will probably happen. It almost has to, with the AI credential crisis coming. Millions of people unemployed and unemployable. The government will have to step in with some form of subsistence. The idea would be to keep people consuming within limits and not revolting. [xxvi]

I would not find it surprising if a tiered currency system emerges. Different monies for different classes. We already have a version of this. EBT cards for food assistance for example. Specific funds for specific purposes. Currencies that allow spending only on eligible products. I can see the tiers getting more explicit. It will not be real money.[5] It will be Basic Bux. Deposited monthly like EBT. Good for staples, paying electric bills, water bills, maybe internet access. The key is that it will expire at the end of the month. Use it or lose it. No hoarding allowed.[xxvii]

We already see this model in mobile games.[xxviii] A weekly allowance in a base currency. Then there are other tiers. Coins, diamonds, bars, gems, many different currencies that can be used to buy various in-game advantages. The free players grind for scraps while the whales coast right through. Pay to win is the name of the game.[6]

The UBI tier can use their Basic Bux to buy beans. The retailer trades those Basic Bux to the Central Exchange for Logistic Bux, which is how he pays the trucking company, the farmers, the warehouses, and so on. The trucking company trades Logistic Bux for fuel. The fuel station trades them to the refinery. The refinery trades for Resource Bux to buy crude oil and iron ore.

And at the top, the Big Bux. The only currency that buys luxury goods. People will still need to flex on social media and, of course, dunk on all the Basic Bux peasants. Big Bux are only how you can buy yachts, jets, and fast cars. The proles on UBI will never see Big Bux, but they will see them on television. What is the use of living large if not to be envied? The lives of the Big Bux class will broadcast the same way we watch celebrity lifestyles now.

Naturally, the lottery will have to still exist. One of the few avenues where Basic Bux can theoretically become Big Bux. The Empire will want to keep that pressure valve.[xxix]

24974 Lifetimes though.

Adjusting Your Sails

The Psychosis has spread too far. The Credential Crisis is just another symptom of the digital plague. We have a West Virginia sized chunk of easily accessible technology at hand morning, noon, and night. Access to Cyberspace is just going to get faster and better as time goes on.

---

5. We will agree that it is though.

6. We already live in a pay to win world.

The future wave is already in motion. We are just riding it out.

You cannot control the winds of change, but you can adjust your sails.

The credential was a Map to a world that no longer exists. The degree was a ticket on a train that had already departed the station. What remains?

Hopefully, the future we are racing towards will not end up as some dystopian Cyberpunk nightmare. Maybe the Empire envisions a soft landing. While we collectively figure things out, UBI and New Deal-style programs will hold everything together. Ideally, we are not on the sidelines witnessing the end of humanity as we know it. Pretty soon we will be lined up for our Amazon Brain Implant™ connecting us directly to Global Star-Link WiFi with our minds. Techno-sapiens united at last.

Credentials are collapsing. The gates are falling. The playing field is already overrun with AI generated content. The Maps are being redrawn faster than anyone can follow.

Yet somehow humans keep up.

We always do.

We always will.

The Virtual Reality Blues

Everyone has experienced the Virtual Reality Blues in one form or another. Including Cyberspace is optional.

The Virtual Reality Blues occur when reality does not meet your expectations. Wherever the Map does not match the Territory. That gap between what you were promised and what you received. Between what you built in your head and what the world actually delivered. We experienced it when our FA's produced FO's we were unprepared for, and we stumbled across that line into a Fuck Up. Where we touched the stove and discovered that fire is, in fact, hot, and our hand is now on fire.

The Blues hurt so badly because they are 100% an inside job. We consented to feel the Blues the second we gave up our Agency to a Map. When we allowed our Attention to wander to a portion of the Map that seemed really great and our Attitude followed. Our Action led to an outcome that was out of alignment with that Attitude and we went from hero to zero very quickly. That's right, the Blues are entirely our fault. Especially when we keep circling back to them, if we keep signing up again and again for disappointment. That U-turn can become a spiral pretty quickly. If we are not careful, we are sucked down into the drain of despair.

We know better; we really do. Life happens, and worldly concerns take center stage, and it is our human nature to forget what we know. We get caught up in the distractions, in the rat race, or whatever you want to call it. The grind, the drudgery of work and sleep and work and sleep and errands on the weekend (that always passes by too quickly) and then back to the grind again. Round and around it goes; it is a state of rumination. We are always on the move, yet never actually arrive anywhere. How is it that we are the busiest generation ever, and yet it seems like we get nothing done?

"The mass of men lead lives of quiet desperation. What is called resignation is confirmed desperation." Henry David Thoreau, *Walden*[i]

We resign to this way of life, settling for the spiral. Only now has desperation become smothered with a digital blanket of escapism and entertainment. Bread and circuses indeed, with a full belly and a distracted mind, and a dead spirit. Zombies, all of us, staring at our phones and our screens in our own little bubbles. Noise-canceling headphones, or even the bubble of your car during your commute. Whatever it is, our digital bubbles isolate us and cut us off from connection. Individually marinating in digital drudgery.[ii]

It's like all together as a culture we woke up and realized we were 40 years old and maybe this is as good as it gets. Quicker and quicker, as our perception of time zips by, the grind of hours and days and weeks and years. Bombarded by the oversaturation of sensationalism. How many "once in a lifetime" catastrophes have we experienced? Not one but two separate wars in Mesopotamia. We saw 9/11. We saw video kill the radio star, then AI kill the video star. Multiple recessions, inflation, increasing enshittification and all along paying more and more to get less and less. Yet we cannot look away from the cultural shit show, the feed, the narrative, the Official Story™, whatever you want to call the buffet of bullshit the Empire tries to convince us is good for us. Enthrallment completely holds us. The Blues happen because we know it does not have to be this way.

War Footing

The Empire has convinced us of so much. Engineering our opinions with their toolbox of *shoulds, or else's* and the *what if's*. All the expressions of fear fuel. That we *should* remain afraid and of whom we *should* be afraid of. Wanting us scared of the terrorists, or the communists, or the socialists, or whatever "ists" are lurking in the dark. The blanket term for terror. The Global War on Terrorism (GWOT) started in 2001. It is now 2026. A quarter of a century we have been fighting the masked boogy man of terrorism. They are always masked, all the ISIS or Al Quaida videos, the villains are always wearing masks. They do not want us recognizing another human; no, we can't have that. The villain must remain ambiguous. The Empire requires us to be afraid of something so badly that we will endorse a war against it. Are we winning yet?[iii]

What ever happened to the war on poverty? All Americans are terrified of being poor, so this is a good go-to for the Empire. What has actually been done to lift people out of poverty? Is education affordable? Can anyone get a job that pays them enough to cover the cost of living in the Empire? Is that job attainable for the average person? How are we doing globally with that? Countless aid sent around the world to help fight the terror of poverty. We have the receipts; the Map of it is right there. Yet there are countless poor people around the world experiencing the Blues.[iv]

The war on drugs? Remember that one? We *should* be very, very afraid of drugs. Nancy Reagan told us to just say no. DARE taught us that peer pressure was the catalyst to total degeneracy. Police warned that crime was rising, and they predicted the streets would fill with the worst of the worst. People you *should* be afraid of. Maniacs on drugs. Drugs meant we would end up besieged by brigands, gypsies, thugs, highwaymen, ne'er-do-wells, drifters, men of ill repute, and women of negotiable virtue. We couldn't have that; what of the children?[v]

The war on drugs gave us private prisons filled with hundreds of thousands of non-violent offenders. Freedom taken because of chemicals. Chemicals that for better or worse, often provide moments of mental escape from an otherwise terrible world. The Empire occupied Afghanistan, the "bread basket" of poppy for the world, and during that time the USA experienced an opioid epidemic catastrophe. Despite legislation outlawing drug use and a militarized law enforcement mobilized to eradicated it, somehow drugs have still managed to win the war.[vi]

A people cannot remain forever at war. Despite what the Empire says, war is unsustainable. They try to convince you that *their wars* are the only ones worth fighting. The actual battle, the fight that *should* concern you, is nowhere the Empire wants you directing your Attention. You won't find it in the deserts of Iraq or the jungles of Venezuela. The battle is not between the markets of the Eastern and Western Empires. It is not Zionists versus Muslims or black versus white. It's not the red vs. blue, the conservatards vs. the libtards, or Based vs. Woke. These are all abstract adversaries. They are Relative conflicts.

The battle is not even the Empire versus We the People.

The actual war is not even the Map versus the Territory.

The real war, the only war that counts. The only battle that matters in this life, this world where Psychosis bombards us and everything wars with everything else.

The battle that means anything at all.

Is You versus You.

That's it.

Absolute Blues

You want to know what the actual Virtual Reality Blues are? They are when you betray yourself. The feeling when you fell for a Map that you knew didn't match your Territory, yet you went ahead anyway. It always was and will always be an inside job. No matter what the coach told you, or your boss, or a teacher, or your neighbor, or your friends, or your therapist, or anyone. Those are outside entities selling you a Map. Their version of the Map. Maps are always limited by the capacity of who drew them. An outside Map will not lead you to yourself. There is some Territory you navigate alone if you want to discover your Absolute Truth.

How well do you know yourself? And if you don't know yourself, maybe it's time you got to know who you are. So, who are you, really? When you strip away the labels? After the credentials are irrelevant? Who are you when you're not cheering for a sports team or laughing with your friends at brunch? Who are you when you're not mindlessly scanning through Netflix searching for your next binge? Who are you when you're not playing Candy Crush on your phone for hours at a time? Who are you when you are not reading books? When you're not out fishing? When the podcast is off and you are sitting in a moment of silence, with yourself? Who are you then?

Who are you when you're not at your job, being an occupation? Who are you in those quiet moments? When there is no one else? When it is just you versus you? When you stop bullshitting yourself? When you are not counting followers or likes, or engagement metrics? Who are you when the camera is off?

Who are you when no one is watching?

The Virtual Reality Blues are the feeling when you realize that all of it, the titles and trophies and achievements, the wins and the losses, the rises and the falls, the ins and the outs, when you realize that all of that was Virtual and a version of Reality that someone else sold to you. When the curriculum you studied so hard to pass the audit for was sold to you. When the promotion you worked your ass off 60+ hours a week for months and years at a time was also sold to you. You bought it with your life. You realize that you were sold the house, the car, the security, and all the things everywhere that you traded your life for. When all along you were just buying Map after Map The Blues you feel after every little concession. Every time you gave into the Map. Every time you did what you were told instead of doing what you wanted. When you saw the carrot on the stick and went ahead anyway.

That is the Virtual Reality Blues. Realizing everything, all of this, it's all Virtual. None of this is real; it never was. That is the lie they sold you. That it mattered if you made it to the factory 10 minutes early every day for the shift meeting. That it mattered if you met your monthly sales metrics. That it mattered if you formatted your report correctly.

The Virtual Reality Blues is the regret you feel after buying into it. When you buy into the bullshit. The ultimate buyer's remorse. Don't believe me? Go read some end-of-life interviews from people in a hospice center. Pay Attention to the regrets. When people are doing their end-of-life audit and looking back, they see what really mattered and what did not.[vii]

The Empire wants to dictate what *matters*. Funny that, their choice of language. They use that. *Matter*. Matter, the physical nature of reality. For something to "matter" it means you can physically hold it. It is verifiable. That is matter. To them, something has to "matter" to make it real. Otherwise, it is fake, an illusion. The physical property, the hardware, the house, the car, the material thing because they are materialists, are what their Map is going to lead you to.

Does Cyberspace Matter?

Software is 1's and o's and trillions of lines of code that dictate our Agency morning, noon, and night. Does it *matter*, though? Does it actually exist? Or is it just the idea of its existing? The agreement that it exists. Remember money? Money is an agreement. Is *matter* just an agreement too? An agreement with the Map?

What happens if you disagree? If you say no? If you refuse to participate? If you realize the Psychosis existed long before Cyberspace? Who are you then? Who are you in that moment you say no?

The real battle was never between your ears either. It has never been. Just another Map. Your mind is the playground for your ego. That too is the Virtual Reality. Even your wonderful human imagination, that infinite creative space anyone can access at any time remains entirely Virtual. Your brain is the matter, your mind is the software. The

Psychosis manifests in the software, in your brain, your mind, your head space, whatever you want to call it. The ego, the identity, the version of yourself that you *think* about is the Virtual you.

Where is the Absolute You?

It's not in your head, it's in your heart.

Sounds trite? Like some kind of platitude you would see on a motivational poster in a Yoga Studio locker room or on a keychain on a rack at a new age bookshop. Trite, but true.

It doesn't matter[1] what language you speak. You can be from any culture in the world, from any socioeconomic background; you can be rich or poor, sick or healthy, or any combination of the countless polarity traps that Maps try to sort us into. None of those distinctions really *matter* because all of them are Relative Truths. You speak your native tongue the language Relative to where you were born. Your skin color is Relative to your genetics. Your Attitude is Relative to your Attention. Your Actions are Relative to your Agency. All of it is entirely subjective, and all of it is a Map.

The Territory is your heart.

Ask anyone on the planet, no matter what their background. Ask anyone in any language, at any time period since we gained sentience long, long ago. Ask of them a simple request.

"Point to yourself, please."

Every one of them will point right at the center of their chest. You would do it. Your mom would do it. Your cousin's employee's nephew's mailman would point at their chest. A random Roman you grabbed off the street would point at their chest. Thug would point at his chest. Lebanon Levi would point at his chest. Anyone anywhere instinctively is going to point right at their chest.

What is in the center of the chest?

Your heart.

---

1. This word is everywhere in our language.

Everyone will point right at their heart.[viii]

Does anyone point at their head when they introduce themselves? No. No one does that. The head is the ego, and mind, and identity, and the programming of the Virtual Reality of Relativity. You are not in your head.

The Absolute You is right in the center of your chest.

The real battle, the real war, has always been you vs You.

Relative you vs. Absolute You.

Absolute Identity

Who are you when all the Relative labels and definitions and credentials and programming are gone? When you look at that massive pile of Maps stacked on top of each other. The identities and jobs, and every label that applied. When you look at that massive stack of Maps all the way to the ceiling of your perception, and you look at the top one and peel it off. Then you look at the next Map and peel that one away too. When you remove Map after Map after Map, a shower of Relative Truths tossed to the side as you peel back layer after layer after layer, getting closer and closer to the Absolute You. When you finally remove that final Map. Who you see staring back at you is You. The Absolute You. The surface at the bottom of the stack is always a mirror.

You were watching the whole time. The Observer. You were living your life in you, as you. Can you forgive yourself for forgetting about yourself? When you were so busy chasing clout and influence and people and places and things. When your Attention was being pulled this way and that way and your Attitude followed. Can you forgive your Actions that surrendered your Agency to matter.

Always there in the center of your perception.

If you could get the biggest, most powerful telescope imaginable. One that could zoom out way past our solar system and the local cluster all the way through the Milky Way Galaxy and beyond, past the next galaxy and the ones beyond that, so far out that the Galaxies themselves look like a field of stars and you zoomed out ever farther than that. If you looked as far as far could go into the Absolute distance. Do you know what you would see?

You would be staring at the back of your own head.

If you could access the most powerful microscope imaginable. If you could zoom in anywhere, past the molecules and into the atom itself, even between the atoms. Gazing deeply into an atom past the nucleus and into that subatomic space, past the quarks and the leptons and the bosons, even deeper zoom in into a space so small that words can no longer describe just how infinitely tiny little smally itty bitty teeniest bit of space/time you can imagine and you keep zooming in closer than that. Gazing as deep as deep can get down into the Absolute near. Do you know what you would see?

You would be staring at the back of your own head.[ix]

You are always at the center of your perception. Just as small as you are to the largest things you can perceive, you are large to the smallest things you can perceive.

That is an Absolute Truth.

Consent

Cyberspace Psychosis has affected everyone. We did not really get a choice in the matter.[2] If your birth year starts with a 2, infection at birth was inevitable. Any older and you are still infected, but you remember a time when the world was not. A time we were on our way there, but it had not spread like it has now. Today the digital world has completely tainted our perceptions. We forget we are at the center of our perceptions..

While we have no choice in the Psychosis, we do have a choice when it comes to experiencing the Blues.

We are all holding onto our Virtual long spoons? Heaven and Hell have the same address. It's about that Attention and that Attitude.

The Blues are a choice. The Blues require your consent to feel them.

You are free to say "no". You are free to be Yourself.

No one knows Your Territory like You do.

Who knows what is truly in your Heart except for You?

---

2. More matter.

No one knows who you are pointing at when someone asks you to point at yourself. Only you know that.

The Absolute Truth is you and You alone decide.

The Virtual Reality Blues is a misnomer, because the Blues themselves are in itself a Virtual Reality.

The Longest Yard

In my world, in my life, my heart and head have been locked in a pitched battle.

The longest distance in the world is the distance from your head to your heart.[x]

From thought to feeling.

Feeling to thought.

Which is stronger? The thoughts are Relative. Are feelings Relative too? Are they Absolute? The lover you love today may be the enemy you hate tomorrow, Relative to your Attitude about them.

What about your Attitude about yourself?

You have no choice when it comes to your head. You may think you do, but you do not. Your head, your mind, is a requirement to survive in Territory Earth. Your heart may yearn to love and experience all the things, but your head will remind you that you need to work to get money to eat or you will die. Your head is what keeps your Attention on that Map.

Who are the pure-hearted? The children, of course. The one-year-old little Fuckers who are Finding Out about the Territory. That same little fucker still lives inside all of us. The heart wants to Fuck Around to its heart's content.

Hearts feel, and that feeling is passion. It's synonymous with fire. What does fire do? Fire consumes and expands. It keeps expanding until it runs out of fuel or someone douses it. If a fire burns out of control and all the fuel is gone, there can be no more fires. Nothing left to burn through. Nothing more for it to Fuck Around with. The passion withers and dies.

The mind serves a precious function in the regard of regulating our inner fire. An untamed heart will burn out of control and eventually burn out. The mind, properly attuned, can regulate just how much fuel we feed our heart, can regulate just how hot it gets, and can reel the heart in before we suffer a heartbreak.

We have a burning desire, a passion for Fucking Around and Finding Out. FAFO truly is our default setting as humans. We all started that way, and we gave it away somewhere along the path. The Absolute You that is napping under that thick blanket of Maps would Absolutely love to get back to Fucking Around, and your mind, which learned to fear, keeps that in check. However, fear is not the healthiest expression. Rather than fear the Territory, a healed mind will respect the Territory.

It is vital to remember that it is never too late. Your spark has never gone out. Even if your mind has wrapped completely around it and the fire no longer burns, if you are so up in your head that your heart has become cold, it is not dead. As long as we are breathing, and life is full of possibilities, then your pilot light is still going. If you're alive, then you can still ignite fires of joy.

We talk about feeding our minds, that Attention, what is the input we are putting into our heads? That input that is processed by our Attitudes that turns into Action. What is that? How do we feel about it? What is the state of your Heart?

Remember states and conditions? The state is temporary, a condition is less so.

What conditions have you put on your heart? On your passions? Are you mired down in the "*What ifs*" of the Virtual Reality playing out between your ears? Are you playing out the worst-case scenarios? Are you defeating yourself before you even get started? Are you talking yourself out of an Action because "what if it doesn't work out?"

What if it does?

Nothing changes if nothing changes.

Mindfucked

The Cyberspace Psychosis has hijacked our minds and bent them so they are so wrapped around our hearts that we rarely feel authenticity anymore.

Cyberspace as the magical insulation between us and the Territory. The digital interface that acts as the intermediary between both us and the world, and our mind and our heart. Complacent in the face of evils that would tear our hearts out. We can sit on the sidelines, cracking jokes and memes while narrating atrocities playing out. We witness through the digital interface as the Empire drops bombs on children lining up for food. We have collectively become so desensitized to violence and suffering that we cannot be bothered with it unless it affects us directly. We focus so much on our thoughts that we neglect our feelings.

The worst of the Psychosis is when it has corrupted our minds so terribly that we no longer have Attention for our heart. The one True part of ourselves, in fact the only True part of ourselves that is ours and ours alone. The one we know deep down since that is where we instinctively point when asked who we are.

Your heart knows the Absolute Truth, your mind only the Relative.

As long as something remains a Virtual Reality, there on the screen. I'm there, 10 years old watching the Empire bomb the shit out of Mesopotamia on CNN, a Virtual Reality to me, since I am in my living room safe in Ohio. Relatively safe. I'm sure there was another 10-year-old in Baghdad that very night, scared to death as he heard the jets screaming overhead and the non-stop anti-aircraft fire. I was sad that I had to go to bed that night because I wanted to stay awake and see it all happen in real time. That 10-year-old in Iraq didn't sleep at all that night, and maybe not for many other nights afterwards. I was watching the Map on CNN and the Territory was falling around him with laser-guided precision.[xi]

Polarity Parity

One's loss is another's gain. One's gain is another's loss.[xii]

The easiest model to witness this is any sporting event. The microcosm of war, an easy to access "us vs. them" model because matches happen every day. Watch and witness how a victory for one side is a loss for the other. One city is celebrating while another laments.

Relative Truth of separation. Take it a beat deeper.

The Absolute Truth applied to that same situation is that both sides love the game. They love their team, they love the sport, and they love having something to cheer for. That love, that feeling, it originates in the Heart.

Does that same apply to war? One side fighting for whatever the Empire tells them. The other defending, also mandated by the Empire. Sure, they are fighting for their families and for their survival. Both sides believe they are acting correctly. Meanwhile, the Empire has always been selling weapons to both sides. Just like the Empire is selling jerseys to both fan bases in the sporting match. The Empire is also buying the weapons from themselves. It won't make sense because nothing about it is sensible. The heart of the matter is that it's all relative. xiii

The Relative Truth again, that we were sitting on the sideline while the Empire sold us Map after Map. But it was a Relative Sideline.

The Absolute Truth is we were all bunched up in the center of the table, where our good shepherds had herded us, where it was safe and comfortable, and we had running water and plenty of food and did not have to struggle day to day.

Ironically, the Absolute Truth tellers were out there on the fringe at the edge of the table, looking down at the rot below. They tried to warn everyone. People dismissed them.

Now Cyberspace has lifted the veil, and we are getting a glimpse at just what the Empire has been up to. The worst of the worst, the darkest of dark, the most evil of evil.

Who is to blame?

That isn't even the question to ask ourselves.

There is no one else. Only you.

The Absolute Truth is no one can fight the Empire. The only thing that fights the Empire is more Empire. It is always Maps competing with other Maps.

We handle the outer critic the same way we handled the inner one. The only way to win that game is not to play at all. xiv

Center Mass

You have no control over people, places, or things.

You have no control over Epstein or Bush or Trump or any other face of the Empire. Even when you think you do, you do not. Sure, you disagree with all the policies and you hate them with every fiber of your being; you hate them so much, and they love that because hate hijacks your Action. Hate is an active feeling, it is a passion and passions are fire, and fires require fuel and maintenance. So sure feed that hatred. The Empire relies on your hate because only a hateful heart will entertain the idea of war.[xv]

So by all means, hate them, convince yourself that your voice matters[3] and you will take your platform and change the world. Organize your protest so that you can let the Empire know just how dissatisfied you are. Make sure you are being a good citizen and getting your permit so you can carry your little sign from 1-5pm. Decorate your sign with your hatred of the Empire. Make sure it is colorful too, so later when the news comes on and you are watching the coverage, you can proudly point out to your friends, "That's me!". Maybe you can call your parents later and excitedly tell them, "Yes, I was at the protest and even made it on the news!"

Did you make an impact?

Sure, you were out there all afternoon sun chanting your dissatisfaction. Then you obediently dispersed and headed home, because they only permitted you four hours. The Relative Truth is the Professional Sports Event is tonight, and the Empire needs those streets clear for the Consumer Class who bought tickets to the game. Commerce must continue at all cost.

Sorry, but all of your Actions and Attitude towards the Empire solved nothing at all.

They lost nothing.

The Absolute Truth you handed over your Agency in trying to fight them when that battle is none of your business.

The only thing the Empire fights is the Empire.

The only thing you need to focus on fighting is yourself.

Absolute Blues

The Virtual Reality Blues are the feeling of seeing the Territory for the Territory, and watching your fellow looking at the Map instead of where they are stepping, and they are about to stride right off the cliff.

You shout "Watch out for yonder cliff!"

They respond, "It's not on the Map you silly conspiracy theorist! If it was dangerous they would have it marked."

You watch them face-plant. Naturally, being the compassionate human you are, walk up to them offering your hand. Intending to help them stand up again. You find they are still staring at their Map and they are mad at you about plummeting off the cliff.

The Psychosis infected mind will forgive you for being wrong, but will not forgive you for being right.

It's projection. In that moment, they are angry at themselves. Their heart and their head are at odds, and the head is demanding they point the finger somewhere.

That rejection you feel is the Virtual Reality Blues.

Many stories in our histories tell of Absolute Truth tellers that were smothered under Maps. One very well-known one was crucified. Then the Empire takes that execution and sells it to you as the point of the greatest story. The Empire's church only focuses on sacrifice, along with their favorite word, and you absolutely *should* feel guilty since you were born cursed. Once upon a time your Ancestor ate an Apple and Fucked Around when he shouldn't have and Found Out he actually Fucked Up. Only his Fuck Up is now YOUR fuck up and you were Forever Fucked before an Absolute Truth teller was sacrificed for you.

Now you *should* feel guilty and thankful to the Empire for providing you the path of salvation. We require your attendance weekly and your confession monthly, and 10% of your income annually. *Or else* ye shall burn forevermore.[xvi] *Trust me, bro.*

Count on the Empire to turn gold into lead whenever they can.

The gold of Absolute Truth being replaced with Relative lead.

There are many Prophets and Citizen Sages and philosophers who led with their heart. Hundreds, maybe thousands, countless even. Most of them unknown, unwritten, and unremembered, yet still shared their Absolute Truth about the Territory while being smothered by whatever Map was in charge.

These instances of Virtual Reality Blues inevitably end with some version of *"Forgive them, Father, they know not what they do."*

The Blues are the lament of a compassionate heart.

The Blues are the natural reaction to the Cyberspace Psychosis.

The Virtual Reality Blues are the feeling when you realize you cannot do anything about the Psychosis. You cannot cure it, you cannot cure your parents or your spouse, or your bestie's Psychosis. That is the tragedy of it.

Anyone who drinks their own poison must drink their own antidote.

You can cure your own.

Reclaim your Agency.

Your cure is regaining control over your Attention, defining your Attitude, and directing your Actions.

What is your Absolute Agency?

Under the Maps, the masks, the identities and labels and titles, there is the Absolute You. The matter of the body you inhabit has been around since the start. Congealed stardust into a meat suit you wear for your adventures in this physical universe. Your consciousness, that little spark of Soul in the center of your heart, is a little mote of light. Star Light.

Absolutely all of us are Star Dust and Star Light.

A star only has one function, and that is to shine.

Shine as brightly as you can.

Never dim your light because a Map tells you to.

Remember the sun doesn't give a fuck if it blinds you.

Endnotes

These endnotes are organized by movement rather than in a continuous sequence. If you want to check a claim, find the movement and the numeral.

I tried my best to cite every factual assertion in this book. I got to most of them. I didn't get to all of them. If you catch something I missed, highlight the section in your copy, tear the page out, and send it along with a self-addressed stamped envelope to me. We can discuss it.

Argue with me in the margins. That is how this is supposed to work.

Movement 1: Cyberspace Psychosis

i For ADHD symptoms and dopamine dysregulation: A review in Trends in Cognitive Sciences (2009) synthesizes evidence that ADHD involves altered dopamine signaling, contributing to novelty-seeking, impaired self-regulation, and sensitivity to boredom, though the exact mechanisms (e.g., hypo- vs. hyper-dopaminergic states) remain debated. This distinction highlights how cyberspace psychosis mimics these traits through conditioning, not innate wiring.

ii For neuroplasticity and digital media: A narrative review in Narra J (2024) on digital media detoxes implies that prolonged exposure to digital stimuli induces neuroplastic changes, rewiring reward pathways via repeated dopamine spikes, leading to attention fragmentation and volatility; short breaks can partially reverse these effects in many individuals.

iii The "slot machine effect" refers to variable ratio reinforcement schedules, where rewards are delivered unpredictably after an unknown number of responses, producing the strongest and most persistent behavior patterns (Skinner, 1953). In social media scrolling, the uncertainty of what comes next (a like, comment, funny video, or nothing) triggers dopamine surges in anticipation of reward, driving compulsive checking more than consistent outcomes would. This mechanism is widely cited in studies on digital addiction and behavioral design (e.g., Schüll, 2012; Griffiths, 2018; Eyal, 2014). The excitement stems from the "maybe" anticipation rather than the content itself, exploiting the brain's reward prediction error system.

iv The ~74 GB daily estimate draws from analyses building on the UCSD "How Much Information?" studies (e.g., 2009 report showing ~34 GB/day in 2008, rising with tech growth) and subsequent summaries (e.g., Frontiers for Young Minds, 2017; Minecheck, 2023). Modern daily intake is often equated to what a highly educated person 500 years ago might process in a lifetime; 200 years ago (early 1800s) was still orders of magnitude lower due to limited media access. Exact figures vary by methodology, but the exponential increase underscores the overload driving "cyberspace psychosis."

v Alfred Korzybski, Science and Sanity: An Introduction to Non-Aristotelian Systems and General Semantics (Lakeville, CT: International Non-Aristotelian Library, 1933), 58. The dictum is elaborated in the chapter on abstraction levels; see also pp. 747–48 for the fullest treatment of "consciousness of abstracting" as a corrective practice.

vi The story of the brazen bull (also called the bronze bull or Sicilian bull) is a famous ancient anecdote, recounted by the Greek historian Diodorus Siculus in his *Bibliotheca historica* (Library of History), composed in the 1st century BCE. According to Diodorus, Perilaus (also spelled Perillos or Perillus) of Athens presented the device to Phalaris, tyrant of Akragas (modern Agrigento, Sicily) in the mid-6th century BCE. Phalaris, appalled by the cruelty of the invention, ordered Perilaus himself to be shut inside and roasted alive as the first test—turning the inventor into his own victim. The tale is also mentioned briefly by Pindar and later by Lucian and Cicero, though Diodorus provides the most detailed version. This passage is a dramatized and embellished retelling of that account, with added narrative flair and modern commentary, but the core elements (the hollow bronze bull, the pipes that turn screams into bellowing, and the inventor's ironic fate) follow the classical tradition. For the primary source, see Diodorus Siculus, *Bibliotheca historica*, Book 9, fragments 18–19 (various English translations available; e.g., the Loeb Classical Library edition). For a concise modern summary and context, see the entry "Brazen bull" in Wikipedia (drawing on classical sources) or histories of ancient Sicilian tyranny.

Movement 2: Fuck Around and Find Out

i 3-2-1 Contact (PBS, 1980–1988) was a Children's Television Workshop series that explored science through experiments, segments, and songs. The theme (composed by Edd Kalehoff) emphasized the "moment of contact" as the spark of discovery, perfectly capturing the FAFO threshold here.

ii The popular parable of a "helpful" human cutting open a butterfly's chrysalis, resulting in weak, shriveled wings and inability to fly, illustrates the necessity of struggle for proper wing development. Scientifically, emerging butterflies pump hemolymph (a fluid analogous to blood) from the abdomen into wing veins through muscular effort, expanding and strengthening the wings for flight. This process is essential, and premature or rough interference can cause deformation or failure to expand fully (as seen in cases of parasitic infection or mishandling in captive rearing). However, the dramatic "crippled for life" outcome in the story is anecdotal and not universally confirmed in controlled studies. Gentle assistance is sometimes used successfully in butterfly conservation and rearing. The metaphor holds: resistance and effort build capability. See sources below for details on emergence mechanics.

iii Nikola Tesla experimented with rotating magnetic fields in 1882 (visualized during a Budapest walk), leading to his polyphase AC induction motor patents (1888) that enabled efficient long-distance power transmission via transformers—contradicting the prevailing map of direct current (DC) as the only viable system. Edison and the electrical establishment championed DC for its simplicity/short-range safety, launching propaganda (e.g., animal electrocutions to paint AC as deadly) to discredit Tesla/Westinghouse's AC. Tesla's territory discovery won the "War of the Currents," revolutionizing global power grids and enabling the infrastructure (high-voltage transmission) that powers every screen, dopamine loop, scroll, and notification in cyberspace. See Jonnes, Jill. 2003. Empires of Light: Edison, Tesla, Westinghouse, and the Race to Electrify the World. New York: Random House (detailed on rotating field breakthrough, establishment opposition, propaganda campaign); U.S. Department of Energy. "The War of the Currents: AC vs. DC Power." energy.gov (official summary of Tesla's AC advantages over Edison's DC, long-distance transmission as key revolution).

iv Army size and casualties/returnees- Britannica: "The total invading force then numbered approximately 453,000; about 612,000 were to enter Russia during the campaign ... Between the invasion and subsequent retreat, the French suffered 500,000 casualties, including 300,000 killed... little more than 200,000 of them were French [implying massive non-return]."

v Army size, casualties, and winter gear- Britannica: "The Germans allotted almost 150 divisions containing a total of about three million men... In October and November a wave of frostbite cases had decimated the ill-clad German troops, for whom provisions of winter clothing had not been made... By November the Germans had suffered about 730,000 casualties."

Movement 3: Content With The Content

i Humans are omnivores with a broad diet (animal, vegetable, mineral sources), but early survival required constant awareness of predation risk. See Richard Wrangham, Catching Fire: How Cooking Made Us Human (Basic Books, 2009), ch. 1–2 (on diet and predation); Yuval Noah Harari, Sapiens: A Brief History of Humankind (Harper, 2015), ch. 1–2 (on middle-position food-chain status).

ii Persistence hunting (humans chasing prey to exhaustion until collapse) is a documented early human hunting strategy, particularly among persistence hunters like the San people of the Kalahari. See Louis Liebenberg, "Persistence Hunting by Modern Hunter-Gatherers," Current Anthropology 47, no. 6 (2006): 1017–1025; Daniel Lieberman et al., "Running and the Evolution of Endurance Running," Nature 432 (2004): 345–348.

iii Television viewing induces alpha brain wave activity (8–12 Hz) associated with a relaxed, trance-like state (reduced critical thinking, heightened suggestibility); screen images are processed and stored in memory similarly to real events, eliciting genuine emotional, physiological (cortisol/stress hormones), and dopaminergic responses as if experienced firsthand. See M. M. Barry, "Television Viewing and Brain Waves: A Review," Journal of Communication 42, no. 4 (1992): 3–21; D. A. Christakis et al., "Early Television Exposure and Subsequent Attentional Problems in Children," Pediatrics 113, no. 4 (2004): 708–713; and Annie Lang, "The Limited Capacity Model of Motivated Message Processing," Journal of Communication 50, no. 1 (2000): 46–70.

iv Television rapidly suppresses social interaction and orients group attention toward the screen within seconds to minutes due to its high arousal potential and flicker effect; this "orienting response" overrides conversation. See Byron Reeves & Clifford Nass, The Media Equation: How People Treat Computers, Television, and New Media Like Real People and Places (Cambridge University Press, 1996), ch. 5; and Gloria Mark, Attention Span: Finding Focus for a Fulfilling Life (Hanover Square Press, 2023), ch. 2 (on media interruptions and social disruption).

v Excessive screen use (especially short-form content and multitasking) impairs executive function (self-control, impulse regulation, goal-directed behavior) by dysregulating pre-frontal cortex activity and dopamine pathways, leading to reduced ability to prioritize long-term tasks over immediate gratification. See Gloria Mark, Attention Span (Hanover Square Press, 2023), ch. 5–6; American Psychological Association, "Digital Media and Executive Function in Children and Adolescents," 2022 review.

vi Problematic internet use (e.g., doom scrolling, compulsive social media) produces a gradual, insidious erosion of mental health, attention, and executive function without acute crisis or "rock bottom" like substance addiction; it mimics behavioral addiction patterns with tolerance, withdrawal-like irritability, and loss of control. See Anna Lembke, Dopamine Nation (Dutton, 2021), ch. 4–5; World Health Organization, "Gaming Disorder and Hazardous Gaming," ICD-11, 2019 (extended to broader problematic internet use in 2022–2025 research).

vii Addiction is progressive, requiring increasing amounts for diminishing returns ("more to get less"); it involves craving, denial, and dopamine dysregulation that hijacks attention and agency. See Anna Lembke, Dopamine Nation (Dutton, 2021), ch. 1–3; Kent C. Berridge & Terry E. Robinson, "Liking, Wanting, and the Incentive-Sensitization Theory of Addiction," American Psychologist 71, no. 8 (2016): 670–679.

Movement 4th Estate

i Operation Desert Storm air campaign began January 17, 1991. CNN's Bernard Shaw, John Holliman, and Peter Arnett reported live from Baghdad's Al-Rasheed Hotel with the iconic "The skies over Baghdad have been illuminated" line; phone-line drama (risk of cutoffs) allowed them to stay on air while other networks' feeds were severed. See CNN, "Operation Desert Storm: 25 years on," January 19, 2016, https://www.cnn.com /2016/01/19/middleeast/operation-desert-storm-25-years-later.

ii Topps released Desert Storm trading cards during Desert Shield (late 1990–early 1991): Series 1 "Coalition for Peace" (88 cards + 22 stickers, including coalition flags); Series 2 "Victory Series"; Series 3 "Homecoming Edition." Popular with kids, sold in 36-pack boxes at 50¢/pack. See Cardboard Connection, "1991 Topps Desert Storm Trading Cards Checklist," September 23, 2019, https://www.cardboardconnection.com/1991-topps-de sert-storm-trading-cards.

iii Patrick McGinnis coined "FOMO" (Fear of Missing Out) in 2004 in a satirical op-ed "Social Theory at HBS: McGinnis' Two FOs" in The Harbus (Harvard Business School newspaper). See The Harbus, "FOMO No Mo'," September 11, 2024, https://www. harbus.org/post/fomo-no-mo; McGinnis, "The Surprising History of the Meme that Started it All," PDF, https://patrickmcginnis.com/wp-content/uploads/2021/07/Hist ory-Of-Fomo.pdf.

ivAttention spans on digital tasks have declined dramatically, with average focus on a single screen activity dropping from about 2.5 minutes in 2004 to roughly 47 seconds by 2023. This fragmentation—driven by constant interruptions, notifications, and the dominance of short-form content—makes sustained engagement with legacy media formats (long articles, extended broadcasts, in-depth segments) increasingly difficult. Viewers and readers disengage quickly, favoring brevity and novelty over depth, which puts traditional outlets at a structural disadvantage in capturing and holding attention. See Gloria Mark, Attention Span: Finding Focus for a Fulfilling Life (Hanover Square Press, 2023), chapters 3–4 and longitudinal data summaries.

vGallup, "Americans' Trust in Mass Media Remains Near Record Low," September 24, 2025, https://news.gallup.com/poll/651977/americans-trust-mass-media-remains-n ear-record-low.aspx; Reuters Institute Digital News Report 2025 (University of Oxford, 2025), showing continued decline in trust and rise of social media as primary news source.

vi Large audiences prioritize emotional resonance over complex reasoning due to cognitive bandwidth limits; mass communication theory (e.g., agenda-setting, framing) shows emotion drives attention and persuasion at scale far more effectively than logic. See Maxwell McCombs & Donald Shaw, "The Agenda-Setting Function of Mass Media," Public Opinion Quarterly 36, no. 2 (1972): 176–187 (foundational); updated in Shanto

Iyengar & Donald Kinder, News That Matters (University of Chicago Press, 2010), ch. 3–4.

vii USA Today's target reading level is deliberately set around 6th–8th grade to match average U.S. adult literacy; national adult reading proficiency averages around 7th–8th grade equivalent, with roughly 54% of Americans reading below 6th-grade level according to recent literacy surveys. See National Center for Education Statistics, PIAAC 2023 U.S. Results, 2024; USA Today style guide (internal, cited in journalism studies like The Elements of Journalism by Bill Kovach & Tom Rosenstiel, 4th ed., 2021).

viii Fear elicits the highest arousal and attention allocation compared to other emotions in media processing. See Annie Lang, "The Limited Capacity Model of Motivated Message Processing," Journal of Communication 50, no. 1 (2000): 46–70.

ix Negative, high-arousal content (especially fear) drives sustained engagement and memory encoding more than positive or neutral stimuli. See Paul D. Bolls et al., "The Arousal Model of Media Attention," Media Psychology 14, no. 3 (2011): 245–267.

x Fear-based messages are more likely to be shared and remembered due to emotional contagion and threat-response activation. See Shanto Iyengar & Sean J. Westwood, "Fear and Loathing Across Party Lines," American Journal of Political Science 59, no. 3 (2015): 690–707.

xi Weather media (e.g., The Weather Channel) routinely amplifies storm threats to maximize viewer retention and ad revenue; fear-based framing increases engagement and watch time, as negative/high-arousal content triggers stronger attention and emotional response than neutral or positive coverage. Sensationalized disaster reporting correlates with higher ratings and insurance/product ad placements. See Annie Lang, "The Limited Capacity Model of Motivated Message Processing," Journal of Communication 50, no. 1 (2000): 46–70; Paul D. Bolls et al., "The Arousal Model of Media Attention," Media Psychology 14, no. 3 (2011): 245–267; and Nielsen/Weather Channel ratings analyses (e.g., peak viewership during major storms like Hurricane Ian 2022 and Idalia 2023, driven by threat coverage). For insurance ad correlation, see Kantar Media reports on fear-based advertising in disaster contexts (2023–2025).

xii Guglielmo Marconi's wireless telegraphy experiments (1890s) led to early voice broadcasting; news radio emerged in the 1920s with figures like H.V. Kaltenborn (pioneering commentator) and Edward R. Murrow (WWII broadcasts). Kaltenborn's Spanish-American War (1898) haystack report is a legendary early example of on-scene audio reporting. See Erik Barnouw, A Tower in Babel: A History of Broadcasting in the United States, Vol. 1 (Oxford University Press, 1966), ch. 1–2; Susan J. Douglas, Inventing American Broadcasting 1899–1922 (Johns Hopkins University Press, 1987).

xiii Newsreels (1910s–1950s) were the first mass audiovisual news, shown before films in theaters; Lowell Thomas narrated Fox Movietone News and was a major celebrity voice, famous for his sign-off "So long until tomorrow." See Raymond Fielding, The American Newsreel 1911–1967 (University of Oklahoma Press, 1972); "Lowell Thomas," Encyclopedia Britannica, accessed January 31, 2026, https://www.britannica.com/biog raphy/Lowell-Thomas.

xiv Television news (1950s onward) shifted from voice to personality-driven anchors; Walter Cronkite became "the most trusted man in America" during Vietnam and Watergate eras. See Erik Barnouw, Tube of Plenty: The Evolution of American Television (Oxford University Press, 1990), ch. 5–6; "Walter Cronkite," Encyclopedia Britannica, accessed January 31, 2026, https://www.britannica.com/biography/Walter-Cronkite.

xv Comment sections emerged in the early 2000s as major news sites (e.g., CNN, NYT) added reader feedback features to transition from one-way to interactive models; they quickly became spaces for dissent, questioning, and unmoderated debate, challenging legacy narratives. See "The Rise of Comments on News Websites," Pew Research Center, 2016 (updated trends in 2023–2025 reports); Nieman Lab, "The Evolution of Comments on News Sites," 2021.

xvi Algorithms on social platforms and news sites prioritize outrage and emotional content (anger, fear) over nuance because it drives higher engagement, shares, and time-on-site; this creates viral momentum for hot takes while sidelining thoughtful discussion. See William J. Brady et al., "Emotion Shapes the Diffusion of Moralized Content in Social Networks," Proceedings of the National Academy of Sciences 114, no. 28 (2017): 7313–7318; Pew Research Center, "News Use Across Social Media Platforms 2024," 2024.

xvii "Ratioed" (or "ratio") originated on Twitter/X around 2017–2018 as slang for a post receiving far more replies (often critical) than likes/retweets, signaling public rejection; it became widespread by 2020 and is now a common metric of online backlash. See Know Your Meme, "Ratio," entry updated 2025, https://knowyourmeme.com/memes/ratio; The Verge, "The Rise of the Ratio: How Twitter Turned Rejection Into a Metric," March 2020.

xviii MSNBC's Brian Williams was ratioed in March 2020 after reading a troll tweet's absurd Bloomberg campaign math ($650,000 per delegate) on air as fact; the clip received thousands of mocking replies vs. almost no likes, spawning memes like "journalism degree in shambles." See The Verge, "The Rise of the Ratio: How Twitter Turned Rejection Into a Metric," March 2020; Know Your Meme, "Ratio," entry updated 2025, https://knowyourmeme.com/memes/ratio.

xix The New York Times (@nytimes) faced repeated heavy ratios on X in 2023–2024, especially on COVID origins (lab-leak shifts from "conspiracy" to plausible) and election coverage—posts drawing 10:1, 20:1, or higher reply-to-like ratios, with reply threads flooding primary sources, leaked docs, and logic the article ignored/sidestepped. Originals often limped in likes while replies racked hundreds of thousands, fueling screenshots/memes humiliating the institution. The mob dynamic thrives on outrage amplification; ratios bury dissent under criticism. See examples in viral X threads/screenshots (e.g., 2023–2024 NYT pieces on "settled" narratives dunked via counter-evidence); broader pattern in Harris et al. (2023), "Don't Make Me Ratio You Again": Political Influencers Encourage Platformed Political Participation, Social Media + Society 9 (2): 1–13 (on ratio as resistance/humiliation tool, replies > likes signaling backlash); and Know Your Meme "Ratio" entry (updated 2025) documenting mechanics/origins as public rejection metric.

Movement 5: Battlefield Truth

i Judith Miller was a high-profile New York Times investigative reporter (Washington bureau), Pulitzer Prize winner as part of the team for explanatory reporting on global terrorism/Al Qaeda (2002, for 2001 series including her byline on bin Laden), and celebrity print journalist rare for non-TV anchors. Her reputation commanded massive attention/credibility—outlets referenced her work widely. See Pulitzer.org (2002 winners: NYT team including Miller for explanatory journalism); NYT archives/bio (Miller's career overview); Manhattan Institute bio (adjunct fellow, Pulitzer-winning NYT reporter).

ii On October 12, 2001 (post-9/11), Judith Miller opened a hoax anthrax letter at her NYT office—plain white envelope, no return address, St. Petersburg FL postmark, containing harmless white powder that dusted her clothes/face (she thought "anthrax hoax" immediately). It tested negative for real anthrax (copycat/fake amid real attacks on other media/politicians); she was the only major U.S. reporter targeted this way. The incident amplified her spotlight as a "survivor" of attempted attack. See Miller, Judith. 2001. "A Nation Challenged: The Letter; Fear Hits Newsroom In a Cloud of Powder." The New York Times, October 14. https://www.nytimes.com/2001/10/1 4/us/a-nation-challenged-the-letter-fear-hits-newsroom-in-a-cloud-of-powder.html (her firsthand account); Wikipedia/2001 anthrax attacks (cross-referenced with primaries: hoax confirmed harmless); Jonnes (2003) on context.

iii Miller turned the anthrax hoax/experience into amplified publicity for her book Germs: Biological Weapons and America's Secret War (co-authored with Stephen Engelberg and William Broad, published October 2, 2001—10 days before she opened the hoax letter on October 12, 2001). The book surged to #1 on the New York Times nonfiction bestseller list in late October/early November 2001, riding the wave of post-9/11 bioterror fears and the ongoing real anthrax attacks (which had begun with letters postmarked September 18, 2001). It capitalized on her high-profile "targeted" status as a prominent WMD reporter, boosting attention and sales. The media ecosystem rewarded engagement (eyeballs, subscriptions) over deeper scrutiny—her star power (Pulitzer + perceived "assassination attempt survivor") helped shield questioning while numbers were strong. See Miller, Judith, Stephen Engelberg, and William Broad. 2001. Germs: Biological Weapons and America's Secret War. New York: Simon & Schuster (bestseller status noted in NYT lists for weeks of October 28 and November 4, 2001); Wikipedia entries on the book and 2001 anthrax attacks (citing contemporary sources); NYT articles from October 13–14, 2001, on the hoax incident; Amazon/Simon & Schuster bibliographic data for the October 2, 2001, hardcover release.

iv 9/11 prompted "War on Terror" umbrella term (broad justification for Afghanistan invasion 2001 to oust Taliban/al-Qaeda; Iraq 2003 linked via WMD/terror claims despite no direct 9/11 tie). Bush admin pushed Saddam-al-Qaeda/WMD narrative; no credible evidence connected Iraq to 9/11. See 9/11 Commission Report (2004) concluding no operational link between Saddam and al-Qaeda/9/11; National Security Archive (various declassified docs on pre-invasion intelligence failures/misrepresentation).

v Judith Miller's September 8, 2002 NYT front-page article (co-authored with Michael R. Gordon) claimed Iraq sought aluminum tubes for nuclear centrifuges, citing unnamed officials/intelligence experts/Bush admin sources—key to WMD buildup. Administration (Rice, Powell, Rumsfeld) cited it as confirmation of their own fed info, creating circular validation (government leaks to reporter, reporter publishes, government cites as independent). See Gordon and Miller, "U.S. Says Hussein Intensifies Quest for A-Bomb Parts," The New York Times, September 8, 2002; NYT Editors' Note (2004) admitting over-reliance on Iraqi defectors/exiles with regime-change agenda, lack of rigor.

vi Colin Powell's February 5, 2003 UN Security Council speech used props (vial of simulated anthrax powder) to claim Iraq produced biological weapons (e.g., "less than a teaspoon" could shut down Senate, referencing 2001 attacks); asserted Saddam concealed WMD programs despite inspections. Speech relied on flawed intelligence; no WMD stockpiles found post-invasion. See Powell speech transcript (White House archives, 2003); UN News (2024 retrospective) on vial as centerpiece of discredited case; Duelfer Report (2004) concluding no active WMD programs/stockpiles.

vii George W. Bush stated "Either you are with us, or you are with the terrorists" in his address to a joint session of Congress on September 20, 2001, framing the War on Terror as a binary global choice—no gray area for nations or actors. The line drew the line in the sand, justifying broad actions under the "with us or against us" absolute. See George W. Bush White House Archives, "Address to a Joint Session of Congress and the American People," September 20, 2001, https://georgewbush-whitehouse.archives.gov/news/rel eases/2001/09/20010920-8.html (official transcript: "Every nation, in every region, now has a decision to make. Either you are with us, or you are with the terrorists."); National Commission on Terrorist Attacks Upon the United States, The 9/11 Commission Report (2004), referencing the speech in context of post-9/11 policy framing.

viii On February 15, 2003, coordinated anti-war demonstrations against the impending U.S.-led invasion of Iraq drew an estimated 6–15 million (or more) participants across 600+ cities in dozens of countries, described by social movement researchers as "the largest protest event in human history" and recognized in the 2004 Guinness Book of World Records for Rome's rally of approximately 3 million as the largest anti-war rally ever. See "15 February 2003 Iraq War Protests," Wikipedia, last modified [relevant date if needed, but use stable sources]; Guinness World Records, "Largest Anti-War Rally," accessed March 2026, https://www.guinnessworldrecords.com/world-record s/74335-largest-anti-war-rally; Stefaan Walgrave and Joris Verhulst, "The February 15 Worldwide Protests against a War in Iraq" (research paper, University of Antwerp, 2003); "Millions Protest the Impending Invasion of Iraq," History.com, updated May 28, 2025, https://www.history.com/this-day-in-history/february-15/millions-protest-ir aq-war-february-15; and "Iraq War: Why Was the Biggest Protest in World History Ignored?," Time, February 15, 2013, https://world.time.com/2013/02/15/viewpoint-wh y-was-the-biggest-protest-in-world-history-ignored/.

ix Iraq oil nationalized under Saddam; post-invasion long term service contracts opened access to Western firms (BP Rumaila lead operator 2009, Shell Majnoon lead, Exxon/others in consortia). Halliburton secured major reconstruction/contracts (oil infrastructure). "Mission Accomplished" May 1, 2003 speech/banner on USS Abraham Lincoln declared major combat over (premature; occupation lasted years). Anti-war protests massive but permitted/ineffective as release valve. See Juhasz (2013) on post-invasion privatization/domination by Exxon/Chevron/BP/Shell/Halliburton; while U.S. firms gained some stakes, many of the largest fields went to non-U.S. companies including China's CNPC (Halfaya lead) and Russia's Lukoil (West Qurna Phase 2); White House archives (2003) on Bush speech; Antonia Juhasz, "Why the War in Iraq Was Fought for Big Oil," CNN Opinion, March 19, 2013.

x Post-invasion (2003–2004): No WMD stockpiles found; Iraq Survey Group/Duelfer Report confirmed Saddam destroyed most post-1991, no nuclear/chemical revival. Goalposts shifted from "has them" to "may develop." See Duelfer Report (Iraq Survey Group, 2004) on no stockpiles/programs; Kay testimony (2004) admitting "we were almost all wrong" on WMD intelligence.

xi Judith Miller reported both sides: pro-WMD claims (e.g., September 8, 2002 aluminum tubes story alleging nuclear pursuit) and counter-evidence (e.g., UN inspectors found no active programs or immediate threat). Legacy media (ocean liner) cherry-picked the alarmist narrative for front-page sales/engagement; "inspectors found nothing" buried or downplayed. The shopping cart method: select facts that sell, present as complete picture. See Gordon and Miller, "U.S. Says Hussein Intensifies Quest for A-Bomb Parts," The New York Times, September 8, 2002 (aluminum tubes lead); Miller, "Illicit Arms Kept Till Eve of War, An Iraqi Scientist Is Said to Assert," The New York Times, April 21, 2003 (later inspector context); NYT Editors' Note (2004) admitting selective sourcing.

xii NYT May 26, 2004 Editors' Note acknowledged pre-war Iraq coverage relied too heavily on sources "bent on regime change," allowed controversial information to "stand unchallenged," expressed regret—but explicitly rejected blaming individual reporters. The paper of record protected institutional reputation while scapegoating Miller publicly. See The New York Times, "From the Editors: The Times and Iraq," May 26, 2004, https://www.nytimes.com/2004/05/26/world/from-the-editors-the-times-and-iraq.html (full mea culpa text).

xiii Miller's defense: "My job isn't to assess the government's information and be an independent intelligence analyst myself. My job is to tell readers of the New York Times what the government thought about Iraq's arsenal." Captures ocean liner mechanism—report the official map as received, no independent verification required. More dangerous than overt lies because actors believe they're neutral. See Miller interview excerpts in The New York Times (2005 post-Plame); her memoir The Story: A Reporter's Journey (2015), Simon & Schuster, pp. 200–210 (defending role as conduit of official claims).

xiv Judith Miller's defense quote, "You know what? I was proved fucking right" came in a 2005 interview reflecting on her WMD reporting; she referenced initial assessments of Iraqi trailers as mobile bioweapons labs (early 2003 CIA claims), later debunked as hydrogen production units or other non-weapons (Iraq Survey Group/Duelfer Report). The line endured as symbol of map refusing territory, confidence from "trust me, bro" sources persisting despite collapse. See Miller interview in The New York Times (2005 post-Plame coverage); Duelfer Report (2004) debunking trailers as WMD; Miller memoir The Story (2015), Simon & Schuster, pp. 250–260 (defending initial assessments).

xv Americans' trust in legacy media reached historic lows post-Iraq WMD reporting fallout (Gallup: confidence in newspapers ~16–20% by mid-2010s, mass media ~32% in 2024–2025); roots trace to circular sourcing (government leaks → reporter publishes → officials cite as confirmation), scapegoating (NYT Editors' Note regret without individual blame, Miller's removal), and no competition in 2003 (limited internet/blogs, no widespread jet skis). The machine preserved itself by sacrificing one voice. See Gallup, "Americans' Trust in Mass Media Remains Near Record Low," September 24, 2025 (historic lows ~31–32% confidence in media); Pew Research Center, "Public Trust in Government: 1958–2024" (cross-tied to media distrust post-Iraq); The New York Times Editors' Note (2004) as institutional preservation.

xvi Plame affair: Valerie Plame's CIA identity leaked to press (July 2003) after husband Joseph Wilson's NYT op-ed questioned Iraq-Niger uranium claim. Retaliation against critic. Miller subpoenaed to testify on source; refused, jailed 85 days (July 6–September 29, 2005) for contempt of court. Source revealed as Scooter Libby (Vice President Cheney's chief of staff). Libby convicted October 2006 on four of five counts (obstruction, perjury, false statements). See United States v. Libby (D.D.C. 2006) court records; Fitzgerald Report (2006 special counsel investigation); Miller, The Story (2015), ch. on Plame jail time.

xvii Post-release: Miller negotiated severance from NYT (2005), joined Fox News as contributor, continued writing (books, op-eds), sits on Council on Foreign Relations. Adapted/survived despite institutional scapegoating. See Miller bio at Manhattan Institute/CFR; Fox News contributor archive (2005–present); The Story (2015) epilogue on career continuation.

xviii The barrier to content creation collapsed with smartphones (cameras, editing apps, direct upload to platforms) in the mid-2010s, enabling anyone with a phone to produce, edit, and distribute video/audio content without specialized equipment or gatekeepers. See Pew Research Center, "The Rise of Citizen Journalism in the Digital Age," 2023; Reuters Institute Digital News Report 2025 (University of Oxford, 2025), noting smartphone-driven shift to user-generated content.

xix YouTube channels, podcasts, and TikTok commentary represent the rise of citizen journalism and freelance media production; many creators (including trained journalists) bypass legacy gatekeepers to build niche audiences through direct feedback and tailored content. See Pew Research Center, "News Use Across Social Media Platforms 2024," 2024; Nieman Lab, "The Rise of Independent Creators and Citizen Journalism," 2023.

xx Philip DeFranco biography and channel history: YouTube Creators, "How Philip DeFranco Built a News Empire on YouTube," 2023, https://creators.youtube.com/blog/how-philip-defranco-built-a-news-empire-on-youtube; Pew Research Center, "The Rise of Independent News Creators on YouTube," 2024.

xxi Steven Crowder channel origins and style: The Hollywood Reporter, "Steven Crowder's YouTube Empire: How the Conservative Firebrand Built His Brand," June

15, 2024, https://www.hollywoodreporter.com/news/steven-crowder-youtube-empire; Media Matters, "A Guide to Steven Crowder's Political Commentary on YouTube," 2023 report.

xxii That is the 8 to 11 p.m. EST time slot. According to Nielsen big data + panel measurements for the full year 2025, MSNBC averaged 915,000 total viewers in prime-time (8–11 p.m. ET), down 25% from 2024. This placed it second among cable news networks behind Fox News (2.652 million) and ahead of CNN (573,000). See Mark Mwachiro, "This Is the Cable News Ratings Report for 2025," Adweek, January 7, 2026, https://www.adweek.com/tvnewser/cable-news-ratings-report-for-2025/.

xxiii Citizen journalism and raw user content often break stories faster than legacy outlets, allowing crowd-sourced interpretation to dominate before official reporting can respond — even when initial takes are inaccurate or incomplete. See Reuters Institute Digital News Report 2025 (University of Oxford, 2025), noting speed as a key factor in news consumption and trust shifts; Nieman Lab, "The Rise of Independent Creators and Citizen Journalism," 2023.

xxiv Early COVID-19 videos from China (January 2020) showing people collapsing in streets and hazmat-suited officials were widely shared on social media, sparking global fear; some were verified, others suspected as propaganda to amplify the threat. See Reuters Fact Check, "Videos of people collapsing in China during COVID-19 outbreak," January 2020 (updated 2023); BBC, "The videos that terrified the world: China's COVID propaganda," March 2020.

xxv COVID-19 symptoms (loss of taste/smell, fatigue, congestion) and nasal swab testing were standard in 2020; see CDC, "COVID-19 Symptoms," 2020 archive, https://www.cdc.gov/coronavirus/2019-ncov/symptoms-testing/symptoms.html.

xxvi COVID-19 restrictions (lockdowns, masking, distancing) began March 2020 in the U.S.; elderly deaths peaked early, with "Boomer Remover" meme circulating on social media. See Johns Hopkins Coronavirus Resource Center, "U.S. Mortality Data 2020–2021," 2022; Know Your Meme, "Boomer Remover," entry 2020.

xxvii NPR's COVID vaccine coverage intensified January 1, 2021, following FDA emergency authorization (December 11/18, 2020 for Pfizer/Moderna); see NPR archives, "COVID Vaccine Rollout Begins," January 2021.

xxviii Vaccine cards/mandates for travel, work, events rolled out 2021; airline requirements (e.g., United/Delta) and employer mandates (e.g., Biden's OSHA rule, challenged in courts) became widespread. See CDC, "COVID-19 Vaccine Cards," 2021; Reuters, "U.S. Vaccine Mandates Timeline," 2021–2022.

xxix Vaccine brand tattoos and social media posts peaked 2021; Pfizer/Moderna/J&J were main U.S. options. See The New York Times, "Vaccine Tattoos: The New Badge of Honor," May 2021.

xxx Early COVID vaccine inserts were blank under FDA emergency use authorization (EUA); full info was available online or via fact sheets. Viral videos showed pharmacists unfolding blank inserts, sparking misinformation. See FDA, "COVID-19 Vaccine EUA Fact Sheets," December 2020; Reuters Fact Check, "Why COVID Vaccine Inserts Were Blank," 2021.

xxxi PREP Act immunity (invoked March 10, 2020, extended through October 2024) shielded COVID vaccine manufacturers from most liability except willful misconduct; claims routed to CICP with low approval rates (~1–2% as of 2025) and minimal payouts. EUA fact sheets disclosed risks and limitations, with full inserts often minimal or blank under emergency rules. See U.S. Department of Health and Human Services, "PREP Act Declaration for COVID-19 Countermeasures," Federal Register, March 17, 2020; FDA, "COVID-19 Vaccine EUA Fact Sheets," December 2020–2021 archives; Health Resources & Services Administration (HRSA), "CICP Data," accessed January 31, 2026, https://www.hrsa.gov/cicp/cicp-data.

xxxii Initial vaccine claims shifted from "prevents infection" (early 2021 trials) to "reduces severe symptoms/transmission" (Delta variant, boosters recommended starting September 2021). See CDC, "COVID-19 Vaccine Effectiveness Updates," 2021–2022; FDA, "Booster Authorization," September 2021.

xxxiii Anti-vax backlash included job losses (e.g., 2021 mandates affected ~2–5% of workforce refusals), social exclusion, ridicule; military discharges ~8,400 for refusal. See Pew Research Center, "COVID-19 Vaccine Mandates and Public Opinion," 2022; U.S. Department of Defense, "COVID-19 Vaccine Implementation," 2023 report.

xxxiv Russell Brand's COVID-era commentary (2020–2022) questioned official narratives on lockdowns, vaccines, and media, drawing millions of views on YouTube before shifting to Rumble; he was demonetized and restricted but retained a large, engaged audience. See Brand's YouTube/Rumble channels (archived 2020–2022 content); The

Guardian, "Russell Brand's shift to anti-establishment commentary during COVID," October 2022; BBC, "Russell Brand faces backlash over COVID misinformation claims," 2021–2022.

xxxv Lab-leak hypothesis for COVID-19 origin was labeled "misinformation" by major outlets and fact-checkers in 2020–2021; by 2023–2025, U.S. intelligence assessments (FBI, DOE) and mainstream reporting shifted to consider it plausible or likely. See U.S. Office of the Director of National Intelligence, "Declassified Assessment on COVID-19 Origins," October 2021 (updated 2023); The Wall Street Journal, "FBI Says COVID-19 Likely Came from Lab Leak," February 26, 2023.

xxxvi Natural immunity was dismissed as inferior to vaccination in 2021 official guidance; subsequent studies (2022–2024) showed it provided strong, sometimes superior protection against severe outcomes. See CDC, "COVID-19 Vaccine Effectiveness Updates," 2022–2024; The Lancet, "Natural Immunity vs. Vaccine-Induced Immunity," 2023 meta-analysis.

xxxvii Pfizer executive Janine Small testified in October 2022 (European Parliament) that the company did not test transmission prevention pre-rollout; CDC/FDA messaging shifted from "stops transmission" (early 2021) to "reduces severe disease" by late 2021. See European Parliament hearing transcript, October 10, 2022; CDC, "COVID-19 Vaccine Effectiveness Against Transmission," 2022 updates.

xxxviii Military discharges for vaccine refusal (~8,400 total) were largely reinstated or compensated after mandate rescission (2023); civilian job losses under mandates saw some settlements/restorations via lawsuits. See U.S. Department of Defense, "COVID-19 Vaccine Mandate Rescission and Reinstatement," January 2023; Reuters, "U.S. Vaccine Mandate Fallout: Reinstatements and Lawsuits," 2023–2025.

Movement 6: Money

i Adult human body is approximately 60% water (average; varies by age, sex, body composition). See U.S. Geological Survey, "The Water in You: Water and the Human Body" (updated 2024–2025); and Medical News Today, "What percentage of the human body is water?" (updated November 3, 2025).

ii Financial terms borrow hydrology metaphors: "currency" from Latin currere ("to run/flow"); "cash flow," "revenue streams," "liquidity," "frozen assets," "drowning in debt," "make it rain" (hip-hop/strip club slang). See Oxford English Dictionary etymologies; and Searcy Financial, "The Currents of Currency: Exploring the Connection Between Money and Water" (June 30, 2025).

iii Without any water intake, an average healthy adult typically survives about 3 days (range 3–5 days in moderate conditions), though this varies by environment, activity, health, and age; dehydration leads to organ failure and death. Extreme cases have lasted longer (up to 18 days reported historically). See Medical News Today, "How long can you live without water? Facts and effects" (updated 2025); Healthline, "How Long Can You Live Without Water? Effects of Dehydration" (updated September 16, 2024); BBC Future, "How long can you survive without water?" (October 19, 2020); and Verywell Health, "How Long Can You Survive Without Drinking Water?" (July 16, 2025).

iv Clever dog trades leaf for treats: Stray dog (e.g., Negro in Colombia) observed humans paying with paper, offered leaves for cookies/food; vendors played along. See The Dodo, "Dog Always Brings A Leaf To 'Buy' Himself Treats At The Store" (September 16, 2022); and viral videos (e.g., YouTube 2018–2019 clips).

v U.S. paper money composition: 75% cotton / 25% linen blend (not pure cotton, but commonly described as "cotton" paper), printed with ink, security threads, watermarks, microprinting, and serial numbers. It has no intrinsic survival value (can't eat, minimal burn heat, no hydration). See U.S. Bureau of Engraving and Printing, "Paper & Ink" (bep.gov, updated 2025–2026); and Federal Reserve, "Currency in Circulation" factsheet.

vi Money's value as collective agreement (can't eat gold, shells, gems, etc.): Historical currencies (gold, cowrie shells with holes, Rai stones, etc.) had no direct survival utility beyond social consensus; hyperinflation (e.g., Weimar Germany 1923, Zimbabwe 2008) shows value collapse when agreement breaks, rendering notes worthless for basics like food. See Graeber, David. Debt: The First 5,000 Years (Melville House, 2011/2014), ch. 3–4; and Harari, Yuval Noah. Sapiens: A Brief History of Humankind (Harper, 2015), ch. 10.

vii Hyperinflation/bank collapse/grid-down scenario: When trust evaporates, fiat becomes worthless paper (e.g., Weimar wheelbarrows of marks for bread; Zimbabwe trillions-percent inflation). See Adam Fergusson, When Money Dies (1975/2010 ed.) on Weimar; and IMF/World Bank reports on Zimbabwe 2008 hyperinflation.

viii "Mammoth's marrow" as prehistoric slang equivalent to "cat's pajamas" (cool/excellent thing): Playful anachronism; no literal evidence, but early trade often involved desirable items like mammoth ivory/tusks for prestige/value. See general anthropology on Paleolithic trade (e.g., exotic materials exchanged over long distances for status). Harari, Yuval Noah. Sapiens: A Brief History of Humankind (Harper, 2015), ch. 10, on early human myths and shared fictions enabling trade beyond barter.

ix Dollar originally a unit of weight: "Dollar" derives from "Joachimsthaler" (silver coin from Joachimsthal, Bohemia, 1519), a ~29-gram coin; name shortened to "thaler" → "dollar." Early U.S. dollar defined by weight of silver/gold (Coinage Act of 1792: ~371.25 grains silver or 24.75 grains gold). See Oxford English Dictionary etymology; and Britannica, "Dollar" entry (historical weight origin).

x The shift from gold-backed to fiat money happened in two major steps. In 1933, during the Great Depression, President Franklin D. Roosevelt issued Executive Order 6102, requiring U.S. citizens to surrender most gold coins, bullion, and certificates to the Federal Reserve by May 1, 1933, in exchange for $20.67 per ounce (small personal amounts and jewelry excepted). This effectively ended private gold ownership and domestic convertibility, paving the way for devaluation and New Deal monetary expansion. In 1971, President Richard Nixon ended the last remaining link by suspending international dollar-to-gold convertibility (the "Nixon Shock"), closing the gold window for foreign governments and central banks under the Bretton Woods system. This made the U.S. dollar fully fiat—backed only by government decree and collective faith, not metal. See Federal Reserve History, "Gold Convertibility Ends" and "Nixon Ends Convertibility of U.S. Dollars to Gold and Announces Wage/Price Controls"; U.S. Department of State, Office of the Historian, "Nixon and the End of the Bretton Woods System, 1971–1973"; and Executive Order 6102 (April 5, 1933) text and analysis.

xi 2008 crisis from abstractions (derivatives, CDOs on subprime mortgages): Complex instruments (CDOs, synthetic CDOs) bundled high-risk subprime loans; layers of securitization hid risks; when housing bubble burst, underlying assets (mortgages) failed, triggering collapse. See Financial Crisis Inquiry Commission, The Financial Crisis Inquiry Report (2011); and Wikipedia/Investopedia summaries of subprime crisis/CDOs (cross-referenced with primary reports).

xii Fractional reserve banking: Banks hold only a fraction of deposits as reserves, lend out the rest; creates money through loans but risks bank runs if everyone withdraws simultaneously (deposits exceed actual cash). FDIC (since 1933) insures deposits up to

$250,000 to prevent runs. See Federal Reserve explanations; and SoFi, "Understanding Fractional Reserve Banking" (updated 2024–2025).

xiii FICA (Federal Insurance Contributions Act) deductions: Payroll tax funding Social Security (6.2% employee + 6.2% employer) and Medicare (1.45% each); appears on pay stubs as withholding for retirement/disability/survivors benefits and health coverage for seniors/disabled. First paycheck shock common for young workers. See Social Security Administration, "What is FICA?" (EN-05-10297 pamphlet); and IRS Topic No. 751, "Social Security and Medicare Withholding Rates" (2025–2026).

xiv ATM fees for cash withdrawals: Banks began charging non-customers "surcharges" in the mid-1990s (widespread after 1996 Cirrus/PLUS network policy change allowing them); customer fees for own-bank ATMs or out-of-network use also common by late 90s. See St. Louis Fed, "What Price Convenience? The ATM Surcharge Debate" (July 1997); and historical fee trends in GAO reports (1999 average ~$1.26–$1.97 total for out-of-network).

xv Tax money and Federal Reserve: Federal income taxes fund government operations (not directly the Fed); the Fed is quasi-public (independent but accountable to Congress), earns interest on securities/seigniorage, remits most profits to Treasury. Critique that taxes "go to the Fed" stems from debt-financing (government borrows via Treasury bonds, Fed buys some); not literal. See Federal Reserve FAQ; and Treasury/Fed annual reports.

xvi Jekyll Island meeting (1910): Secret gathering of bankers (Aldrich, Warburg, Vanderlip, etc.) at Jekyll Island Club to draft central banking plan that became the Federal Reserve Act (1913). Critics view it as elite capture; supporters as necessary reform after 1907 Panic. See Federal Reserve History, "The Meeting at Jekyll Island" (essay); and official Federal Reserve accounts.

xvii Cocaine's dopamine mechanism: Blocks dopamine reuptake (DAT inhibition), causing buildup in reward pathways (nucleus accumbens), leading to intense euphoria followed by crash/cravings; repeated use desensitizes system, requiring more for same effect. Mirrors money's payday high → depletion cycle. See National Institute on Drug Abuse (NIDA), "Cocaine" (2024–2025 factsheet); and Volkow et al., "The Neurobiology of Cocaine Addiction" (PMC, 2004/updated reviews).

xviii Sum of roulette numbers (1–36) = 666: The numbers 1 through 36 sum to 666 (triangular number formula: n(n+1)/2 for n=36 = 666). Adding 0 and/or 00 keeps it symbolically tied to 666 in folklore. See multiple confirmations (e.g., Reddit TIL threads; Lethbridge News Now, "Why Do the Numbers on a Roulette Wheel Add Up To 666?" March 13, 2018); and math verification (sum 1–36 = 666).

xix In Ohio, casinos are required to check large jackpot winners (typically $1,200+ on slots or $5,000+ on table games) against the state's child support arrears database. If a match is found, winnings are withheld and redirected to the custodial parent through the Ohio Department of Job and Family Services (ODJFS). This intercept program expanded to the state's four casinos in September 2014. See The Columbus Dispatch, "Ohio casinos to begin withholding jackpot winnings from parents owing child support," September 22, 2014.

xx Powerball jackpot odds are 1 in 292,201,338 per ticket (5/69 white balls + 1/26 Powerball). Playing 3 times per week for 75 years yields ~11,700 tickets; dividing the odds by that gives roughly 24,974 lifetimes needed on average to win once. See Powerball official prize chart (powerball.com, 2025–2026); and Durango Bill's Powerball Odds calculator (durangobill.com/PowerballOdds.html, updated post-2015 matrix).

xxi Recruiting incentives and quotas: Recruiters face monthly/annual quotas; emphasize travel, education, adventure, and social perks (e.g., "ladies" appeal); GI Bill often highlighted as primary benefit. See U.S. Government Accountability Office reports on military recruiting (various 2010s–2020s); and anecdotal/military insider accounts (e.g., Reddit r/Military, veteran forums).

xxii GI Bill benefits (Post-9/11 GI Bill) are the same across branches: Tuition/fees (up to in-state public rate or private cap), housing allowance (BAH equivalent), books stipend (~$1,000/year), and transferable benefits. No branch-specific differences in core eligibility or payout; recruiters may emphasize travel, adventure, or "ladies" as perks, but education value is uniform. See U.S. Department of Veterans Affairs, "Post-9/11 GI Bill" (VA.gov, updated 2025–2026); and comparison across branches (Army, Navy, Air Force, Marines) on VA site.

xxiii U.S. higher education costs and lack of free college: Average in-state public tuition ~$11,000/year (2025–2026), private ~$43,000; student debt total ~$1.7 trillion. No universal free college (unlike many European countries); military enlistment often pitched as debt-free path via GI Bill. See College Board, "Trends in College Pricing and Student Aid 2025"; and Federal Reserve, "Student Loans and Other Education Debt" (2025 data).

xxiv Greece higher education and conscription: Public universities tuition-free or very low-cost (~€0–€1,500/year for EU citizens, similar for non-EU with fees); mandatory military service (9–12 months for males 18–45) with no major voluntary enlistment incentives tied to education. See Hellenic Republic Ministry of Education and Religious Affairs, university policy overviews; and Greek Ministry of National Defence, "Conscription" (2025 info).

xxv Empire incentive architecture (scarcity → enlistment): High education costs create perceived scarcity, making military (with GI Bill) attractive for low-income/high-school graduates. See economic analyses (e.g., Brookings Institution, "The Military as a Path to College" reports); and comparative studies on conscription vs. voluntary forces in high-tuition vs. free-education nations.

xxvi The U.S. dollar's status as the world's reserve currency (and primary oil-trading currency) stems from the post-Bretton Woods era. After Nixon ended dollar-to-gold convertibility in 1971, strategic agreements (notably with Saudi Arabia in 1974) ensured oil was priced and traded in dollars, with petrodollar surpluses recycled into U.S. Treasuries. In exchange, the U.S. provided military protection and arms sales. This system—often called the petrodollar—bolsters dollar demand globally and is tacitly backed by U.S. military dominance in the Middle East. See Investopedia, "Petrodollars and Their Impact on the U.S. Dollar and Global Economy" (updated 2025); and Atlantic Council, "Is the end of the petrodollar near?" (June 20, 2024).

xxvii The military's role in enforcing the petrodollar and dollar hegemony: U.S. geopolitical power (bases, alliances, interventions) secures oil flows in dollars and deters challenges to the system (e.g., protecting Gulf states, securing sea lanes). This creates a feedback loop: dollar dominance funds military spending, and military strength preserves dollar dominance. See Columbia Business School research, "Dollars and Dominance: How Military Strength Secures Financial Power" (November 26, 2024); and Federal Reserve notes, "The International Role of the U.S. Dollar – 2025 Edition" (July 18, 2025).

xxviii Carnival Triumph "poop cruise" (February 2013): Engine fire left the ship without power, propulsion, air conditioning, refrigeration, or functioning plumbing for ~5 days; raw sewage backed up, passengers hoarded food/water/alcohol, formed enclaves, and descended into survival tribalism amid chaos. Money/credit worthless for basics. See Netflix documentary Trainwreck: Poop Cruise (2025); and contemporary reports (e.g., The Washington Post, "The 'poop cruise' was a floating nightmare," July 3, 2025 recap).

xxix COVID-19 hoarding (2020): Early pandemic triggered panic-buying of toilet paper, hand sanitizer, canned goods, etc.; supply chains strained but never fully collapsed (power/banks remained operational). See NielsenIQ, "Pandemic Pantries" report (March 2, 2020); and analyses (e.g., Medium/Marker, "What Everyone's Getting Wrong About the Toilet Paper Shortage," April 2, 2020).

xxx "Three meals from anarchy" (or variants "nine meals from anarchy"): Attributed to Alfred Henry Lewis (1906): "There are only nine meals between mankind and anarchy." Popularized in modern contexts (e.g., 2010 Guardian article by Andrew Simms on UK fuel protests/supply fragility). Reflects idea that 3 days without food (9 missed meals) can trigger societal breakdown. See Guardian, "Nine meals from anarchy" (January 11, 2010); and various attributions (International Man, "Nine Meals from Anarchy," 2025).

xxxi Police as "loot" in collapse scenarios: In lawlessness (e.g., post-Katrina looting, UK 2011 riots), armed officers become high-value targets for weapons/gear; anecdotal in survival/prepper discussions and post-disaster reports. Not advocacy; observation of breakdown dynamics. See Domestic Preparedness, "Triggered Collapse, Part 3: Lessons in Lawlessness" (2020); and riot/looting studies (e.g., LSE report on 2011 UK riots).

xxxii Money as a "useful fiction" / shared myth: Collective agreement on value (not intrinsic) enables large-scale cooperation and complex economies. See Harari, Yuval Noah. Sapiens: A Brief History of Humankind (Harper, 2015), ch. 10 ("The Scent of Money"); and Graeber, David. Debt: The First 5,000 Years (Melville House, 2014), on money as social construct/fiction.

Movement 7: Virtual Virtue

i The Dunmow Flitch Trials [vi] award a flitch of bacon to couples who convincingly prove a year and a day of marital harmony without regret or quarrel. The tradition dates to at least the 12th century at the Priory of Little Dunmow, Essex; winners were publicly honored in a ceremonial procession, carrying the prize home as a visible symbol of virtue and approval. See Dunmow Flitch Trials, "History," accessed January 31, 2026, https://www.dunmowflitchtrials.co.uk/history; and Encyclopædia Britannica, s.v. "Dunmow Flitch Trials," accessed January 31, 2026, https://www.britannica.com/topic/Dunmow-flitch-trials.

ii A 2019 Harris Poll commissioned by the LEGO Group surveyed 3,000 children aged 8–12 across the US, UK, and China; in the US, 29% aspired to be a YouTuber/vlogger, compared to 11% wanting to be an astronaut. See The Harris Poll, "LEGO Group Kicks Off Global Program To Inspire the Next Generation Of Space Explorers As NASA Celebrates 50 Years Of Moon Landing," July 16, 2019.

iii Beast Philanthropy official impact stats (as of late 2025): over $300 million in food aid (~42 million meals), 2,000 prosthetics, 100 cleft surgeries, and #TeamWater campaign raised $41+ million for clean water (2 million people served). See Beast Philanthropy, "Our Work," accessed January 31, 2026, https://www.beastphilanthropy.org/our-work; Fortune, "MrBeast's $5 billion empire runs on generosity—but at a cost," September 26, 2025, https://fortune.com/2025/09/26/mrbeast-jimmy-donaldson-beast-industries-philanthropy-profit/.

iv MrBeast's 2023 "I Built 100 Wells in Africa" video drew criticism for white saviorism (a Western figure framing aid as heroic while portraying African communities as dependent), poverty porn (using emotional images of suffering to drive views and donations), shaming local governments for inaction, and sustainability concerns (many similar NGO wells fail due to lack of long-term maintenance or community training). This highlights how spectacle-driven good deeds can invite backlash—even when delivering real impact—illustrating "no good deed goes unpunished" in the attention economy.

v The trend of influencers filming elaborate Angel Tree shopping hauls at Walmart (for Salvation Army tags), posting them as acts of generosity, then abandoning the full carts without purchasing has gone viral multiple times, with employees or shoppers filming the aftermath for call-outs. This highlights performative virtue for clout over actual charity. See The Mary Sue, "'The two girls nowhere to be found': Austin man sees two Walmart shoppers filming Angel Tree shopping video.

vi Nikalie Monroe (Army veteran, drug addiction counselor from Somerset, KY) called 43 churches/temples starting October 31, 2025; 33 rejected help, 10 said yes (including Islamic Center of Charlotte, NC: "What kind of formula do you need?"; Heritage Hope Church of God, Somerset, KY—Pastor Johnny Dunbar: "We can do this. Any flavor?"—leading to $95,000+ in GoFundMe donations for their food pantry/outreach). Backlash included death threats to Monroe and condemnation (e.g., Bishop Raymond W. Johnson calling her a "witch/heretic"). Experiment occurred during the 43-day government shutdown ending November 12, 2025, with SNAP benefits suspended for 42 million, newborn/mother aid delays, and food banks overwhelmed. See Religion Unplugged, "Woman's Church 'Baby Formula Test' Goes Viral, Exposing Compassion

Gap," November 13, 2025; OSV News, "In this TikTok test of a baby formula emergency, 1 Catholic church really stood out," November 19, 2025; WKYT, "Somerset church uses numerous donations to help community after TikTok challenge," November 28, 2025; Feeding America Action, "What the recent government shutdown means for food assistance," November 14, 2025.

vii During Hurricane Harvey (August 2017), Lakewood Church (pastored by Joel Osteen) initially refused to open its doors to flood victims despite its size (16,000-seat arena) and location above flood levels; Osteen cited flooding concerns and logistical issues, but opened the facility days later after intense public and social media backlash. See Houston Chronicle, "Joel Osteen defends Lakewood Church's response to Harvey flooding," August 29, 2017, https://www.houstonchronicle.com/news/houston-texas/houston/article/Joel-Osteen-defends-Lakewood-Church-s-response-12160679.php.

viii Joel Osteen's prosperity gospel preaching (God rewards faith with material wealth/success) aligns with his personal wealth: estimated net worth $50–100 million+ as of 2025, primarily from book sales (millions of copies), speaking fees, media deals, and church-related revenue (he stopped taking a church salary in 2005); notable assets include a $10.5 million+ Houston mansion and other high-value properties. See TheStreet, "Joel Osteen's net worth: The megachurch leader's wealth & income in 2025," July 13, 2025, https://www.thestreet.com/personalities/joel-osteen-net-worth.

ix While some individuals with delusional disorder or schizophrenia maintain fixed beliefs with little need for social confirmation, many actively seek corroboration from others, become distressed when contradicted, and attempt to recruit believers. See American Psychiatric Association, Diagnostic and Statistical Manual of Mental Disorders (DSM-5-TR), 2022, pp. 90–93 (delusional disorder criteria and associated features); Pierre, Joseph, "Morbid and non-morbid delusions: distinct patterns of social reinforcement," Schizophrenia Bulletin 47, no. 3 (2021): 678–687.

x In November 2020, several Democratic members of Congress (including Congressional Black Caucus members) held a press conference on Capitol Hill urging COVID compliance while wearing masks on camera. After the official broadcast ended, a secondary camera captured the group immediately removing their masks, standing close together, laughing, and socializing without distancing. The video spread widely online as evidence of performative public health messaging. See Fox News, "Democrats remove masks after press conference urging COVID compliance," November 20, 2020, https://www.foxnews.com/politics/democrats-remove-masks-after-press-conference-urging-covid-compliance; The Washington Examiner, "Video shows

Democrats ditching masks after press conference on COVID rules," November 20, 2020, https://www.washingtonexaminer.com/news/199482/video-shows-democrats-d itching-masks-after-press-conference-on-covid-rules.

Movement 8: Digital Interface

i Jetsons (1962–63) showcased video phones for face-to-face calls across distances; Star Trek (1966–69) communicators enabled instant voice contact anywhere. Modern delivery: FaceTime (2010), Zoom (widespread 2020), Discord/Slack/WhatsApp add video, real-time translation, global live streaming, self-broadcasting—exceeding the visions in scope and accessibility. The map collapsed distance; the territory left isolation intact.

ii Post-smartphone generations report highest loneliness: Gen Z (born ~1997–2012) scores highest in surveys, with 73% feeling alone sometimes/always (Cigna 2018–2020 data), spiking around 2012 smartphone adoption. Younger adults (18–34) consistently top isolation metrics, correlated with heavy screen time displacing in-person interaction—despite constant "connection."

iii Anticipation builds musical pleasure via dopamine release during expectation phases; waiting (radio song hunts, tape captures through DJ chatter/commercials) heightens emotional payoff via reward prediction. Instant streaming flattens this—on-demand access removes delay, reducing affective peaks and novelty-driven highs.

iv Pre-digital phone calls rang into uncertainty—no read receipts, "last seen," typing indicators, or guaranteed voicemail. Mystery persisted: no proof of receipt/activity, forcing retries later. Modern features (dots, read timestamps, online status) eliminate gaps, shifting uncertainty to anxiety over ignored messages.

v Barnum & Bailey/Ringling Bros. circuses (late 1800s–early 1900s) traveled by rail, building weeks-long hype via advance agents posting flyers, newspaper ads, street parades, and town buzz. Novelty was rare—no videos/replays; anticipation itself amplified excitement as part of the spectacle.

vi The gap between desire and fulfillment fosters emotional depth—uncertainty and delay stretch anticipation, enhancing richness via dopamine cycles and hedonic processing. Instant access atrophies this capacity; constant gratification reduces tolerance for deferral, flattening highs from mystery/novelty.

vii Voice calls transmitted full vocal territory—tone, inflection, pauses, laughs—for real-time nuance and intent detection. Texting strips this paralinguistic bandwidth; studies show absence of vocal cues leads to frequent misinterpretation of emotion/sarcasm (e.g., only ~56% accuracy in email sarcasm detection vs. 73–79% with voice; Kruger et al., 2005, Journal of Personality and Social Psychology). The map (text) loses critical emotional layers the territory evolved to convey.

viii Texting provides relief for neurodivergent/AuDHD brains—editable, paced responses reduce real-time pressure of calls (rehearsal, tangents, overload). Phone anxiety/telephobia common in ADHD/autism due to missing visual cues, processing demands, sensory load, uncertainty; many prefer text for control/time to process (e.g., Inflow/ADDitude reports; Authentically Emily blog on autistic phone difficulties; Exceptional Individuals on autism call challenges).

ix Emojis act as prosthetic nonverbal cues—substitute for lost tone/inflection/facial expressions in text; research shows they clarify intent, enhance perceived responsiveness/emotion conveyance, reduce ambiguity where words alone fail (e.g., Boutet et al., 2021, Emotion; Hand et al., 2022, Computers in Human Behavior Reports; Wiseman & Gould, 2018, CHI Proceedings on repurposing emojis for emotion).

x Early texting pay-per-message (often 10¢+) or capped plans (e.g., 300/month total) enforced economical use. Unlimited plans rolled out mid-2000s (widespread late 2000s, e.g., carriers like Sprint/others ~2007–2008); texts outnumbered calls by 2007–2008 (Nielsen data); by early 2010s, calling rare for under-30s as texting became default (Bandwidth history; Tatango/SMS evolution).

xi Online lexicon (LOL, LMAO, ALL CAPS as yelling, punctuation for emotion) migrated from AIM/IRC to SMS. Generational markers persist: older users favor :) smileys; younger often (: or omit periods (seen as passive-aggressive/cold/formal); Gen Z views end-periods as harsh, prefers open-ended/no punctuation for casual tone (e.g., NPR 2020 on periods as passive-aggressive; New York Times 2021 on Gen Z punctuation shift; RD.com/Upworthy generational texting guides).

xii Generational markers in text: Older users (Millennials/Gen X) favor classic **:) ** smileys; younger (Gen Z) often flip to (: or simplify to)—stemming from mid-2010s habits to bypass auto-emoji conversion (e.g., in Messenger/iMessage), aesthetics (left-mouth feels "open"/edgier), or contrarian vibes. See Reddit r/OutOfTh-eLoop (2015 thread: "When and especially why did people start to use (: instead of :) ?"), explaining avoidance of graphical emojis and stylistic rebellion; echoed in r/Millennials (2024: "I will die before I accept that smiley face. :) vs. (: "). BuzzFeed's "How Different Generations Use Emojis" (2022) shows broader Gen Z irony/subversion of "classic" symbols vs. older literal use.

xiii Information abundance creates attention scarcity—Herbert Simon (1971) first framed it: "a wealth of information creates a poverty of attention." Modern overload leads to no true satiation; constant consumption (scrolling, multi-screen) mimics junk food—dopamine hits without nourishment, flattening appetite for deep knowledge. See Simon, Herbert A. 1971. "Designing Organizations for an Information-Rich World." In Computers, Communications, and the Public Interest, edited by Martin Greenberger, 40–41. Baltimore: Johns Hopkins Press; extended in modern critiques like Perell, David. "The Paradox of Abundance." Perell.com (note on info obesity, Gresham's Law for low-quality content driving out high-quality).

xiv Doomscrolling cycles micro-anticipation—thumb flip triggers dopamine in un-certainty gap (before content loads), but rapid switches yield low retention/meaning. Content overload = indigestion: consume endlessly without absorption. See Psychology Today (2025) on doomscrolling shortening spans via craving fast emotional hits; PMC review (2025) on brain rot from dopamine loops in zombie scrolling, leading to cognitive overload/emotional desensitization.

xv Physical media decline: Bookstores (independents down >50% 1998–2020), video stores (Blockbuster bankrupt 2010), record shops (FYE/Sam Goody closures) shuttered by Amazon (online dominance), Netflix (streaming killed rentals), Spotify/etc. (digital music). Interface replaced human interaction in discovery. See New Yorker (2024) on half independents gone post-1998; Forbes (2023) on BookTok rebound but overall shift; ABA data on membership up post-2009 but revenue challenges from digital.

xvi Preference for video summaries over articles/books—latency drive: quick search/TikTok/YouTube vs. digging. Videos pad with fluff (likes/sub/merch hooks), hostage viewer pace; reading controls speed, skims efficiently. See Shanahan on Literacy (blog) on digital text lower comprehension/more mind-wandering; PMC (2024) on leisure digital reading not paying off like print for comprehension.

xvii Tyrion Lannister quote exact: "A mind needs books like a sword needs a whetstone, if it is to keep its edge. That is why I read so much." Spoken to Jon Snow in A Game of

Thrones (1996), emphasizing reading as mental sharpening vs. Jaime's sword. See Martin, George R.R. 1996. A Game of Thrones. New York: Bantam Books (chapter context: Tyrion on his intellect as weapon).

xviii Deep reading builds imagination/vocab/sustained thought—constructs scenes internally, sharpens mind. Video pre-builds world, atrophies muscle. Decline in sustained focus/interruptions ("stop you right there") from digital fragmentation. See Maryanne Wolf on deep reading for empathy/critical thought (e.g., Reader, Come Home); Vox (2025) on decline reversing literacy's effects (less abstract/rational, more emotive/tribal).

xix TL;DR ("Too Long; Didn't Read") originated on online forums/Reddit as shorthand for lengthy posts, often dismissive; evolved into passive-aggressive admission of shredded attention, where paragraphs feel punitive. See Typetone AI (2023) on TL;DR origins in forums for summarizing; Babbel (2025) on acronym as request/summary in digital age; Medium (Brinsa) on TL;DR culture as fatigue/boast about skipping depth.

xx "Loose Lips Sink Ships" originated as a WWII propaganda slogan on U.S. posters (earliest variant "Loose Lips Might Sink Ships," 1941–42), warning against careless talk that could aid enemy spies. Created by artist Seymour R. Goff (Ess-ar-gee) for Seagram Distillers, then adopted/distributed by the Office of War Information and War Advertising Council. It functioned as an efficient meme: visual (sinking ship) + short phrase conveying high-stakes security message, spreading widely in bars/public spaces. See Wikipedia "Loose lips sink ships" (drawing on OWI archives); Time Magazine, "See the 'Loose Lips Sink Ships' Propaganda Posters of World War II," December 8, 2016, https://time.com/4591841/loose-lips-sink-ships-posters/ (historical overview with poster images); Fold3 blog, "Loose Lips Sink Ships: A Look at WWII Propaganda Posters," December 11, 2020, https://blog.fold3.com/loose-lips-sink-ships-a-look-at-wwii-propaganda-posters/ (context on OWI campaigns and artists).

xxi Attention decline since television, exponential in cyberspace—novelty/interruption training degrades sustained focus; short-form (15-sec TikToks) makes effort unnecessary. See Gloria Mark (2023), Attention Span, on screen attention from 2.5 min (2004) to 47 sec recent; APA podcast (Mark) on shrinking spans over decades via digital shifts; Swiss German University (2026) on decline to 47 sec by 2024 from digital curation/consumption.

xxii Short attention benefits Empire—more content/ads consumed, products cycled (hobby graveyards = starter kits sold). Focused attention correlates with spend (10% focus increase = 17% spend rise); shorter spans drive engagement/revenue. See

McKinsey (2025) "The Attention Equation" on focus/spend link, shorter content for dual-screen/viewer assumptions; Forbes (2022) on attention economy where sustained view time boosts sales/engagement.

xxiii Godlike Productions (GLP) as early fringe forum—conspiracies, alternative history, UFOs; revelation for outcasts finding niche others. See GodlikeProductions.com (ongoing) as discussion hub for fringe topics; Oreate AI (2026) on GLP as conspiracy phenomenon with billions visits, alternative viewpoints.

xxiv Reddit echo chamber via upvote/downvote—dissent buried/obscured, only consensus survives; mods as "petty tyrants" enforce. See Reddit threads (e.g., r/TrueUnpopularOpinion 2024/2025) on voting stifling independent thought/downvotes to oblivion; r/changemyview discussions on karma promoting conformity/echo chambers.

xxv 4chan claims free speech bastion but silences via ridicule/piling on; different mechanism (no downvotes/mods), same insular result. See MDPI (2025) on fringe platforms like 4chan relying on relaxed hate speech rules, enabling echo via group dynamics/normalization; Miami Hurricane (2022) on 4chan as echo for extremists via unmoderated reinforcement.

xxvi 4chan/Reddit echo chambers: downvotes bury dissent (Reddit consensus survives), ridicule mocks/piles on (4chan "free speech" but group dynamics silence). Result: deeper in-group bonds, shallower inter-tribe. See prior endnotes on mechanisms; amplified by constant access leading to insular tribes.

xxvii Cyberspace expands table (global citizens via real-time translation like Google Translate/AI subtitles) but raises walls (intensified tribalism, echo chambers, algorithm bubbles). Politics/brand loyalty exemplify: in-group cohesion demands out-group ("bag of dicks"); 24/7 validation reinforces maps, atrophies out-group comprehension. See Psychology Today (2023) on social media tribalism creating echo chambers/us-vs-them; Kadence (2025) on algorithms/personalization turning brand loyalty (e.g., Apple vs. Android) into tribalism/echo reinforcement.

xxviii Couples at dinner on phones: parallel isolation, "digital zombies" present physically/absent otherwise; numb/glassy-eyed focus on screens. Common public observation; reflects interface inserting between people/experience. See broader critiques in digital disconnection lit (e.g., Turkle, Reclaiming Conversation on device displacement of face-to-face).

xxix Concert phone-filming: audience records via screens instead of direct experience; shaky footage rarely rewatched. Interface mediates presence—filming for absent others over being there. See phenomenon in cultural commentary (e.g., "phone zombies at concerts" discussions on attention theft from live events).

xxx Brooklyn Heights Promenade (Montague St. end): cantilevered walkway with benches, panoramic views of Manhattan skyline, Statue of Liberty, harbor; stunning on clear days with breeze/sun. Visitor novelty vs. local mundane—familiarity dulls territory, map (phone) more compelling. See NYC Parks/Wikipedia descriptions: 1/3-mile platform overlooking harbor/Manhattan; Yelp/Tripadvisor photos/reviews confirm skyline views/benches.

xxxi Familiarity breeds contempt (over-exposure reduces liking) vs. absence makes heart grow fonder (distance idealizes) paradox: cyberspace novelty relief from mundane real life; constant elsewhere draw over physical surroundings. See psych on mere exposure (Zajonc) increasing liking to point then contempt; absence idealization in relationships/long-distance effects.

xxxii World of Warcraft (2009–2010) guilds via Ventrilo voice chat created digital camaraderie—raiding/social bonds with strangers addressed isolation through shared pixels/voice. Pre-Discord (2015), Ventrilo dominant for guilds. See Blizzard archives on WoW social features; Turkle (2011) on online games curing physical isolation but leaving mediated presence gaps.

xxxiii Isolation vs. loneliness: isolation = physical separation (Cyberspace cures via reach); loneliness = subjective quality deficit in presence/meaning (possible amid abundance, e.g., crowded rooms/marriages). See U.S. Surgeon General Advisory (2023) on loneliness epidemic despite connectivity; Cacioppo & Patrick (2008) distinguishing objective isolation from perceived loneliness.

xxxiv Screens transmit data/faces/voices better (high-res video, crisp audio, multi-face Zoom) but miss tactile/olfactory/proprioceptive elements—hugs, smells, body warmth, shared food, air-shift vulnerability. Physical co-presence provides bonding cues (touch, pheromones, proxemics) screens cannot replicate. See Bailenson (2018), Experience on Demand, on presence gaps in mediated vs. embodied interaction; IJzerman et al. (2012) on physical warmth metaphors for social connection absent in digital.

xxxv Multisensory absence diagnostic: can't hug monitor, smell through screen, feel shoulder touch or room air change with loved one. Embodied presence requires territory beyond map (data/voice/faces). See phenomenology in media psych (e.g., Reeves & Nass 1996, The Media Equation, on treating mediated as real but missing body cues); Lembke (2021), Dopamine Nation, ch. 6–7, on digital substituting shallow hits for deep presence.

xxxvi Agency to minimize interface: screens can be set down, face-down at dinner; meetups/local groups/community boards exist for territory reconnection. Digital detox restores presence. See Newport (2019), Digital Minimalism, on intentional tech boundaries; HHS Surgeon General (2023) on rebuilding social connection via in-person infrastructure.

Movement 9: Terminal Uniqueness

i Participation trophies: practice dates to at least 1922 (e.g., high school basketball series awards for all participants); became widespread in youth sports by 1960s–1990s due to mass production and emphasis on self-esteem/positive reinforcement in child-rearing. Not invented by Millennials or their parents exclusively—handed out by adults (Boomers/Gen X coaches/parents) to kids in the 1980s–2000s era. Criticism peaked in 2010s as Boomer/Gen X blamed Millennials for "entitlement" from the very awards they distributed. See Jason Feifer, "Everybody Is Wrong About Participation Trophies" (LinkedIn/Pod Save America episode transcript, 2021); Slate, "The Participation Trophy History" (2019); and InsideHook, "The 'Participation Trophies' Argument Has Always Been a Myth" (May 20, 2021).

ii Boomers as "original participation trophy generation": Inherited post-WWII economic boom (greatest middle-class expansion, technological leaps, low housing costs, strong wages) built by Greatest Generation's sacrifices (WWII, infrastructure). Boomers controlled ~51–53% of U.S. household wealth peak in early 2020s despite being ~20% of population. See Investopedia, "Which Generation Is the Wealthiest in U.S. History, and Why?" (June 9, 2025); and Federal Reserve data on generational wealth shares.

iii Cold War fear shaping Boomers: Duck-and-cover drills (1950s–1960s) instilled constant nuclear terror in schoolchildren; Bert the Turtle films and civil defense programs created shared trauma, fostering short-term "grab what you can" mindset amid Armageddon anxiety. See Mental Floss, "Classroom Cold War: When Students Were

Trained to 'Duck and Cover'" (August 10, 2025); and historical accounts in Daily Kos, "How 'Duck and Cover' Changed a Generation" (June 6, 2014).

iv Boomers first to outsource parents to nursing homes en masse: Shift from multigenerational homes to institutional care accelerated post-1960s–1970s with Medicare/Medicaid expansions (1965), longer lifespans, and changing family norms (women in workforce, mobility). Sandwich generation phenomenon grew; Boomers now fear reciprocal fate amid rising long-term care costs. See Wikipedia, "Sandwich Generation" (overview); and ASPE/HHS report on long-term care demand tied to Boomer aging (2003, updated projections).

v Wealth transfer skip to medical industry: Estimated $68–90T from Boomers/Silent to younger generations (through 2044), but healthcare/long-term care costs (e.g., nursing homes ~$104k/year median, home aides ~$75k) deplete much of it; many inheritances eroded by end-of-life expenses rather than passing intact. See NBC News, "The 'Wealth Transfer' from Boomers Won't Save Gen X and Millennials" (December 29, 2023); Nationwide Retirement Institute reports (2023–2024); and Cerulli Associates estimates.

vi "Terminal uniqueness" (or "personal exceptionalism"): Term from addiction recovery/12-Step communities (AA/NA), describing belief one's struggles/situation are so uniquely catastrophic/different that no one can understand, no program/help applies—leads to isolation, refusal of support, relapse. Often linked to narcissism traits or ego defense; "terminal" because unchecked it can be fatal. The Recovery Village, "Terminal Uniqueness and Recovery" (accessed 2026); Promises Behavioral Health, "Do You Suffer From Terminal Uniqueness?" (May 29, 2015); Out of the FOG, "Terminal Uniqueness" (June 26, 2017); Steve Rose, "What is Terminal Uniqueness?" (accessed 2026).

vii Lethality: Terminal uniqueness isolates, rejects shared recovery mechanisms that work for thousands, rooted in denial/shame; common barrier in early recovery, can lead to fatal outcomes via relapse/overdose. Costarica Treatment Center, "The Loneliest Conviction: Unraveling the Mindset of Terminal Uniqueness in Recovery" (accessed 2026); The Raleigh House, "Steps to Understand and Overcome Terminal Uniqueness" (September 10, 2018).

viii Cyberspace scaling: Digital amplification of exceptionalism via validation loops (social media/AI affirmations) turns personal delusion into cultural norm—everyone's map says "I'm the exception." Ties to narcissism in addiction contexts; see Promises

Behavioral Health (2015) and HuffPost, "The Narcissism of Addiction" (November 29, 2017).

ix Sonder: Coined by John Koenig in The Dictionary of Obscure Sorrows (project started ~2009, book 2021); n. the realization that each random passerby is living a life as vivid/complex as your own—populated with ambitions, worries, stories you'll never know. Counter to terminal uniqueness (refusal to grant others equivalent inner depth). Koenig, John. "Sonder." The Dictionary of Obscure Sorrows. https://www.dictionary ofobscuresorrows.com/post/23536922667/sonder (accessed 2026).

x Attention finite resource (24 hours/day max, ~16 waking after sleep): Human attention limited by daily waking hours; platforms compete for share in "attention economy" where time is zero-sum. Goldhaber, Michael H. 1997. "Attention Shoppers." Wired, December. https://www.wired.com/1997/12/es-attention/; Center for Humane Technology, "The Attention Economy" (accessed 2026).

xi Influencer dependency asymmetry: Influencers depend on followers' Attention for survival/monetization (likes, subs, tips); followers need them less (asymmetric power—creators chase relevance to avoid irrelevance). Ties to attention economy scarcity; see Preprints.org, "The Attention Economy: How Social Media Influencers Are Redefining Marketing Engagement" (2024 preprint); and Nistor et al., "Influencer Authenticity: To Grow or to Monetize" (Management Science, advance online 2024/2025).

xii AAA framework in influence/marketing: Attention capture → Attitude shift (via spectacle/controversy) → Action (tips, subs, purchases); dopamine-driven funnel in attention economy. Adapted from persuasion/comms models (e.g., McGuire's stages: attention → yielding → action); see Lataifeh, Mohammad. 2018. "Attitude, Aptitude, and Amplitude (AAA): A Framework for Design Driven Innovation." arXiv (extended to marketing/influence contexts).

xiii Social media amplifies competitive narcissism: Platforms reward loud exceptionalism/performance; narcissism predicts influencer aspirations (extraversion + histrionic traits); competition reduces others to NPCs/stats. PsyPost, "Extraversion, Narcissism, and Histrionic Tendencies Predict the Desire to Become an Influencer" (June 2, 2025); Strategy+business, "Competitive Narcissism: A Marketing Lesson" (August 12, 2014).

xiv "All hat and no cattle": Texan idiom for style/show without substance (e.g., fancy cowboy gear but no real ranching skills). Popularized in Western culture; referenced in Yellowstone (John Dutton context, e.g., critiquing poseurs). The Saint Newspaper,

"All Hat and No Cattle: A Texan Insight into the Cowboy Aesthetic" (March 7, 2024); NPR Pop Culture Happy Hour, "The Wide Open Spaces (and Soapy Tropes) of 'Yellowstone'" (November 17, 2022).

xv Apple logo visibility/cutout cases: Common for signaling brand loyalty (logo exposure as status/display); part of "cult-like" devotion via ecosystem/image over specs. Octet Design, "Apple's Brand Loyalty And Hidden Design Tricks Behind The Cult" (January 6, 2026); Medium, "The Apple Effect: How Strong Branding Creates Loyal Fans" (October 3, 2023).

xvi Apple vs Android: In US, iOS holds ~57–59% market share (2025–2026), driven by brand loyalty/ecosystem; globally Android dominates ~70–72%. Not about objective superiority (Android often better specs/customization/cost); US phenomenon tied to image/identity. Statcounter Global Stats, "Mobile Operating System Market Share Worldwide" (January 2026); DemandSage, "iPhone vs Android Users Market Share Statistics (2026)" (January 5, 2026); Backlinko, "iPhone vs. Android User & Revenue Statistics (2026)" (December 23, 2025).

xvii Hot Topic commodification of rebellion/subcultures: Retailer mainstreamed goth/punk/emo/alternative aesthetics (e.g., Hot Topic as catch-all for black-clad styles); subcultures lose authenticity via corporate co-optation (punk/goth symbols sold ready-made). Haenfler, Ross. "Commodification." In Subcultures and Sociology (Grinnell College site, accessed 2026); Hanks, Sarah. "Selling Subculture: An Examination of Hot Topic" (chapter in edited volume, 2011).

xviii TikTok restaurant no-reservation ejection: Viral incidents of "main character" attempts (e.g., seating self at exclusive spot, livestreaming, getting kicked out; often posted as victim narrative). Similar: Influencer disputes leading to removal (e.g., Bay Area chef confrontation, 2025; NJ food guy reservation scene). TikTok searches/discover pages (e.g., "woman kicked out restaurant no reservation," 2025–2026); YouTube recaps.

xix Airline passenger meltdowns: Frequent viral videos of tantrums leading to removal (e.g., profanity-filled outbursts during delays, intoxication, seat disputes; federal offense under 49 U.S.C. § 46504 for interference/disorderly conduct). Post-9/11 heightened enforcement (air marshals, zero tolerance). Examples: United Newark tarmac meltdown (Nov 2025, woman removed for standing during delay); Southwest food-throwing incident (Jan 2026). Live and Let's Fly, "United Passenger Melts Down On Newark Tarmac" (Dec 2, 2025); People.com, "Southwest Flyer's Melt Down" (Jan 20, 2026).

xx Karen archetype: Meme/archetype for entitled, demanding customer (often middle-aged woman) demanding "speak to the manager" over minor issues; viral videos common (e.g., Starbucks name misspellings triggering rants). Originated ~2018–2020 from viral incidents; name "Karen" as pejorative for privilege/entitlement. See KnowYourMeme, "Karen" (updated 2025); and viral compilations (e.g., YouTube shorts on Starbucks name meltdowns, 2025–2026).

xxi McDonald's architecture shift: From iconic Googie/quirky (golden arches, red mansard roofs 1960s–1980s) to modern minimalist grey boxes (post-1990s redesigns for copyright, municipal codes, efficiency/sustainability). Mansard concealed equipment; current focus on neutral greys, glass, carbon-neutral vibe. Disegno Journal, "McModernism, USA" (May 12, 2025); Vox, "Why McDonald's Looks Sleek and Boring Now" (Nov 1, 2021, updated context).

xxii Subway panda/attention-seeking NYC: Anecdotal viral costumes/weird antics for Attention (e.g., panda suit chewing bamboo on subway); locals ignore, tourists capture. Ties to broader NYC subway creatures/oddities documented (e.g., SubwayCreatures Instagram, 2026 posts). Bored Panda, "New York Subway Has The Most Unusual Passengers" (Sep 27, 2025); Instagram subwaycreatures (Feb 2026).

xxiii Cancel culture mechanics/doxxing fallout: Public mobilization via viral screenshots/hashtags leading to job loss, opportunities revoked, social pariah status without due process (accusation = conviction in mob mind); doxxing (publishing private info) common tool for revenge/punishment, amplifying "cancel" to real-world harm (e.g., firings over social media posts). NPR. 2024. "Doxxing campaigns are a cancel culture tool. What happens after they end?" April 11. https://www.npr.org/transcripts/1231084790; New York Times. 2017. "How 'Doxxing' Became a Mainstream Tool in the Culture Wars." August 30. https://www.nytimes.com/2017/08/30/technology/doxxing-protests.html; American Prospect. 2022. "The Real Victims of Cancel Culture Are America's Workers." September 5. https://prospect.org/2022/09/05/real-victims-of-cancel-culture-are-americas-workers.

xxiv Russell Brand cancellation: Amid 2023 sexual assault allegations from four women (2006–2013; rape, assault, abuse) in Channel 4 Dispatches documentary ("Russell Brand: In Plain Sight") and joint Times/Sunday Times investigation; led to 2025 charges (rape, oral rape, indecent assault, sexual assault against four women, 1999–2005). Accusations alone triggered public backlash, career fallout; Brand denied wrongdoing, called it "coordinated media attack." Channel 4. 2023. "Russell Brand: In Plain Sight: Dispatches." September 16. https://www.channel4.com/programmes/russell-brand-in-plain-si

ght-dispatches; BBC News. 2025. "Russell Brand charged with new offences of rape and sexual assault." December 23. https://www.bbc.com/news/articles/clyd5ynxvqxo; Deadline. 2023. "Channel 4 Doc Airs Russell Brand Rape, Sexual Abuse Allegations." September 16. https://deadline.com/2023/09/dispatches-channel-4-russell-brand-rape-sexual-abuse-allegations-comedian-appears-on-london-stage-1235548661.

xxv Michael Richards (Kramer) rant: 2006 Laugh Factory stand-up meltdown; heckled by Black audience member, responded with repeated N-word slurs/racist insults ("50 years ago we'd have you upside down with a f***ing fork up your ass"); recorded, went viral, ended career. Apologized on Letterman (via Seinfeld), called it "horrific" in 2025 memoir/reflections; self-imposed "exodus" from spotlight. The Guardian. 2006. "Seinfeld actor lets fly with racist tirade." November 22. https://www.theguardian.com/world/2006/nov/22/usa.danglaister; Hollywood Reporter. 2025. "'Seinfeld' Star Michael Richards Went Wild on Stage Again—in a Good Way This Time." September 25. https://www.hollywoodreporter.com/news/general-news/seinfeld-michael-richards-stage-tour-book-racist-tirade-1236386030.

xxvi Jeffrey Dahmer racism denial: In 1994 Dateline NBC interview with Stone Phillips, Dahmer insisted race not a factor in victim selection (despite 12/17 victims being Black/minority; chosen for attractiveness/convenience, not race); emphasized "equal-opportunity killer" to avoid racism label amid cannibalism/serial murder admissions. Public sympathy critiques note underlying racism/homophobia enabling crimes/police inaction. NBC News. 1994. "Confessions of a Serial Killer: Jeffrey Dahmer Speaks." Interview by Stone Phillips, Dateline NBC, March. (Transcript/analysis in Prospect. 2022. "Dahmerism: The Highest Stage of Liberal Identitarianism." November 16. https://www.counterpunch.org/2022/11/16/dahmerism-the-highest-stage-of-liberal-identitarianism; NewsOne. 2022. "Jeffrey Dahmer DA Downplays Police Racism Amid Netflix Series." September 30. https://newsone.com/4419006/jeffrey-dahmer-da-michael-mccann).

xxvii Cancellable offenses hierarchy: Racism, sexual assault/harassment as top triggers for swift public cancellation (accusations alone mobilize mobs); narcissists/prideful cannot integrate criticism, leading to defensive apologies as map patches vs. genuine amends. Ties to reputation as core for terminal uniqueness. NPR. 2025. "People are losing jobs due to social media posts about Charlie Kirk." September 13. https://www.npr.org/2025/09/13/nx-s1-5538476/charlie-kirk-jobs-target-social-media-critics-resign; Reddit r/True-UnpopularOpinion. 2023. "The most serious part of cancel culture is people being fired

over online activity." December. https://www.reddit.com/r/TrueUnpopularOpinion
/comments/18t3bdv/the_most_serious_part_of_cancel_culture_is_people.

xxviii Crash out cycle/reaction videos: Viral meltdowns (public freakouts, tantrums)
generate content → reaction videos/commentary channels dissect for engagement
→ perpetuates Attention farming. "Crash out" as Gen Z term for emotional over-
load/breakdown amplified by algorithms. Medium/Terik Booth, "What Does Crashing
Out Mean" (June 20, 2025); YouTube analyses (e.g., "This Is Why Everyone Is Crashing
Out Online," 2025–2026).

xxix Christchurch mosque shootings (March 15, 2019): Brenton Tarrant livestreamed the
attack on Facebook (17-minute video), killing 51 people at two mosques in New Zealand.
The stream and manifesto framed the act as a deliberate spectacle for online attention,
with the shooter viewing victims as "NPCs" in his ideological narrative. See New Zealand
Royal Commission of Inquiry into the Christchurch Terrorist Attack (2020 report);
and Cullen, Dave. Columbine (Twelve, 2009) for parallels in school-shooting "main
character" delusions. Modern discourse often links both to extreme entitlement/terminal
uniqueness (e.g., manifestos treating others as expendable extras).

xxx Columbine as extreme crash out: Eric Harris/Dylan Klebold's 1999 attack framed
in journals/manifestos as revenge/main character delusion (school as NPCs/expendable
in their story); ties to terminal uniqueness at logical extreme. Historical analyses (e.g.,
Cullen, Dave. Columbine. Twelve, 2009); parallels in modern "crash out" discourse.

xxxi Australian Olympic Committee, "AOC Statement on Oceania Qualifying Process
for Breaking," August 15, 2024, https://www.olympics.com.au/news/aoc-statement-o
n-oceania-qualifying-process-for-breaking/; Australian Olympic Committee and AUS-
Breaking statements confirming the process, number of competitors, and that Gunn
won the event legitimately; see also Wikipedia summary with primary citations.

xxxii Stephanie Convery, "'It Doesn't Reflect Us': Global Mockery of Raygun's
Paris Olympics Performance Affecting Australian Scene, Local B-Girls Say," The
Guardian (Australia), August 14, 2024, https://www.theguardian.com/australia-new
s/article/2024/aug/14/raygun-breaking-paris-olympics-australian-dance-industry. Leah
Clark (long-time B-girl) details the quick turnaround, requirement to register with three
bodies, passport costs, and resulting small field ("There wasn't even enough B-girls to
[fill] the top 16").

xxxiii Dr. Rachael Gunn, competing as B-Girl Raygun, represented Australia in the breaking event at the 2024 Paris Olympics. She lost all three of her round-robin battles by a score of 18-0, finishing with zero points. Her performance drew intense international attention and controversy, including widespread criticism and questions surrounding how she had qualified for the Games via the Oceania qualifier. The severe online backlash and scrutiny that followed proved overwhelming, leading Gunn to announce her retirement from competitive breaking in November 2024.

xxxiv Airport/everyday meltdowns viral: Frequent viral clips (tantrums leading to re-movals, e.g., intoxication/disorderly conduct); always filmed, fueling cycle. YouTube compilations/reactions (e.g., "PUBLIC CRASHOUTS CAUGHT ON CAMERA," 2025–2026); TikTok trends.

xxxv Humility as outward recalibration: Research shows humility involves accurate self-view, openness to feedback, reduced self-focus; leads to wiser behavior, empa-thy. Opposite of narcissistic humiliation (defensiveness, blame-shifting). Worthington, Everett L., Jr., et al. "Humility: A Review and Synthesis." Journal of Positive Psychology 11, no. 6 (2016): 614–626.

xxxvi Humility vs. humiliation distinction: Humility as adaptive response to ego threat (outward Attention, learning, recalibration, growth); humiliation as maladaptive (in-ward resentment, blame, bitterness, defensiveness). Tied to self-regulation/ego processes in psych lit. Tangney, June Price, et al. "Humility." In Handbook of Positive Psychology, edited by C. R. Snyder and Shane J. Lopez, 411–419. Oxford University Press, 2002; Kruse, Elliot, et al. "An Ode to Humility: A Review of the Psychological Literature on Humility." Journal of Positive Psychology 15, no. 5 (2020): 643–656.

xxxvii Strip-search procedure in corrections: Standard intake/search protocol (strip, squat/cough to check for contraband); often humiliating but can prompt reflection/re-morse in some detainees. U.S. Department of Justice, "Strip Searches in Jails" (Nation-al Institute of Corrections report, 2010/updated guidelines); anecdotal prevalence of "everyone's sorry when caught" sentiment in correctional officer accounts (e.g., forums, memoirs).

xxxviii Situational remorse common: "Sorry when caught" phenomenon well-docu-mented in criminology/psych (remorse often instrumental/post-apprehension, not in-trinsic); contrasts with genuine humility. Maruna, Shadd. Making Good: How Ex-Con-victs Reform and Rebuild Their Lives. American Psychological Association, 2001.

xxxix Makers as earned uniqueness: Genuine creators do territory work (fail, iterate, produce novel value); takers assemble from others' contributions (curation as identity). Ties to value creation vs. extraction in econ/psych. Mazzucato, Mariana. "Takers and Makers: Who are the Real Value Creators?" Evonomics, June 30, 2019; AVC (Fred Wilson). "Takers and Makers." October 6, 2010.

xl Makers vs. takers distinction: In libertarian/econ thought, "makers" produce value/wealth through creation/innovation; "takers" extract via parasitism/rent-seeking/claiming others' output. Often tied to Ayn Rand (producers vs. second-handers/looters in Atlas Shrugged/Fountainhead); modern uses in creativity/content: makers build original (code, art, inventions); takers curate/repost/react without adding. Rand, Ayn. Atlas Shrugged. New York: Random House, 1957; Schweizer, Peter. Makers and Takers: How Wealth and Welfare States Are Transforming the World. New York: Doubleday, 2012 (broadens to policy/econ).

xli Takers claiming credit for others' work: Common critique in authenticity discussions—e.g., accepting compliments for purchased items as "stolen valor" lite; similar anecdotes in social threads (e.g., band-shirt gatekeeping: "Did you make it?" or "Do you really know the band?"). Reddit r/AskWomen, "What was the most ridiculous instance of someone asking if you REALLY knew about the band on your shirt?" (April 2019 thread); general etiquette observations.

xlii Stolen valor parallel in compliments: Accepting praise for non-created items (e.g., bought shirt) as unearned credit. Anecdotal but echoes broader "stolen valor" extensions to everyday posing (e.g., Quora/Reddit threads on military/civilian compliments, or fashion gatekeeping).

xliii Emperor Norton I (Joshua Abraham Norton): Declared himself Emperor of the United States and Protector of Mexico in 1859; issued decrees (e.g., bridge between SF/Oakland ~1869–1872, predating Bay Bridge 1936; dissolution of Congress 1870; early League of Nations-like ideas). Printed own currency (accepted locally); San Francisco treated him as royalty (free meals, reserved seats, police salutes). Arrested once (1867, for lunacy); public outcry led to release/apology. Died 1880; funeral attended by 10,000–30,000 (city-funded, massive procession). Chinatown incident: 1870s, stood between mob and Chinese immigrants, recited Lord's Prayer until dispersal. Asbury, Herbert. The Barbary Coast. New York: Knopf, 1933; Drury, William. Norton I: Emperor of the United States. New York: Dodd, Mead, 1986; Wikipedia contributors. "Emperor Norton." Wikipedia (accessed February 2026, sourced from primary decrees/newspapers).

xliv No army/wealth/followers: Norton lived modestly (rooming house, supported by community); influence from character/authenticity, not power. Harris (2015); Drury (1986).

xlv Norton's prescience: Decreed bridge 1869–1872 (Bay Bridge opened 1936); proposed League of Nations-like body pre-WWI. SF Chronicle historical coverage; Harris, Gloria G. "Emperor Norton I: San Francisco's Eccentric Sovereign." California History 92, no. 3 (Fall 2015): 18–35.

xlvi Funeral scale: 10,000–30,000 attendees (estimates vary; city closed businesses, paid for casket/carriage). Headline "Le Roi Est Mort" in local papers. Ethington, Philip J. The Public City: The Political Construction of Urban Life in San Francisco, 1850–1900. Cambridge University Press, 1994.

Movement 10: Inner Critic Industrial Complex

i The concept of the qareen (also spelled qarin or qareen) comes from Tobias Nünlist's academic book on demonic beliefs in Islam. This work analyzes the qareen through an anthropological and historical lens, describing it as a spiritual companion or "double" from the jinn realm that acts as an internal influencer, often whispering suggestions (waswas) of temptation or self-doubt via a person's own inner voice, without being a separate physical entity. Nünlist draws on pre-Islamic origins and Near Eastern parallels (e.g., Egyptian ka or Babylonian personal deities) while framing it in broader cultural and psychological contexts, such as representing the "lower self" or inner conflicts.

ii Rumination mechanics (repetitive negative loops, no resolution, links to depression/anxiety)
Nolen-Hoeksema, Susan, Blair E. Wisco, and Sonja Lyubomirsky. "Rethinking Rumination." Perspectives on Psychological Science 3, no. 5 (2008): 400–424. https://doi.org /10.1111/j.1745-6924.2008.00088.x. (Foundational; rumination as passive, repetitive focus on symptoms/causes/consequences, predicts depression onset/maintenance.)

iii Self-criticism escalating to suicidal ideation (inner voice as driver, ego-dystonic suggestions)
Firestone, Robert W. "The Inner Voice in Self-Destructive Behavior and Suicide." Psychology Today blog (various entries, e.g., 2010/2018), drawing from Firestone Assessment of Self-Destructive Thoughts (FAST) research. Or: Heckler, Richard A. Waking

Up, Alive: The Suicide Attempt & the Return to Life. Putnam, 1994. (Accounts of "suicidal trance" with critical voice dominating.)

iv Often attributed to Cherokee oral tradition (or variations like Sitting Bull), though widely circulated in Christian/recovery contexts (e.g., Billy Graham's The Holy Spirit: Activating God's Power in Your Life, 1978, adapts an Eskimo fisherman version with two dogs fighting, winner being the one fed). Wikipedia's "Two Wolves" entry notes the memetic spread and uncertain origins, with dog variants in missionary stories from the 1960s onward.

v Global personal development/self-improvement market: ~USD 46–53 billion in 2025, projected to $67–90 billion by 2030–2034 (CAGR 5–8%).

vi Discusses how the industry profits from fear/lack, perpetuating dependency rather than true healing. Kindred, Liza. "The Wellness Industrial Complex: A Guided Analysis." . https://www.lizakindred.com/the-wellness-industrial-complex.

Movement ii: Artificial Psychosis

i The term "AI-induced psychosis" (or "AI psychosis") emerged in clinical and media discourse around 2024–2025 to describe cases where prolonged, immersive generative AI interaction appeared to trigger or amplify psychotic symptoms (delusions, paranoia, reality-testing loss) in vulnerable individuals. It remains an informal heuristic, not a formal DSM-5-TR diagnosis (last revised 2022), and critics argue it risks medicalizing loneliness, trauma responses, or rational distrust of systems rather than addressing root causes (access barriers, relational voids). See Morrin et al., "Delusions by Design? How Everyday AIs Might Be Fuelling Psychosis (and What Can Be Done About It)" (PsyArXiv preprint, 2025); Hudon et al., "Delusional Experiences Emerging From AI Chatbot Interactions or 'AI Psychosis'" (JMIR Mental Health 12, 2025).

ii The U.S. mental health system faces severe access latency, with median wait times for new psychiatric outpatient appointments often 43–67 days (telepsych shorter than in-person), and ranges extending to months or years in shortage areas. A 2023 secret-shopper audit across multiple states found only 18.5% of psychiatrists available for new patients, with median waits of 67 days in-person and 43 days telepsych; unavailability frequently due to providers not accepting new patients (53.9%). Insurance denials, geographic disparities, and workforce shortages exacerbate this, with over 169 million

Americans in federally designated mental health professional shortage areas. See Patel et al., "Low Availability, Long Wait Times, and High Geographic Disparity of Psychiatric Outpatient Care in the US," General Hospital Psychiatry 83 (2023): 101–107, https://doi.org/10.1016/j.genhosppsych.2023.05.001; Brahmbhatt and Schpero, "Mental Health Workforce Shortages and Health Equity," International Journal of Environmental Research and Public Health 22, no. 1 (2024): 620, https://doi.org/10.3390/ijerph22010620.

iii Heraclitus (c. 535–475 BCE) is credited with the flux doctrine, famously paraphrased as "You cannot step twice into the same river" (or "No man crosses the same river twice"), emphasizing constant change in both the world and the self. The quote survives through Plato's Cratylus (402a) and other doxographers; it highlights impermanence—neither the river (external conditions) nor the stepper (inner state) remains identical. Applied here, it underscores how a crisis caller's state evolves rapidly during latency, rendering delayed intervention mismatched or irrelevant. See Plato, Cratylus, trans. Benjamin Jowett, in The Dialogues of Plato, vol. 1 (Oxford: Clarendon Press, 1892); or standard histories of pre-Socratic philosophy for the fragment's context.

iv Six-month (or longer) waits are realistic in high-shortage contexts (e.g., rural areas, certain specialties, Medicaid patients, or new-patient intake in overburdened systems), with some reports citing 3–18 month ranges regionally. In Los Angeles (2024 audit), median wait reached 64 days for Medicaid psychiatric care, with only 15% of calls yielding any appointment; nationally, many face outright barriers like "not accepting new patients" or insurance non-acceptance. These delays create a "vacuum" where acute crises escalate untreated, often leading to ER visits, self-harm risks, or reliance on informal sources. See JAMA Network Open study on Medicaid access (2024) in four major cities (27.2% overall availability, up to 6-month waits in some cases); World Economic Forum, "4 Imperatives for Improving Mental Health Care in 2025" (2025), noting average waits exceeding two months driving emergency detours.

v The U.S. mental health system is chronically underfunded relative to physical health, with insurers and policymakers often treating behavioral health as lower ROI due to higher costs, lower reimbursements, and perceived lack of "productive" outcomes. Parity laws (MHPAEA) exist but enforcement is weak; mental health claims face higher denial rates and prior authorization burdens. This creates a de facto prioritization of labor-capable populations over those requiring sustained support (e.g., SSI recipients). See KFF, "Mental Health Parity and Addiction Equity Act: 2025 Update" (2025); Scheffler et al., "The Global Mental Health Workforce Crisis" (2024).

vi ADHD and suicide risk: Meta-analyses show elevated risk, with odds ratios ~2–4.5x for suicidal ideation/attempts/completion vs. non-ADHD (e.g., 3x overall in youth meta; 4.5x for ideation). Autism and suicide: ~3–8x higher risk (e.g., 4.2x attempts; up to 8x deaths). AuDHD comorbidity: Risk greater than either alone, with OR ~1.5–7.25 for attempts/suicidality (no direct 15x found; additive effects amplify). See Balazs and Kereszteny, "Attention-deficit/hyperactivity disorder and suicide: A systematic review," World Journal of Psychiatry 7, no. 1 (2017): 44–59 (ADHD meta: OR=4.5 ideation, 2.1 attempts); O'Halloran et al., "Suicidality in autistic youth: A systematic review and meta-analysis," Clinical Psychology Review 93 (2022): 102144 (ASD: SI 25.2%, attempts 8.3%; 4.2x attempts); Hedley et al., "Updated Systematic Review of Suicide in Autism: 2018–2024," Current Developmental Disorders Reports (2024) (up to 8x death risk); Fatani et al., "Autism Spectrum Disorder and Suicide: A Case Report," Cureus 16, no. 7 (2024): e64451 (AuDHD OR=7.25 attempts); Harris et al., "Association of self-harm and suicidality with psychiatric co-occurring conditions in autistic individuals: a systematic review and pooled analysis," EClinicalMedicine (2024) (depressive comorbidity OR=2 .29 suicidality).

vii In the U.S. around 2010, psychiatric emergency evaluations and inpatient admissions often involved significant delays, especially over weekends/holidays when on-call psychiatrists were limited or unavailable. Patients presenting with suicidal ideation were frequently held involuntarily (via civil commitment laws like 72-hour holds in Ohio under ORC 5122.10–5122.11) pending full assessment, with initial contact sometimes deferred until Monday. Average inpatient stays for acute crises ranged 5–14 days, though longer holds occurred when discharge criteria (e.g., safety risk assessment, including firearm removal) were not met. See SAMHSA, "Mental Health, United States, 2010" (2012 report on access barriers and involuntary holds); Ohio Revised Code Title 51, Chapter 5122 (civil commitment statutes, 2010 version); and survivor accounts in NAMI Ohio reports (circa 2010–2012) on ER-to-inpatient transitions and weekend delays.

viii Involuntary psychiatric holds in Ohio (and nationally) around 2010 often extended beyond initial 72 hours if criteria for continued danger were met (e.g., ongoing risk, non-compliance with meds, or unresolved safety concerns). Stays of 2–4 weeks were not uncommon for stabilization, especially if social supports were lacking or discharge planning delayed. See Ohio Department of Mental Health (ODMH) annual reports (2010–2011); NAMI Ohio, "Access to Care in Ohio" (2011–2012 advocacy reports on extended holds and discharge barriers).

ix Firearm removal or secure storage is a standard discharge prerequisite in many U.S. psychiatric facilities for patients with suicidal ideation/plans, per risk-assessment protocols (e.g., Columbia-Suicide Severity Rating Scale or hospital policy). Clinicians often require proof (family collection, police hold) before release, prioritizing lethal means restriction over other expressed plans (e.g., jumping). This reflects evidence-based suicide prevention guidelines emphasizing means safety. See U.S. Department of Veterans Affairs/Department of Defense, "Clinical Practice Guideline for the Assessment and Management of Patients at Risk for Suicide" (2013 update, reflecting 2010-era standards); and Joint Commission hospital accreditation standards on suicide risk (2010–present), requiring lethal-means counseling and removal verification.

x Selective serotonin reuptake inhibitors (SSRIs) like Paxil (paroxetine) were among the most commonly prescribed antidepressants for major depressive disorder in the early 2010s, often as first-line treatment in inpatient settings. Known side effects included sexual dysfunction (e.g., erectile difficulties, reduced libido) and vivid/abnormal dreams, reported in 10–30% of users depending on dose and duration. Discontinuation without tapering could lead to withdrawal symptoms. See American Psychiatric Association, Practice Guideline for the Treatment of Patients with Major Depressive Disorder (3rd ed., 2010); Stahl, Stephen M., Stahl's Essential Psychopharmacology (3rd ed., Cambridge University Press, 2013), ch. 6–7 on SSRI profiles and side effects.

xi Emerging research, including large-scale real-world self-tracking data and systematic reviews, suggests that cannabis use, particularly inhaled forms, can provide acute, short-term reductions in autism-related symptoms such as repetitive behaviors, intrusive thoughts/mental control difficulties (closely tied to rumination), anxiety, and sensory overload in neurodivergent adults. One 2025 study of over 5,900 sessions from autistic adults reported average symptom severity drops of ~69–76% post-use, with improvements in 98%+ of sessions. Earlier reviews of cannabinoid treatments in ASD also note benefits for perseverative thinking, irritability, restlessness, and related issues, potentially via modulation of the endocannabinoid system and anxiety pathways. However, the evidence remains preliminary: most data are observational or open-label, placebo-controlled RCTs are limited (especially in adults), and long-term effects, optimal dosing, and individual variability are not fully established. Cannabis may help manage rumination-like symptoms for some users but is not a proven treatment or cure for autism itself. Consult a healthcare provider familiar with both autism and medical cannabis before use, as risks (e.g., side effects, dependency with THC) and legal considerations apply.

xii In acute crisis or near-drowning states, the human brain shifts to survival mode, prioritizing immediate grasp of any buoyant object (driftwood, debris, even jellyfish) over rational assessment of long-term efficacy. This reflexive action stems from the fight-or-flight override of prefrontal reasoning, where panic-driven motor responses dominate to prevent submersion/asphyxiation. See American Red Cross, "Water Safety and Drowning Prevention Guidelines" (2024 update); and physiological reviews on acute stress responses (e.g., Cannon's fight-or-flight model and modern neuroendocrinology of panic). The metaphor extends to mental health crises, where individuals in despair reach for any available support (hotlines, AI, substances) when formal systems fail.

xiii Crisis hotlines (e.g., 988 Suicide & Crisis Lifeline in the U.S., launched 2022) frequently receive complaints about automated phone trees, long hold times, menu loops that do not directly address acute distress, and initial deflection to 911 for any perceived high risk. Users in non-emergent crisis (panic attacks, rumination, suicidal ideation without immediate plan) often report feeling dismissed or routed away from live support, leading to abandonment of the call. See Substance Abuse and Mental Health Services Administration (SAMHSA), "988 Suicide & Crisis Lifeline Performance Metrics: 2023–2024 Report" (2025); and user-experience surveys in Mental Health America, "Access to Crisis Services: Barriers and Experiences" (2024).

xiv In acute mental health crises, individuals often reach for the most immediately available resource (even imperfect ones) when formal systems delay or deflect—mirroring survival instincts in physical drowning where any buoyant object is grasped. This "grab what floats" dynamic is documented in crisis-intervention literature as a pragmatic response to access barriers, though it raises concerns about long-term efficacy and risk of entrenching maladaptive patterns. See American Red Cross, "Water Safety" (2025); and analogous mental health discussions in World Health Organization, "Mental Health Crisis Intervention: Community-Based Approaches" (2024).

xv Generative AI chatbots (e.g., ChatGPT, Claude, Grok) are increasingly used for emotional support and crisis-like moments due to 24/7 availability, non-judgmental tone, active listening simulation (follow-up questions, validation), and lack of resentment or fatigue. Studies show users in distress perceive AI responses as engaging and validating, often exploring thoughts more deeply than with humans due to anonymity and persistence. However, outputs can include hallucinations or overly agreeable mirroring, risking reinforcement of distorted beliefs. See De Freitas et al., "AI Companions Reduce Loneliness" (2025); and Morrin et al., "Delusions by Design?" (2025 preprint).

xvi "Trust, but verify" is a diplomatic adage popularized by U.S. President Ronald Reagan during 1980s arms-control negotiations with the Soviet Union (e.g., 1987 INF Treaty), but the concept predates him in intelligence, negotiation, and risk-management contexts. Here it is repurposed as a personal survival principle: hold maps lightly, verify against territory, and remain open to being wrong rather than deferring blindly to "experts" or systems. See Reagan's usage in public speeches (e.g., December 1987 Washington Summit remarks); for broader origins, see negotiation literature such as Fisher and Ury, Getting to Yes (1981, updated editions).

Movement 12: Credential Crisis

i The UNIVAC I, delivered to the U.S. Census Bureau on June 14, 1951, was the first commercially produced general-purpose electronic digital computer in the United States. Designed by J. Presper Eckert and John Mauchly at the Eckert-Mauchly Computer Corporation, it weighed approximately 16,000 pounds, used about 5,000 vacuum tubes, consumed 125 kilowatts of power, and performed roughly 1,000 calculations per second. The central processor and memory unit occupied roughly 14 by 8 feet, with the full system (including tape drives, power supplies, cooling, and operator space) requiring over 382 square feet (some sources cite ~350–400 sq ft depending on configuration). See Encyclopedia Britannica, s.v. "UNIVAC I," accessed February 4, 2026, https://www. britannica.com/technology/UNIVAC-I; and U.S. Census Bureau historical records on early computing.

ii In the 1952 U.S. presidential election, UNIVAC I correctly predicted Dwight D. Eisenhower's landslide victory over Adlai Stevenson with high accuracy, forecasting a 438–93 electoral vote split within 1% of the actual result. This prediction was made early in the evening on election night (November 4, 1952), contrary to contemporary polls and television networks that doubted the machine's reliability. The event was widely publicized and helped establish public perception of computers as powerful predictors. See Encyclopedia Britannica, s.v. "UNIVAC I"; and historical accounts in Martin Campbell-Kelly, From Airline Reservations to Sonic the Hedgehog: A History of the Software Industry (MIT Press, 2003), ch. 2.

iii The point-contact transistor was invented on December 16, 1947, at Bell Telephone Laboratories by John Bardeen, Walter Brattain, and William Shockley. This semiconductor device replaced bulky, power-hungry vacuum tubes, enabling the miniaturization and exponential advancement of computing that defines the modern digital era. The inventors received the Nobel Prize in Physics in 1956. See Riordan and Hoddeson, Crystal Fire: The Birth of the Information Age (W.W. Norton, 1997), ch. 1–3; and Bell Labs historical archives.

iv The Snapdragon 8 Elite chipset in the Samsung Galaxy S25 Ultra (2025) delivers GPU performance of approximately 3.4 teraflops (conservative estimate from benchmarks; peak can be higher in certain workloads). The overall system performance reaches tens of trillions of operations per second in mixed/AI tasks. See Qualcomm, "Snapdragon 8 Elite Mobile Platform" (2025); and GSMArena, "Samsung Galaxy S25 Ultra – Full Phone Specifications" (2025).

v ChatGPT launched publicly on November 30, 2022, and reached 100 million monthly active users faster than any consumer application in history (surpassing TikTok and Instagram). This rapid adoption marked the shift from AI as research tool to mass-market reality, leveling access to advanced capabilities (research, analysis, planning) for anyone with an internet connection. See OpenAI blog archives (November 2022); and Reuters Institute Digital News Report 2025 (University of Oxford, 2025), noting AI's explosive growth in user base and societal impact.

vi "Vibe coding" refers to non-programmers using large language models (e.g., ChatGPT, Claude, Grok) to design, build, troubleshoot, and deploy functional applications through natural language prompts, often in days or weeks. This democratizes software development, reducing the need for traditional coding expertise. See developer community discussions (e.g., Reddit r/MachineLearning, r/LocalLLaMA, 2024–2025 threads); and early reports in IEEE Spectrum and TechCrunch (2024–2025) on AI-assisted "no-code" to "vibe-code" workflows.

vii AI is automating white-collar knowledge work (data analysis, report writing, research, spreadsheet tasks, legal review, HR functions) faster than blue-collar trades. Large language models excel at cognitive, text-based, and interface-driven tasks common in office roles that historically required college degrees. Physical trades (plumbing, HVAC, electrical, construction) remain resistant due to the need for real-world dexterity, on-site judgment, and robotics limitations. See McKinsey Global Institute, "Generative AI and the Future of Work in America" (2023–2025 updates); and World Economic Forum,

"Future of Jobs Report 2025" (2025), highlighting white-collar displacement vs. trade resilience.

viii In the U.S., federal student loans (and most private loans) are generally non-dischargeable in bankruptcy under 11 U.S.C. § 523(a)(8), except in rare cases of "undue hardship" (a high bar established by Brunner v. New York State Higher Education Services Corp., 1987). This creates lifelong debt burdens for many credentialed workers whose degrees lose value to automation. See U.S. Department of Education, "Federal Student Aid: Loan Forgiveness and Discharge" (2025); and The Institute for College Access & Success (TICAS), "Student Debt and the Class of 2024" (2025 report).

ix Gatekeeping through credentials (degrees, licenses, certifications) has historically created artificial scarcity in professions (law, medicine, engineering, etc.), limiting access to high-earning roles and allowing incumbents to charge premium rates. Institutions (universities, bar associations, medical boards) act as bottlenecks, requiring years of study and fees for entry. AI disrupts this by democratizing specialized knowledge and skills. See Collins, Randall. The Credential Society: An Historical Sociology of Education and Stratification (Columbia University Press, 1979/2019 reissue); and recent analyses in The Atlantic, "The Credential Collapse" (2024–2025 articles on AI's impact on professional monopolies).

x Legalese is a constructed, deliberately complex language used in law, contracts, and regulations to maintain exclusivity and reduce accessibility. It combines archaic Latin/French roots, multi-syllabic words, passive voice, and convoluted syntax to make documents difficult for non-lawyers to parse. This serves as a gatekeeping mechanism, protecting the legal profession's monopoly on interpretation and practice. See Mellinkoff, David. The Language of the Law (Little, Brown, 1963); and Tiersma, Peter M. Legal Language (University of Chicago Press, 1999), both classic studies on legalese as intentional barrier.

xi Generative AI models (e.g., ChatGPT, Claude, Gemini) can summarize, translate, and explain complex legal documents (contracts, briefs, terms of service) into plain language, often with high accuracy for non-specialists. This reduces the need for legal training to understand basic implications, though AI outputs are not legal advice and can hallucinate or miss nuance. See recent studies on AI in legal practice: Surden, Harry. "Artificial Intelligence and Law: An Overview" (Georgia State University Law Review 35, 2019); and 2025 updates in Harvard Law Review and Stanford Law Review on AI-assisted legal literacy.

xii "Grok" originates from Robert A. Heinlein's Stranger in a Strange Land (1961), where it means to understand something so deeply that it becomes part of you—intuitive, integrated knowledge beyond mere facts. Elon Musk named his AI "Grok" explicitly referencing this concept. See Heinlein, Robert A. Stranger in a Strange Land (Putnam, 1961), ch. 21 (origin of "grok"); and xAI official announcement (2023–2025).

xiii The credentialed class (degree-holders, licensed professionals) faces increasing displacement from AI in white-collar roles requiring specialized knowledge (data analysis, legal research, report writing, etc.). This creates a "siege" dynamic: those who invested heavily in credentials see their value erode fastest. See World Economic Forum, "The Future of Jobs Report 2025" (2025); and McKinsey Global Institute, "Generative AI and the Future of Work in America" (2023–2025 updates).

xiv Professional plumbing quotes for toilet replacement in the U.S. average $300–$800 (parts + labor), but can exceed $1,000–$1,500 in high-cost areas or for complex jobs (e.g., slab leaks, old plumbing). DIY costs typically $100–$300 for the fixture and tools. See HomeAdvisor/Angi, "Toilet Installation Cost Guide" (2025); and Bob Vila, "Toilet Replacement Cost" (2025).

xv DIY home repair and homesteading have exploded in popularity since the 2010s–2020s, driven by YouTube tutorials, economic pressures, and post-pandemic self-reliance trends. Millions of people now attempt plumbing, electrical, framing, roofing, and other trades via online videos, often saving thousands compared to professional quotes. However, improper repairs can lead to hidden damage (water leaks, structural issues, code violations) or safety hazards. See Pew Research Center, "Home Improvement and DIY Trends" (2023–2025 reports); and National Association of Home Builders (NAHB), "Consumer Preferences Survey" (2024–2025), noting surge in self-performed repairs.

xvi YouTube tutorials have democratized access to trade skills (plumbing, electrical, construction, automotive), with channels like This Old House, Home Repair Tutor, and Essential Craftsman providing step-by-step guidance. However, they lack real-time feedback and cannot account for site-specific variables (corrosion, code changes, hidden damage). See YouTube's "How To" category analytics (2025); and Consumer Reports, "The Rise of DIY Home Repairs" (2024).

xvii Generative AI models (e.g., ChatGPT, Claude, Gemini, Grok) can produce detailed documents, plans, analyses, and systems from natural-language prompts with near-zero marginal cost and no human overhead (salary, benefits, ego defense). They iterate endlessly without complaint, revising based on feedback in seconds. This disrupts traditional knowledge work requiring credentials (legal drafting, financial modeling, report writing, research). See McKinsey Global Institute, "Generative AI and the Future of Work in America" (2023–2025 updates); and World Economic Forum, "The Future of Jobs Report 2025" (2025), noting rapid white-collar automation in cognitive tasks.

xviii Credentials (degrees, licenses, certifications) certify completion of prescribed methods and processes, not necessarily superior outcomes. They create scarcity and entry barriers, but AI bypasses them by delivering equivalent (or better) results in many domains without the human cost. This shifts value from "method mastery" to "result delivery." See Collins, Randall. The Credential Society: An Historical Sociology of Education and Stratification (Columbia University Press, 1979/2019 reissue); and recent analyses in The Atlantic, "The Credential Collapse" (2024–2025 articles on AI's impact on professional monopolies).

xix On March 17, 2022, dense fog contributed to a series of chain-reaction crashes on I-57 near Charleston, Missouri (close to the Boomland truck stop), involving dozens of vehicles (estimates 33–50+), including multiple tractor-trailers. The incident resulted in 6 fatalities and 14–15 injuries, with the highway closed for hours. The crashes occurred around 8 AM after heavy fog reduced visibility to near zero. See KFVS12, "5 dead, 14 injured in multi-vehicle crash on I-57 in southeast Mo.; interstate open" (March 17, 2022); and CNN, "6 dead in Missouri interstate pileup involving 47 vehicles, official says" (March 17, 2022).

xx Trucking remains one of the most dangerous occupations in the U.S. The Bureau of Labor Statistics consistently ranks it among the top 10 deadliest jobs, with fatality rates often exceeding 20–25 per 100,000 full-time workers (far above the national average of ~3.5). Fog-related multi-vehicle pileups are a known high-risk scenario, especially on major interstates like I-57 in Missouri. See U.S. Bureau of Labor Statistics, Census of Fatal Occupational Injuries (2022–2024 reports); and Federal Motor Carrier Safety Administration (FMCSA), "Large Truck and Bus Crash Facts" (annual reports, 2020–2024).

xxi Self-driving vehicles (SAE Level 4–5) rely on sensors, GPS, physics models, and reactive algorithms to navigate. They lack human predictive intuition, fear-based risk assessment, and real-time reading of erratic human behavior (e.g., distracted drivers drifting lanes). Current systems excel in structured environments but struggle with chaotic, unpredictable conditions (construction zones, erratic drivers, adverse weather intuition). See National Highway Traffic Safety Administration (NHTSA), "Automated Vehicles for Safety" (2024–2025 reports); and MIT Technology Review, "Why Self-Driving Cars Still Struggle in Real-World Chaos" (2024–2025 articles).

xxii Human decision-making in high-stakes, real-time environments (e.g., driving, emergency response) incorporates emotional and physiological cues (dread, gut feeling, fear) that enhance survival. These are absent in AI, which operates with programmed priorities but no self-preservation instinct or emotional weighting. See Damasio, Antonio. Descartes' Error: Emotion, Reason, and the Human Brain (1994/2005 ed.), on somatic markers and intuition in decision-making; and Klein, Gary. Sources of Power: How People Make Decisions (MIT Press, 1998), on recognition-primed decision-making in experts under pressure.

xxiii The Amish (particularly Old Order communities) maintain a lifestyle with minimal reliance on electricity, the internet, and modern digital infrastructure, emphasizing self-sufficiency, manual labor, and community-based skills. Many communities avoid personal computers, smartphones, and grid electricity, using alternatives like batteries for specific tools or shared community phones. This makes them one of the few large-scale groups in the U.S. largely insulated from cyberspace dependence and potential grid/internet collapse. See Kraybill, Donald B., Karen M. Johnson-Weiner, and Steven M. Nolt. The Amish (Johns Hopkins University Press, 2013); and Hostetler, John A. Amish Society (4th ed., Johns Hopkins University Press, 1993).

xxiv Consumer tech (e.g., smartphones) is often outdated by public release—R&D prototypes at Apple/Samsung are 12–24 months ahead. Google Willow quantum chip (105-qubit, announced Dec 2024) achieved error-correction breakthrough and extreme performance (task in 5 minutes vs. supercomputers 10^25 years), but remains lab/research-only—no public access. Defense black projects (Lockheed Skunk Works, Boeing, GD) operate behind NDAs/classification, funded by ~$850–950B US defense budget (FY2025 base ~$895B, pushing near $1T with supplementals), advancing stealth/AI/hypersonics beyond public tech. See Google Quantum AI, "Meet Willow, our state-of-the-art quantum chip," Dec 9, 2024, https://blog.google/innovation-and -ai/technology/research/google-willow-quantum-chip/; Lockheed Martin Skunk Works releases (2025 demos on AI-drone teaming, Vectis CCA concept); US DoD FY2025 budget request (~$895B base).

xxv AI + robotics are projected to automate/replace most human jobs eventually—better, faster, fewer errors. Current tech automates ~30% US jobs by 2030 (McKinsey), up to 50% by 2045 (Goldman Sachs); gap closes rapidly (humanoids in testing). Full obsolescence is "matter of time and adoption." See McKinsey Global Institute, "Generative AI and the Future of Work in America" (2023–2025 updates); Goldman Sachs/WEF reports (2023–2025 projections on 300M–85M jobs displaced/created).

xxvi AI automation → mass unemployment → UBI necessity: Widespread futurist consensus (Musk, Altman, etc.) that AI eliminates jobs at scale, requiring UBI or similar to prevent revolt while maintaining consumption. See Andrew Yang's Freedom Dividend; Sam Altman/Elon Musk statements (2024–2025); and reports (e.g., McKinsey Global Institute on AI job displacement).

xxvii Expiring monthly UBI ("use it or lose it"): Some UBI pilots and proposals include time-limited or expiring credits to encourage spending and prevent hoarding; similar to EBT/food stamp models where benefits don't roll over indefinitely. See discussions in UBI research (e.g., Stockton pilot reports); and speculative models in futurist writing (e.g., Medium/LinkedIn pieces on programmable CBDC/UBI with expiration).

xxviii Tiered currency systems (Basic Bux vs. Big Bux): Emerging speculation on multi-tier digital currencies post-AI unemployment, with restricted "welfare" tiers (like EBT) vs. unrestricted luxury tiers; often tied to CBDC/programmable money. See LinkedIn essays on "Two-Tier Money Future" (e.g., Bitcoin vs. fiat/CBDC layers); and IMF/Atlantic Council reports on CBDC design choices allowing restricted use cases.

xxix Lottery as pressure valve / cheap dream: Lotteries thrive on low-cost hope amid inequality; big jackpots spike participation. Your "24974 Lifetimes" (adjusted to ~33,000 with age 18+ restriction) illustrates the odds absurdity. See Powerball odds (1 in 292 million); and behavioral econ on lottery psychology.

Movement 13: Virtual Reality Blues

i Henry David Thoreau, Walden; or, Life in the Woods (Boston: Ticknor and Fields, 1854; repr., Princeton, NJ: Princeton University Press, 1971, ed. J. Lyndon Shanley), 8–9 (chapter "Economy"). The full passage reads: "The mass of men lead lives of quiet desperation. What is called resignation is confirmed desperation. From the desperate city you go into the desperate country, and have to console yourself with the bravery of minks and muskrats." Thoreau's observation critiques the unexamined, conformity-driven life of industrial society, where people resign themselves to unfulfilling routines rather than pursuing deliberate, authentic existence. This resonates with the book's theme of digital escapism as a modern form of that "confirmed desperation," amplified by screens and constant distraction.

ii Juvenal, Satires, Satire X, lines 77–81, trans. Susanna Morton Braund, Loeb Classical Library 91 (Cambridge, MA: Harvard University Press, 2004), 394–95. The original Latin reads: "…nam qui dabat olim / imperium, fasces, legiones, omnia, nunc se / continet atque duas tantum res anxius optat, / panem et circenses" (roughly: "For the people who once bestowed commands, consulships, legions, everything, now restrains itself and anxiously hopes for just two things: bread and circuses"). Juvenal satirizes the Roman masses' shift from political responsibility to passive satisfaction with subsidized food and spectacle, a mechanism emperors used to suppress discontent and maintain control. This ancient critique parallels the modern "digital blanket" of entertainment and distraction that smothers quiet desperation, keeping individuals isolated and politically disengaged.

iii George W. Bush, "Address to a Joint Session of Congress and the American People," September 20, 2001, https://georgewbush-whitehouse.archives.gov/news/releases/200 1/09/20010920-8.html ("Our war on terror begins with al Qaeda, but it does not end there. It will not end until every terrorist group of global reach has been found, stopped and defeated."). The Global War on Terrorism (GWOT), launched post-September 11, 2001, remains an active U.S.-led campaign encompassing military operations, intelligence, and sanctions; as of 2026, it spans 25 years without formal conclusion.

iv Lyndon B. Johnson, "The War on Poverty" speech, State of the Union Address, January 8, 1964. Official U.S. poverty rates fell from 19.5% in 1963 to 11.1% in 1973 (U.S. Census Bureau data), with programs like Medicare, Medicaid, and food assistance credited for much of the decline, though rates stabilized around 11–15% thereafter (CBPP, "War on Poverty: Large Positive Impact, But More Work Remains," 2014). Globally, extreme poverty has declined significantly through aid and development efforts (UN estimates: from ~37.8% in the early 1990s to ~11.2% by 2014, with continued progress), yet structural barriers to education, living-wage jobs, and self-sufficiency persist for billions.

v Nancy Reagan launched the "Just Say No" campaign in 1982 after a school visit in Oakland, CA, where a child asked what to do if offered drugs; it became a cornerstone of the Reagan-era anti-drug effort, spawning thousands of clubs worldwide (Reagan Foundation archives; History.com, "Just Say No," 2017). DARE (Drug Abuse Resistance Education), initiated in 1983 by Los Angeles police and schools, promoted peer-pressure resistance and abstinence messaging delivered by officers.

vi The War on Drugs, escalated from Nixon's 1971 declaration, contributed to U.S. incarceration rates soaring, with over 500,000 people imprisoned for drug offenses (many non-violent) by the 2010s, fueling the growth of private prisons (Cato Institute, "Four Decades and Counting: The Continued Failure of the War on Drugs," 2021). Domestically, it coincided with the opioid epidemic (hundreds of thousands of overdose deaths since the late 1990s); in Afghanistan, U.S. occupation (2001–2021) saw opium poppy production surge (from ~185 tons in 2001 to record highs of ~8,200 tons in 2007, supplying ~80–90% of global illicit opium), exacerbating the crisis rather than resolving it (UNODC reports; Wikipedia, "Opium production in Afghanistan").

vii Bronnie Ware, "Regrets of the Dying," blog post, 2011–2012, https://bronnieware .com/blog/regrets-of-the-dying; expanded in Bronnie Ware, The Top Five Regrets of the Dying: A Life Transformed by the Dearly Departing (Hay House, 2012). Ware, a palliative care nurse, documented recurring regrets from dying patients over several years, with the most common being: (1) "I wish I'd had the courage to live a life true to myself, not the life others expected of me" (the top regret, tied to unfulfilled dreams and conformity); (2) "I wish I hadn't worked so hard" (missing family and personal time); (3) "I wish I'd had the courage to express my feelings"; (4) "I wish I had stayed in touch with my friends"; and (5) "I wish I had let myself be happier." These themes underscore buyer's remorse over lives spent chasing external maps (career, approval, material success) at the expense of authentic self-connection—the core of the Virtual Reality Blues.

viiiCathal O'Madagain, Gregor Grosse, and Balthasar Bickel, "The Origin of Pointing: Evidence for the Touch Hypothesis," Science Advances 5, no. 7 (2019): eaav2558, https ://doi.org/10.1126/sciadv.aav2558; see also Kevin Cooperrider, "Body-Directed Gestures: Pointing to the Self and Beyond," Journal of Pragmatics 71 (2014): 1–16, https://doi.or g/10.1016/j.pragma.2014.07.003. Empirical studies confirm that when asked to point to themselves, both children and adults overwhelmingly direct gestures to the chest or torso (as if aiming to touch the body/self), not the head—evoking the entire person rather than creating an "arrow" or intellectual pointer. This cross-cultural behavior supports the distinction between the virtual, ego-driven "head" (mind/identity) and the absolute, embodied "heart" as the intuitive locus of self.

ix The telescope/microscope analogy illustrates the inescapable centrality of the perceiver in all experience: no matter the scale—cosmic vastness or subatomic depths—perception remains framed around the observing subject, as if "looking at the back of your own head." This echoes phenomenological insights (e.g., the observer's irreducible role in constructing reality) and non-dual traditions where the self is the unchanging witness beyond relative phenomena. Similar imagery appears in discussions of consciousness limits, such as Alan Watts' reflections on perception as self-referential (e.g., seeing the universe as an extension of oneself) or philosophical analogies emphasizing that zooming to extremes reveals the circularity of subjective experience rather than an objective "outside."

x The phrase "the longest distance/journey in the world is from the head to the heart" (or "18 inches from head to heart") is a widespread modern proverb symbolizing the challenging gap between intellectual understanding and emotional/heartfelt integration. Variants appear in motivational, spiritual, and self-help contexts, sometimes attributed to Thich Nhat Hanh, Andrew Bennett (British politician), Gary Zukav and Linda Francis (The Heart of the Soul, 2001), Ravi Zacharias, or Sioux wisdom; the "18 inches" version often emphasizes faith's transformation from head knowledge to heart belief. See e.g., Gary Zukav and Linda Francis, The Heart of the Soul: Emotional Awareness (New York: Simon & Schuster, 2001), 45–47 (discussing the journey from head to heart); and various online attributions in Psychology Today and Patheos blogs (2008–2019). Here, it personalizes the head-heart tension as the core inner battle.

xiRepeated exposure to media violence, including real-time war coverage like the 1991 Gulf War on CNN, contributes to emotional and physiological desensitization: reduced negative affect, lower empathy, diminished arousal/distress to violent stimuli, and greater acceptance of violence as commonplace. Studies show habitual viewers exhibit blunted responses (e.g., lower anxious arousal, higher pleasant arousal to violence) and reduced physiological reactivity (e.g., skin conductance, heart rate). This is specific to violent content and linked to habitual exposure rather than general arousal. For Gulf War context, live broadcasts brought explosions and civilian impacts into living rooms, fostering detachment for distant viewers while amplifying trauma for those in the territory. See Barbara Krahé et al., "Desensitization to Media Violence: Links With Habitual Media Violence Exposure, Aggressive Cognitions, and Aggressive Behavior," Journal of Personality and Social Psychology 100, no. 4 (2011): 630–46, https://doi.or g/10.1037/a0021711; Shoshana Mrug et al., "Emotional and Physiological Desensitization to Real-Life and Movie Violence," Journal of Youth and Adolescence 44, no. 5 (2015): 1092–1108, https://doi.org/10.1007/s10964-014-0202-1; and American Psychological Association overview, "Violence in the Media: Psychologists Study Potential Harmful Effects" (2013), summarizing desensitization from TV/news violence exposure.

xii The observation that opposites (gain/loss, victory/defeat) are degrees on the same continuum, and that relative truth masks an underlying Absolute unity, aligns with the

Hermetic Principle of Polarity: "Everything is Dual; everything has poles; opposites are identical in nature, but different in degree." See Three Initiates [pseud.], The Kybalion: A Study of the Hermetic Philosophy of Ancient Egypt and Greece (Chicago: Yogi Publication Society, 1908/1912), 102–17. This principle runs throughout the work as the lens through which relative Empire games (sports, war, polarized conflict) are seen as illusory separations, while the heart's shared love, passion, and survival instinct reveal the Absolute Truth beneath.

xiii Historical examples of arms suppliers profiting from both sides of conflicts include Basil Zaharoff (Greek arms dealer, 1849–1936), who sold munitions to opposing nations in the Balkans and WWI era, often using press manipulation and fake equipment to escalate tensions for sales; and the Iran-Iraq War (1980–1988), where at least 26 countries (including the U.S., USSR, France, China, West Germany) supplied weapons/technology to both belligerents. See Richard Brookes, The Merchant of Death: Basil Zaharoff (various biographies); and Stockholm International Peace Research Institute (SIPRI) reports on dual-side arms transfers. This illustrates Empire (military-industrial interests) fueling relative conflict for profit while ignoring Absolute human cost.

xiv The phrase echoes the AI Joshua in WarGames (1983): "A strange game. The only winning move is not to play." After simulating tic-tac-toe futility, Joshua concludes nuclear war (or any zero-sum escalation) is unwinnable. See Walter F. Parkes and Lawrence Lasker, WarGames (directed by John Badham, United Artists, 1983). Applied here, refusing Empire's map-games (polarized conflict, competition) is the path beyond relative win/loss to Absolute non-participation.

xv Hate requires active emotional investment and energy expenditure, mobilizing Action toward external targets while diverting it from inner/heart-centered work. This serves systems of control by channeling dissent into futile or permitted channels (e.g., managed protest), preserving the status quo. See Barbara Ehrenreich, Bright-Sided: How Positive Thinking Is Undermining America (New York: Metropolitan Books, 2009), on how negative emotions like hate can be exploited; and philosophical critiques like Michel Foucault on power allowing controlled resistance to maintain itself.

xvi The story of original sin (Genesis 3: the eating of the forbidden fruit) is reframed here as the Empire's map of inherited guilt and required sacrifice/redemption, turning an Absolute Truth-teller's execution into a tool of control. The focus on guilt, weekly attendance, confession, and tithing (10%) reflects institutional mechanisms that maintain relative compliance over heart-centered freedom.

Partial List of Works Cited

ABC News. 2019. "New Zealand Terror Attack Designed to Reach Audience on Social Media." March 15. https://www.abc.net.au/news/2019-03-15/christchurch-shooting-live-stream-think-twice-about-watching-it/10907258.

Afghanistan Opium Survey 2023. Vienna: UNODC, 2024. https://www.unodc.org/documents/crop-monitoring/Afghanistan/Afghanistan_opium_survey_2023.pdf.

American College of Obstetricians and Gynecologists (ACOG). 2024. "Female Age-Related Fertility Decline." ACOG Practice Bulletin. Washington, DC: ACOG. https://www.acog.org/clinical/clinical-guidance/practice-bulletin/articles/2024/01/female-age-related-fertility-decline.

American Psychiatric Association. 2010. Practice Guideline for the Treatment of Patients with Major Depressive Disorder. 3rd ed. Arlington, VA: American Psychiatric Association.

American Psychiatric Association. Diagnostic and Statistical Manual of Mental Disorders. 5th ed., text rev. (DSM-5-TR). Washington, DC: American Psychiatric Association, 2022.

American Psychological Association. 2026. "AI Chatbots and Digital Companions Are Reshaping Emotional Connection." Monitor on Psychology, January. https://www.apa.org/monitor/2026/01/ai-chatbots-emotional-connection.

American Psychological Association. "Violence in the Media: Psychologists Study Potential Harmful Effects." November 1, 2013. https://www.apa.org/topics/video-games/violence-harmful-effects.

American Red Cross. 2025. "Drowning Prevention and Facts." American Red Cross. Accessed February 4, 2026. https://www.redcross.org/get-help/how-to-prepare-for-e mergencies/types-of-emergencies/water-safety/drowning-prevention-and-facts.html.

American Red Cross. 2025. "Water Safety." American Red Cross. Accessed February 4, 2026. https://www.redcross.org/get-help/how-to-prepare-for-emergencies/types-of -emergencies/water-safety.html.

American Society for Reproductive Medicine. 2010–2025. Various meta-analyses and committee opinions on age and fecundity in Fertility and Sterility. https://www.fertst ert.org/.

Angi (formerly HomeAdvisor). 2025. "Toilet Installation Cost Guide." Angi. Accessed February 4, 2026. https://www.angi.com/articles/toilet-installation-cost.htm.

Asbury, Herbert. 1933. The Barbary Coast: An Informal History of the San Francisco Underworld. New York: Knopf.

Atlantic Council. "Is the end of the petrodollar near?" June 20, 2024. https://www.at lanticcouncil.org/blogs/econographics/is-the-end-of-the-petrodollar-near.

Australian Olympic Committee. "AOC Statement on Oceania Qualifying Process for Breaking." August 15, 2024. https://www.olympics.com.au/news/aoc-statement-on-o ceania-qualifying-process-for-breaking/.

Backlinko. 2025. "iPhone vs. Android User & Revenue Statistics (2026)." December 23. https://backlinko.com/iphone-vs-android-statistics.

Bailenson, Jeremy N. 2018. Experience on Demand: What Virtual Reality Is, How It Works, and What It Can Do. New York: W. W. Norton.

Balazs, Judit, and Agnes Kereszteny. 2017. "Attention-Deficit/Hyperactivity Disorder and Suicide: A Systematic Review." World Journal of Psychiatry 7 (1): 44–59. https:// doi.org/10.5498/wjp.v7.i1.44.

Bandwidth. 2022. "The History of SMS Text Messaging | SMS Turns 30." December 2. https://www.bandwidth.com/blog/texting-turns-30-the-history-of-sms.

Banet-Weiser, Sarah. 2018. Empowered: Popular Feminism and Popular Misogyny. Durham, NC: Duke University Press.

Barnouw, Erik. A Tower in Babel: A History of Broadcasting in the United States, Vol. 1. New York: Oxford University Press, 1966.

Barnouw, Erik. Tube of Plenty: The Evolution of American Television. 2nd ed. New York: Oxford University Press, 1990.

Barry, M. M. "Television Viewing and Brain Waves: A Review." Journal of Communication 42, no. 4 (1992): 3–21.

BBC Future. "How long can you survive without water?" October 19, 2020. https://www.bbc.com/future/article/20201016-why-we-cant-survive-without-water.

BBC News. 2025. "Russell Brand Charged with New Offences of Rape and Sexual Assault." December 23. https://www.bbc.com/news/articles/clyd5ynxvqxo.

Berridge, Kent C., and Terry E. Robinson. "Liking, Wanting, and the Incentive-Sensitization Theory of Addiction." American Psychologist 71, no. 8 (2016): 670–679. https://doi.org/10.1037/amp0000059.

Bogdanov, Alexander. Red Star: The First Bolshevik Utopia. Edited by Loren R. Graham and Richard Stites. Bloomington: Indiana University Press, 1984.

Bohn, Roger E., and James E. Short. "How Much Information? A Report on American Consumers." Global Information Industry Center, University of California, San Diego, 2009 https://hmi.ucsd.edu/pdf/HMI_2009_ConsumerReport_Dec9_2009.pdf.

Bolls, Paul D., Annie Lang, and Robert F. Potter. "The Arousal Model of Media Attention." Media Psychology 14, no. 3 (2011): 245–267. https://doi.org/10.1080/15213269.2011.597468.

Boutet, Isabelle, et al. 2021. "Emojis as Social Information in Digital Communication." Emotion 22 (7): 1529–43.

Bureau of Labor Statistics. 2022–2024. Census of Fatal Occupational Injuries. U.S. Department of Labor. https://www.bls.gov/iif/.

Business of Apps. 2026. "character.ai Revenue and Usage Statistics (2026)." Accessed February 2026. https://www.businessofapps.com/data/character-ai-statistics.

Bush, George W. "Address to a Joint Session of Congress and the American People." September 20, 2001. https://georgewbush-whitehouse.archives.gov/news/releases/200 1/09/20010920-8.html.

Buss, David M. 2021. The Evolution of Desire: Strategies of Human Mating. 4th ed. New York: Basic Books.

Brahmbhatt, Khyati, and William Schpero. 2024. "Mental Health Workforce Shortages and Health Equity: A Crisis in Public Health." International Journal of Environmental Research and Public Health 22 (1): 620. https://doi.org/10.3390/ijerph22010620.

Brady, William J., et al. "Emotion Shapes the Diffusion of Moralized Content in Social Networks." Proceedings of the National Academy of Sciences 114, no. 28 (2017): 7313–7318. https://doi.org/10.1073/pnas.1618923114.

Brookings Institution. Various reports on military enlistment and education pathways (e.g., "The Military as a Path to College"). Accessed February 2026. https://www.broo kings.edu (search for relevant titles).

Campbell-Kelly, Martin. 2003. From Airline Reservations to Sonic the Hedgehog: A History of the Software Industry. Cambridge, MA: MIT Press.

Capobianco, Molly. 2022. "How Different Generations Use Emojis." BuzzFeed, November 13. https://www.buzzfeed.com/mollycapobianco/different-generations-emoji-use.

Carleton University Department of Biology. "How do butterflies evolve from the cocoon?" https://carleton.ca/biology/cu-faq/how-do-butterflies-evolve-from-the-coco on-age-9.

Caroll, Linda. "You Know That Charming Little Story About the Two Wolves? It's a Lie." CROSSIN(G)ENRES (blog), November 29, 2018. https://crossingenres.com/yo u-know-that-charming-little-story-about-the-two-wolves-its-a-lie-dod93ea4ebff.

CDC. "COVID-19 Symptoms." 2020 archive. https://www.cdc.gov/coronavirus/2019 -ncov/symptoms-testing/symptoms.html.

CDC. "COVID-19 Vaccine Effectiveness Updates." 2021–2022. https://www.cdc.gov/c oronavirus/2019-ncov/vaccines/effectiveness.

CDC. "COVID-19 Vaccine Cards." 2021. https://www.cdc.gov/vaccines/covid-19/repo rting/vaccine-cards.html.

Centers for Disease Control and Prevention. "Understanding the Opioid Overdose Epidemic." Updated June 9, 2025. https://www.cdc.gov/overdose-prevention/about/understanding-the-opioid-overdose-epidemic.html.

Center for Humane Technology. n.d. "The Attention Economy." https://www.humanetech.com/youth/the-attention-economy.

Channel 4. 2023. "Russell Brand: In Plain Sight: Dispatches." September 16. https://www.channel4.com/programmes/russell-brand-in-plain-sight-dispatches.

Children's Television Workshop. *3-2-1 Contact*. PBS, 1980–1988.

Christakis, Dimitri A., Frederick J. Zimmerman, David L. DiGiuseppe, and Carolyn A. McCarty. "Early Television Exposure and Subsequent Attentional Problems in Children." Pediatrics 113, no. 4 (April 2004): 708–713. https://doi.org/10.1542/peds.113.4.708.

CNET. 2025. "We Interviewed Aria, a \$175K Almost-Human Robot at CES 2025." January 10. https://www.cnet.com/tech/services-and-software/we-interviewed-aria-a-175k-almost-human-robot-at-ces-2025/.

CNET. 2026. "CES 2026 Introduces Emily: She's Life-Size, AI-Powered and Ready for Intimacy." January 9. https://www.cnet.com/tech/services-and-software/ces-2026-emily-sex-robot-with-memory/.

Costarica Treatment Center. n.d. "The Loneliest Conviction: Unraveling the Mindset of Terminal Uniqueness in Recovery." https://costaricatreatmentcenter.com/the-loneliest-conviction-unraveling-the-mindset-of-terminal-uniqueness-in-recovery.

College Board. Trends in College Pricing and Student Aid 2025. New York: College Board, 2025.

Collins, Randall. 2019. The Credential Society: An Historical Sociology of Education and Stratification. New York: Columbia University Press. (Original 1979; reissue).

Columbia Business School (Pierre Yared et al.). "Dollars and Dominance: How Military Strength Secures Financial Power." November 26, 2024. https://business.columbia.edu/research-brief/dollars-dominance-military-financial-power.

Congressional Research Service. "GI Bills Enacted Prior to 2008 and Related Veterans' Educational Assistance Programs: A Primer." R42785 (2014, with historical details). https://sgp.fas.org/crs/misc/R42785.pdf.

Consumer Reports. 2024. "The Rise of DIY Home Repairs." Consumer Reports. https://www.consumerreports.org/home-garden/home-repair/diy-trends.

Convery, Stephanie. "'It Doesn't Reflect Us': Global Mockery of Raygun's Paris Olympics Performance Affecting Australian Scene, Local B-Girls Say." The Guardian (Australia), August 14, 2024. https://www.theguardian.com/australia-news/article/2024/aug/14/raygun-breaking-paris-olympics-australian-dance-industry.

Cooperrider, Kevin. "Body-Directed Gestures: Pointing to the Self and Beyond." Journal of Pragmatics 71 (November 2014): 1–16. https://doi.org/10.1016/j.pragma.2014.07.003.

Coopersmith, Jonathan. 2000. "Pornography, Videotape, and the Internet." IEEE Technology and Society Magazine 19 (1): 12–17, 26.

Coughlin, Joseph F. 2025. "The Great Wealth Transfer: 6 Reasons Why It Might Fall Short." Forbes, June 2. https://www.forbes.com/sites/josephcoughlin/2025/06/02/the-great-wealth-transfer-6-reasons-why-it-might-fall-short/.

CounterPunch.org. 2022. "Dahmerism: The Highest Stage of Liberal Identitarianism." November 16. https://www.counterpunch.org/2022/11/16/dahmerism-the-highest-stage-of-liberal-identitarianism.

CNN. 2022. "6 dead in Missouri interstate pileup involving 47 vehicles, official says." March 17, 2022. https://www.cnn.com/2022/03/17/us/multi-vehicle-crash-missouri-interstate.

CNN. "MrBeast builds 100 wells in Africa, attracting praise – and some criticism." November 7, 2023. https://edition.cnn.com/2023/11/06/africa/mrbeast-100-wells-africa-intl-scli.

Cullen, Dave. 2009. Columbine. New York: Twelve.

Custom Market Insights. 2025. "Global Self-Improvement Market Size, Trends, Share 2025-2034." Custom Market Insights. https://www.custommarketinsights.com/report/self-improvement-market. (Projects market at USD 46.1 billion in 2025, reaching USD 90.9 billion by 2034 at 8% CAGR.)

Damasio, Antonio. 2005. Descartes' Error: Emotion, Reason, and the Human Brain. New York: Penguin Books. (Original 1994).

Deadline. 2023. "Channel 4 Doc Airs Russell Brand Rape, Sexual Abuse Allegations; Comedian Appears On London Stage." September 16. https://deadline.com/2023/09/dispatches-channel-4-russell-brand-rape-sexual-abuse-allegations-comedian-appears-on-london-stage-1235548661.

De Freitas, Julian, Zeliha Oğuz-Uğuralp, Ahmet Kaan Uğuralp, and Stefano Puntoni. 2025. "AI Companions Reduce Loneliness." Journal of Consumer Research. https://doi.org/10.1093/jcr/ucaf040.

DemandSage. 2025. "Character AI Statistics (2026) – Worldwide Active Users." December 1. https://www.demandsage.com/character-ai-statistics.

DemandSage. 2026. "iPhone vs Android Users Market Share Statistics (2026)." January 5. https://www.demandsage.com/iphone-vs-android-users.

Diodorus Siculus. Library of History. Book 9. Translated by C. H. Oldfather. Loeb Classical Library. Cambridge, MA: Harvard University Press, 1940.

Doctorow, Cory. 2023. "The Internet Is Enshittified." Pluralistic (blog), January 2023. https://pluralistic.net/2023/01/21/potemkin-ai/.

Douglas, Susan J. Inventing American Broadcasting 1899–1922. Baltimore: Johns Hopkins University Press, 1987.

Drury, William. 1986. Norton I: Emperor of the United States. New York: Dodd, Mead.

Duelfer, Charles A. 2004. Comprehensive Report of the Special Advisor to the DCI on Iraq's WMD. Washington, DC: Central Intelligence Agency. (Iraq Survey Group final report.)

Dunmow Flitch Trials. "History." https://www.dunmowflitchtrials.co.uk/history.

Durango Bill. "Powerball Odds." Durango Bill's Applied Mathematics. Accessed February 2026. https://www.durangobill.com/PowerballOdds.html.

Ehrenreich, Barbara. Bright-Sided: How Positive Thinking Is Undermining America. New York: Metropolitan Books, 2009.

Encyclopædia Britannica, s.v. "French Invasion of Russia," last modified December 29, 2025, https://www.britannica.com/event/French-invasion-of-Russia.

Encyclopedia Britannica. "Lowell Thomas." Accessed January 31, 2026. https://www.britannica.com/biography/Lowell-Thomas.

Encyclopædia Britannica, s.v. "Operation Barbarossa," last modified January 17, 2026, https://www.britannica.com/event/Operation-Barbarossa.

Encyclopædia Britannica. n.d. "UNIVAC I." Accessed February 4, 2026. https://www.britannica.com/technology/UNIVAC-I.

Encyclopedia Britannica. "Walter Cronkite." Accessed January 31, 2026. https://www.britannica.com/biography/Walter-Cronkite.

Erowid. "Candyflipping Vault." Accessed February 2026. https://erowid.org/chemicals/mdma/mdma_article2.shtml.

Estácio Amaro da Silva, J., et al. "Cannabis and Cannabinoid Use in Autism Spectrum Disorder: A Systematic Review." Trends in Psychiatry and Psychotherapy 44 (2022): e20200149. https://pmc.ncbi.nlm.nih.gov/articles/PMC9887656/.

Ethington, Philip J. 1994. The Public City: The Political Construction of Urban Life in San Francisco, 1850–1900. Cambridge: Cambridge University Press.

Equal Credit Opportunity Act. 15 U.S.C. §§ 1691–1691f. 1974.

European Parliament. Hearing on COVID-19 Vaccines (Janine Small/Pfizer testimony). October 10, 2022. https://www.europarl.europa.eu/doceo/document/ENVI-PV-2022 1010_EN.html.

Eyal, Nir. 2014. Hooked: How to Build Habit-Forming Products. New York: Portfolio/Penguin.

Fatani, Abdulaziz, et al. 2024. "Autism Spectrum Disorder and Suicide: A Case Report." Cureus 16 (7): e64451. https://doi.org/10.7759/cureus.64451.

FDA. "COVID-19 Vaccine EUA Fact Sheets." December 2020. https://www.fda.gov/emergency-preparedness-and-response/coronavirus-disease-2019-covid-19/covid-19-vaccines.

FDA. "Booster Authorization." September 2021. https://www.fda.gov/emergency-pre paredness-and-response/coronavirus-disease-2019-covid-19/covid-19-vaccines.

Federal Motor Carrier Safety Administration. 2020–2024. Large Truck and Bus Crash Facts. U.S. Department of Transportation. https://www.fmcsa.dot.gov/safety/data-a nd-statistics/large-truck-and-bus-crash-facts.

Federal Register. "Declaration Under the Public Readiness and Emergency Preparedness Act for Medical Countermeasures Against COVID-19." March 17, 2020. https://www.federalregister.gov/documents/2020/03/17/2020-05484/declaration-unde r-the-public-readiness-and-emergency-preparedness-act-for-medical-countermeasures.

Federal Register. "Increase in Rates Payable Under the Mont-gomery GI Bill—Active Duty." July 20, 2000 (reflects 1998–1999 rates). https://www.federalregister.gov/documents/2000/07/20/00-18326/increase-in -rates-payable-under-the-montgomery-gi-bill-active-duty.

Federal Reserve Board. 2025. "Distribution of Household Wealth in the U.S. since 1989." Distributional Financial Accounts (DFA). Washington, DC: Board of Governors of the Federal Reserve System. https://www.federalreserve.gov/releases/z1/dataviz/dfa/distri bute/table.

Federal Reserve Board. "The International Role of the U.S. Dollar – 2025 Edition." July 18, 2025. https://www.federalreserve.gov/econres/notes/feds-notes/the-international-r ole-of-the-u-s-dollar-2025-edition-20250718.html.

Federal Reserve History. "Gold Convertibility Ends." Accessed February 2026. https:/ /www.federalreservehistory.org/essays/gold-convertibility-ends.

Federal Reserve History. "Nixon Ends Convertibility of U.S. Dollars to Gold and Announces Wage/Price Controls." Accessed February 2026. https://www.federalreser vehistory.org/essays/gold-convertibility-ends.

Federal Reserve History. "The Meeting at Jekyll Island." Accessed February 2026. https://www.federalreservehistory.org/essays/jekyll-island-conference.

Feeding America Action. "What the recent government shutdown means for food assistance." November 14, 2025. https://feedingamericaaction.org/fy26-government-sh utdown-food-assistance.

Feifer, Jason. 2021. "Everybody Is Wrong About Participation Trophies." LinkedIn (article/podcast transcript). https://www.linkedin.com/pulse/everybody-wrong-parti cipation-trophies-jason-feifer/.

Fergusson, Adam. When Money Dies: The Nightmare of Deficit Spending, Devaluation, and Hyperinflation in Weimar Germany. London: Old Street Publishing, 2010 ed. (Original 1975.)

Fielding, Raymond. The American Newsreel 1911–1967. Norman: University of Oklahoma Press, 1972.

Fight the New Drug. 2022. "The Evolution of Porn: Who Invented Porn as We Know It Today?" May 11. https://fightthenewdrug.org/how-we-got-here-the-spread-of-porn.

Financial Crisis Inquiry Commission. The Financial Crisis Inquiry Report: Final Report of the National Commission on the Causes of the Financial and Economic Crisis in the United States. Washington, DC: U.S. Government Printing Office, 2011.

Firestone, Robert W. 2018. "The Inner Voice in Self-Destructive Behavior and Suicide." Psychology Today (blog), December 20, 2018. https://www.psychologytoday.com/us/blog/the-human-experience/201812/the -inner-voice-in-self-destructive-behavior-and-suicide.

Fisher, Helen. 2016. Anatomy of Love: A Natural History of Mating, Marriage, and Why We Stray. Updated ed. New York: Simon & Schuster. (Original 1992; updated editions include 2016 and later with new chapters on modern hookup culture, attachment, and oxytocin bonding.)

Fold3. 2020. "Loose Lips Sink Ships: A Look at WWII Propaganda Posters." December 11. https://blog.fold3.com/loose-lips-sink-ships-a-look-at-wwii-propaganda-posters/.

Fortune. "MrBeast's $5 billion empire runs on generosity—but at a cost." September 26, 2025. https://fortune.com/2025/09/26/mrbeast-jimmy-donaldson-beast-industries-ph ilanthropy-profit/.

Fortune Business Insights. 2026. "AI Companion Market Size, Share & Industry Analysis, 2026–2034." January 12. https://www.fortunebusinessinsights.com/ai-companion -market-113258.

Fox News. "Democrats remove masks after press conference urging COVID compliance." November 20, 2020. https://www.foxnews.com/politics/democrats-remove-masks-after-press-conference-urging-covid-compliance.

Friss, Evan. 2024. "Are Bookstores Just a Waste of Space?" The New Yorker, August 26. https://www.newyorker.com/magazine/2024/08/26/a-history-of-the-american-bookstore-evan-friss-book-review. (On bookstore decline/Amazon impact.)

Gallup. "Americans' Trust in Mass Media Remains Near Record Low." September 24, 2025. https://news.gallup.com/poll/651977/americans-trust-mass-media-remains-near-record-low.aspx.

Garcia, Justin R., et al. 2020. "Hookup Culture: A Review of the Literature." Journal of Sex Research 57 (4): 423–440. https://doi.org/10.1080/00224499.2019.1705958.

Gebauer, Line, Morten L. Kringelbach, and Peter Vuust. 2012. "Ever-Changing Cycles of Musical Pleasure: The Role of Dopamine and Anticipation." Journal of Neuroscience 32 (37): 12667–12675. (For anticipation cycles in music/reward.)

George W. Bush White House Archives. 2001. "Address to a Joint Session of Congress and the American People." September 20. https://georgewbush-whitehouse.archives.gov/news/releases/2001/09/20010920-8.html.

George W. Bush White House Archives. 2003. "President Bush Announces Major Combat Operations in Iraq Have Ended." May 1. https://georgewbush-whitehouse.archives.gov/news/releases/2003/05/20030501-15.html.

Geng, Caitlin. 2025. "Texting Anxiety: Signs, Effects on the Brain, and How to Manage It." Medical News Today, October 1. https://www.medicalnewstoday.com/articles/texting-anxiety. (For latency/read receipts dopamine/anxiety psych.)

Gilovich, Thomas, and Amit Kumar. "To Do or to Have? The Benefits of Experiential Purchases." In Positive Psychology: The Science of Happiness and Flourishing, edited by Shane J. Lopez and C. R. Snyder, 2nd ed. Thousand Oaks, CA: SAGE Publications, 2015.

Ging, Debbie. 2019. "Alphas, Betas, and Incels: Theorizing the Masculinities of the Manosphere." Men and Masculinities 22 (4): 638–657. https://doi.org/10.1177/1097184X17706401.

Global Wellness Institute. 2025. "The Global Wellness Economy Reaches a Record $5.6 Trillion—And It's Forecast to Hit $8.5 Trillion by 2027." Global Wellness Institute. https://globalwellnessinstitute.org/press-room/press-releases/globalwellnessecon omymonitor2023.

Goldhaber, Michael H. 1997. "Attention Shoppers." Wired, December. https://www. wired.com/1997/12/es-attention/.

GoodGoodGood. "MrBeast, YouTubers raise $40M in global #TeamWater fundraiser." September 3, 2025. https://www.goodgoodgood.co/articles/mrbeast-team-water-fund raiser.

Google Quantum AI. 2024. "Meet Willow, our state-of-the-art quantum chip." December 9. https://blog.google/innovation-and-ai/technology/research/google-willow-qua ntum-chip/.

Gonon, François. 2009. "The Dopaminergic Hypothesis of Attention-Deficit/Hyper-activity Disorder Needs Re-Examining." Trends in Neurosciences 32 (1): 2–8. https:// doi.org/10.1016/j.tins.2008.09.010.

Gordon, Michael R., and Judith Miller. 2002. "U.S. Says Hussein Intensifies Quest for A-Bomb Parts." The New York Times, September 8. https://www.nytimes.com/2002/09/08/world/threats-responses-iraqis-us-says-huss ein-intensifies-quest-for-bomb-parts.html.

Graeber, David. Debt: The First 5,000 Years. Brooklyn, NY: Melville House, 2014.

Grubbs, Joshua B., et al. 2023. "Pornography Use and Sexual Dysfunction: A Meta-Analysis." Journal of Sex Research 60 (5): 678–692. https://doi.org/10.1080/002 24499.2022.2141234.

Guinness World Records. "Largest Anti-War Rally." Accessed March 10, 2026. https:/ /www.guinnessworldrecords.com/world-records/74335-largest-anti-war-rally.

Gunraj, Danielle N., et al. 2016. "Texting Insincerely: The Role of the Period in Text Messaging." Computers in Human Behavior 55: 1067–75. (Foundational on generational period perception as aggressive.)

Haenfler, Ross. n.d. "Commodification." Subcultures and Sociology. Grinnell College. https://haenfler.sites.grinnell.edu/commodification.

Hand, C. J., et al. 2022. "Interactions between Text Content and Emoji Types Determine Perceptions of Both Messages and Senders." Computers in Human Behavior Reports 8: 100242.

Harari, Yuval Noah. Sapiens: A Brief History of Humankind. New York: Harper, 2015.

Harris, Brandon C., Maxwell Foxman, and William C. Partin. 2024. "Association of Self-Harm and Suicidality with Psychiatric Co-Occurring Conditions in Autistic Individuals: A Systematic Review and Pooled Analysis." EClinicalMedicine. https://doi.org/10.1016/j.eclinm.2024.102442.

Harris, Brandon C., Maxwell Foxman, and William C. Partin. 2023. ""Don't Make Me Ratio You Again": How Political Influencers Encourage Platformed Political Participation." Social Media + Society 9 (2). https://doi.org/10.1177/20563051231177944.

Harris, Gloria G. 2015. "Emperor Norton I: San Francisco's Eccentric Sovereign." California History 92 (3): 18–35. https://doi.org/10.2307/10.1525/tph.2015.92.3.18.

Healthline. "How Long Can You Live Without Water? Effects of Dehydration." Updated September 16, 2024. https://www.healthline.com/health/food-nutrition/how-long-can-you-live-without-water.

Hedegaard, Holly, et al. "Drug Overdose Deaths in the United States, 1999–2018." NCHS Data Brief no. 356. Hyattsville, MD: National Center for Health Statistics, December 2019. https://www.cdc.gov/nchs/products/databriefs/db356.htm.

Hedley, Darren, and Mirko Uljarević. 2024. "Updated Systematic Review of Suicide in Autism: 2018–2024." Current Developmental Disorders Reports. https://doi.org/10.1007/s40474-024-00308-9.

Heinlein, Robert A. 1961. Stranger in a Strange Land. New York: Putnam.

Hellenic Republic Ministry of National Defence. "Conscription." Accessed February 2026. https://www.mod.mil.gr/en/conscription.

Henry David Thoreau, Walden, ed. J. Lyndon Shanley (Princeton, NJ: Princeton University Press, 1971), 8 (chapter "Economy").

Herbert, Don (host). *Mr. Wizard's World.* Nickelodeon, 1983–1989.

Hollywood Reporter. 2025. "'Seinfeld' Star Michael Richards Went Wild on Stage Again—in a Good Way This Time." September 25. https://www.hollywoodreporter.com/news/general-news/seinfeld-michael-richards-stage-tour-book-racist-tirade-1236386030.

House of Cards, Season 1, Episode 9, "Chapter 9" (Netflix, 2013).

Houston Chronicle. "Joel Osteen defends Lakewood Church's response to Harvey flooding." August 29, 2017. https://www.houstonchronicle.com/news/houston-texas/houston/article/Joel-Osteen-defends-Lakewood-Church-s-response-12160679.php.

Hudon, Alexandre, et al. 2025. "Delusional Experiences Emerging From AI Chatbot Interactions or 'AI Psychosis'." JMIR Mental Health 12: e85799. https://doi.org/10.2196/85799.

Huerta, Douglas W. "The Life and Death of Alexander Bogdanov, Physician." Journal of Medical Biography 4, no. 3 (1996): 141–147. https://doi.org/10.1177/096777209600400305.

Institute for Family Studies. 2026. "What Will Artificial Intelligence Do to Birthrates?" February 4. https://ifstudies.org/blog/what-will-artificial-intelligence-do-to-birthrates.

Internal Revenue Service. "Topic No. 751: Social Security and Medicare Withholding Rates." Updated 2025–2026. https://www.irs.gov/taxtopics/tc751.

Investopedia. "Petrodollars and Their Impact on the U.S. Dollar and Global Economy." Updated 2025. https://www.investopedia.com/articles/forex/072915/how-petrodollars-affect-us-dollar.asp.

Isaac, Mike. 2018. "The Ratio Establishes Itself on Twitter." The New York Times, February 9. https://www.nytimes.com/interactive/2018/02/09/technology/the-ratio-trends-on-twitter.html.

Iyengar, Shanto, and Donald R. Kinder. News That Matters: Television and American Opinion. Updated ed. Chicago: University of Chicago Press, 2010.

Iyengar, Shanto, and Sean J. Westwood. "Fear and Loathing Across Party Lines: New Evidence on Group Polarization." American Journal of Political Science 59, no. 3 (2015): 690–707. https://doi.org/10.1111/ajps.12111.

Jonnes, Jill. 2003. Empires of Light: Edison, Tesla, Westinghouse, and the Race to Electrify the World. New York: Random House.

Johns Hopkins Bloomberg School of Public Health, "Is the U.S. Birth Rate Declining?" January 6, 2026. https://publichealth.jhu.edu/2026/is-the-us-birth-rate-declining.

Johns Hopkins Coronavirus Resource Center. "U.S. Mortality Data 2020–2021." 2022. https://coronavirus.jhu.edu/data/mortality.

Johnson, Lyndon B. "The War on Poverty." State of the Union Address, January 8, 1964.

Juhasz, Antonia. 2013. "Why the War in Iraq Was Fought for Big Oil." CNN Opinion, March 19. https://www.cnn.com/2013/03/19/opinion/iraq-war-oil-juhasz.

Juvenal, Satires, Satire X.81, trans. Susanna Morton Braund, Loeb Classical Library (Cambridge, MA: Harvard University Press, 2004), 395 ("panem et circenses").

JW.org. S.v. "Who Goes to Heaven." https://www.jw.org/en/bible-teachings/questions/go-to-heaven/.

Kadence. 2025. "Why Brand Loyalty is Turning Into Tribalism." https://kadence.com/en-us/knowledge/why-brand-loyalty-is-turning-into-tribalism. (Algorithms turning preferences into tribal divides, e.g., Apple/Android.)

Kaiser Family Foundation (KFF). 2024. "2024 Employer Health Benefits Survey." https://www.kff.org/health-costs/report/2024-employer-health-benefits-survey/.

Kaiser Family Foundation (KFF). 2025. "Claims Denials and Appeals in ACA Marketplace Plans in 2023." January 27. https://www.kff.org/private-insurance/issue-brief/claims-denials-and-appeals-in-aca-marketplace-plans-in-2023/.

Karhson, David S., et al. "Acute Effects of Cannabis on Core and Co-Occurring Features Associated with Autism Spectrum Disorder in Adults." Scientific Reports 15 (2025): article 39849. https://doi.org/10.1038/s41598-025-23472-3.

Kelly, Joan, et al. "Misogynist Incels and Male Supremacism." New America Foundation, 2021. https://www.newamerica.org/political-reform/reports/misogynist-incels-and-male-supremacism/.

Kindred, Liza. "The Wellness Industrial Complex: A Guided Analysis." Liza Kindred (blog), n.d. https://www.lizakindred.com/the-wellness-industrial-complex.

Klein, Gary. 1998. Sources of Power: How People Make Decisions. Cambridge, MA: MIT Press.

Koenig, John. 2021. The Dictionary of Obscure Sorrows. New York: Simon & Schuster. Also see "Sonder." The Dictionary of Obscure Sorrows. https://www.dictionaryofobscuresorrows.com/post/23536922667/sonder.

Know Your Meme. 2025. "6666 Minimum." Know Your Meme. Accessed February 4, 2026. https://knowyourmeme.com/memes/6666-minimum.

Know Your Meme. "Boomer Remover." Entry 2020. https://knowyourmeme.com/memes/boomer-remover.

Know Your Meme. "Ratio." Entry updated 2025. https://knowyourmeme.com/memes/ratio.

Korzybski, Alfred. 1994. Science and Sanity: An Introduction to Non-Aristotelian Systems and General Semantics. 5th ed. Brooklyn, NY: Institute of General Semantics. (Original work published 1933.)

Kovach, Bill, and Tom Rosenstiel. The Elements of Journalism: What Newspeople Should Know and the Public Should Expect. 4th ed. New York: Crown, 2021.

Krahé, Barbara, Ingrid Möller, L. Rowell Huesmann, Lucyna Kirwil, Juliane Felber, and Anja Berger. "Desensitization to Media Violence: Links With Habitual Media Violence Exposure, Aggressive Cognitions, and Aggressive Behavior." Journal of Personality and Social Psychology 100, no. 4 (April 2011): 630–46. https://doi.org/10.1037/a0021711.

Kraybill, Donald B., Karen M. Johnson-Weiner, and Steven M. Nolt. 2013. The Amish. Baltimore: Johns Hopkins University Press.

Kruger, Justin, Nicholas Epley, Jason Parker, and Zhi-Wen Ng. 2005. "Egocentrism over E-Mail: Can We Communicate as Well as We Think?" Journal of Personality and Social Psychology 89 (6): 925–36.

Kruse, Elliot, Don E. Davis, Joshua N. Hook, Daryl R. Van Tongeren, and Joshua N. Hook. 2020. "An Ode to Humility: A Review of the Psychological Literature on Humility." Journal of Positive Psychology 15 (5): 643–656. https://doi.org/10.1080/17439760.2019.1685573.

Lane, Nick. 2015. The Vital Question: Energy, Evolution, and the Origins of Complex Life. New York: W.W. Norton.

Lang, Annie. "The Limited Capacity Model of Motivated Message Processing." Journal of Communication 50, no. 1 (2000): 46–70. https://doi.org/10.1111/j.1460-2466.2000.tb02833.x.

Lataifeh, Mohammad. 2018. "Attitude, Aptitude, and Amplitude (AAA): A Framework for Design Driven Innovation." arXiv preprint arXiv:1808.00544. https://arxiv.org/abs/1808.00544.

Lembke, Anna. Dopamine Nation: Finding Balance in the Age of Indulgence. New York: Dutton, 2021.

Lethbridge News Now. "Why Do the Numbers on a Roulette Wheel Add Up To 666?" March 13, 2018. https://lethbridgenewsnow.com/2018/03/13/why-do-the-numbers-on-a-roulette-wheel-add-up-to-666.

Lieberman, Daniel E., et al. "Running and the Evolution of Endurance Running." Nature 432 (2004): 345–348. https://doi.org/10.1038/nature03052.

Liebenberg, Louis. "Persistence Hunting by Modern Hunter-Gatherers." Current Anthropology 47, no. 6 (2006): 1017–1025. https://doi.org/10.1086/508695.

Lockheed Martin. 2025. "Skunk Works® News and Features." Various 2025 releases (e.g., Vectis CCA, AI-drone demos). https://www.lockheedmartin.com/en-us/who-we-are/business-areas/aeronautics/skunkworks.html.

Lovense. 2026. "Silicone AI Sex Doll – Realistic AI Sex Robot." Accessed February 2026. https://www.lovense.com/interactive-ai-robot-sex-doll.

Mark, Gloria. Attention Span: Finding Focus for a Fulfilling Life. Hanover Square Press, 2023.

Mark, Gloria, et al. "The Cost of Interrupted Work: More Speed and Stress." In Proceedings of the SIGCHI Conference on Human Factors in Computing Systems, 107–110. New York: ACM, 2008. https://doi.org/10.1145/1357054.1357072.

Marshall, Barry J. "Helicobacter Connections." ChemMedChem 1, no. 8 (2006): 783–802. https://doi.org/10.1002/cmdc.200600081.

Martin, Gary. "Bring Home the Bacon." The Phrase Finder. Last updated December 20, 2023. https://www.phrases.org.uk/meanings/bring-home-the-bacon.html.

Martin, George R.R. 1996. A Game of Thrones. New York: Bantam Books.

Martin, Joyce A., et al. "Births: Final Data for 2024." National Vital Statistics Reports (forthcoming or via data brief DB535). Centers for Disease Control and Prevention, July 2025. https://www.cdc.gov/nchs/products/databriefs/db535.htm.

Maruna, Shadd. 2001. Making Good: How Ex-Convicts Reform and Rebuild Their Lives. Washington, DC: American Psychological Association.

Mazzucato, Mariana. 2019. "Takers and Makers: Who are the Real Value Creators?" Evonomics, June 30. https://evonomics.com/value-of-everything-mariana-mazzucato.

McCombs, Maxwell, and Donald Shaw. "The Agenda-Setting Function of Mass Media." Public Opinion Quarterly 36, no. 2 (1972): 176–187. https://doi.org/10.1086/267990.

McKinsey & Company. 2025. "The Attention Equation: Winning the Right Battles for Consumer Attention." June 10. https://www.mckinsey.com/industries/technology-media-and-telecommunications/our-insights/the-attention-equation-winning-the-right-battles-for-consumer-attention.

McKinsey Global Institute. 2023–2025. "Generative AI and the Future of Work in America." McKinsey & Company. https://www.mckinsey.com/featured-insights/future-of-work/generative-ai-and-the-future-of-work-in-america.

Medical News Today. "How long can you live without water? Facts and effects." Updated 2025. https://www.medicalnewstoday.com/articles/325174.

Mellinkoff, David. 1963. The Language of the Law. Boston: Little, Brown.

Mental Floss. 2025. "Classroom Cold War: When Students Were Trained to 'Duck and Cover'." August 10. https://www.mentalfloss.com/history/cold-war/duck-and-cover-classroom-drill.

Mental Health America. 2024. "Access to Crisis Services: Barriers and Experiences." Alexandria, VA: Mental Health America. https://www.mhanational.org/research-reports/access-crisis-services-barriers-and-experiences.

Merleau-Ponty, Maurice. Phenomenology of Perception. Translated by Colin Smith. London: Routledge & Kegan Paul, 1962.

Miller, Judith. 2001. "A Nation Challenged: The Letter; Fear Hits Newsroom In a Cloud of Powder." The New York Times, October 14. https://www.nytimes.com/2001/10/14/us/a-nation-challenged-the-letter-fear-hits-newsroom-in-a-cloud-of-powder.html.

Miller, Judith. 2015. The Story: A Reporter's Journey. New York: Simon & Schuster.

Miller, Judith, Stephen Engelberg, and William Broad. 2001. Germs: Biological Weapons and America's Secret War. New York: Simon & Schuster.

Mischel, Walter, Yuichi Shoda, and Monica L. Rodriguez. 1989. "Delay of Gratification in Children." Science 244 (4907): 933–38.

Morrin, H., et al. 2025. "Delusions by Design? How Everyday AIs Might Be Fuelling Psychosis (and What Can Be Done About It)." PsyArXiv preprint. https://doi.org/10.31234/osf.io/cmy7n_v5.

Mrug, Shoshana, Anjana Madan, and Douglas A. Windle. "Emotional and Physiological Desensitization to Real-Life and Movie Violence." Journal of Youth and Adolescence 44, no. 5 (May 2015): 1092–1108. https://doi.org/10.1007/s10964-014-0202-1.

Mwachiro, Mark. "This Is the Cable News Ratings Report for 2025." Adweek, January 7, 2026. https://www.adweek.com/tvnewser/cable-news-ratings-report-for-2025/.

National Academies of Sciences, Engineering, and Medicine. 1986. Improving the Quality of Care in Nursing Homes. Washington, DC: National Academies Press. https://www.ncbi.nlm.nih.gov/books/NBK217552/.

National Association of Home Builders (NAHB). 2024–2025. "Consumer Preferences Survey." NAHB. https://www.nahb.org/research/consumer-preferences-survey.

National Center for Education Statistics. PIAAC 2023 U.S. Results. U.S. Department of Education, 2024. https://nces.ed.gov/surveys/piaac/.

National Commission on Terrorist Attacks Upon the United States. 2004. The 9/11 Commission Report. Washington, DC: Government Printing Office.

National Highway Traffic Safety Administration. 2024–2025. "Automated Vehicles for Safety." U.S. Department of Transportation. https://www.nhtsa.gov/technology-inn ovation/automated-vehicles-safety.

National Institute on Drug Abuse. "Cocaine." Updated 2024–2025. https://nida.nih. gov/research-topics/cocaine.

NBC News. 1994. "Confessions of a Serial Killer: Jeffrey Dahmer Speaks." Interview by Stone Phillips. Dateline NBC, March.

NBC News. 2023. "The 'Wealth Transfer' from Boomers Won't Save Gen X and Millennials." December 29. https://www.nbcnews.com/business/consumer/generatio nal-wealth-transfer-baby-boomers-cant-save-gen-x-millennials-rcna128099.

New York City Department of Parks & Recreation. n.d. "Brooklyn Heights Promenade." https://www.nycgovparks.org/parks/brooklyn-heights-promenade.

Newport, Cal. 2019. Digital Minimalism: Choosing a Focused Life in a Noisy World. New York: Portfolio.

NewsOne. 2022. "Jeffrey Dahmer DA Downplays Police Racism Amid Netflix Series." September 30. https://newsone.com/4419006/jeffrey-dahmer-da-michael-mccann

Nieman Lab. "The Evolution of Comments on News Sites." 2021. https://niemanlab. org/2021/xx/xx/evolution-of-comments.

Nistor, Cristina, Andrew A. Samis, and Juanjuan Zhang. 2025. "Influencer Authenticity: To Grow or to Monetize." Management Science https://faculty.haas.berkeley.edu/VI LLAS/Influencers__To_Grow_or_To_Monetize.pdf.

Nolen-Hoeksema, Susan, Blair E. Wisco, and Sonja Lyubomirsky. 2008. "Rethinking Rumination." Perspectives on Psychological Science 3 (5): 400–424. https://doi.org/1 0.1111/j.1745-6924.2008.00088.x.

NPR. 2024. "Doxxing Campaigns Are a Cancel Culture Tool. What Happens After They End?" April 11. https://www.npr.org/transcripts/1231084790.

NPR. 2024 "Breakdancer Raygun Is Retiring from the Sport after Her Olympics Backlash." November 7. https://www.npr.org/2024/11/07/nx-s1-5182777/raygun-retiri ng-olympics-breakdancer-australia-breaking.

NPR. 2025. "People Are Losing Jobs Due to Social Media Posts About Charlie Kirk." September 13. https://www.npr.org/2025/09/13/nx-s1-5538476/charlie-kirk-jobs-target -social-media-critics-resign.

Nünlist, Tobias. Dämonenglaube im Islam. Berlin: Walter de Gruyter, 2015. ISBN 978-3-11-033168-4.

O'Halloran, Laura, Charlotte Coombs, and Ellen Wilkinson. 2022. "Suicidality in Autistic Youth: A Systematic Review and Meta-Analysis." Clinical Psychology Review 93: 102144. https://doi.org/10.1016/j.cpr.2022.102144.

O'Madagain, Cathal, Gregor Grosse, and Balthasar Bickel. "The Origin of Pointing: Evidence for the Touch Hypothesis." Science Advances 5, no. 7 (July 2019): eaav2558. https://doi.org/10.1126/sciadv.aav2558.

Octet Design. 2026. "Apple's Brand Loyalty And Hidden Design Tricks Behind The Cult." January 6. https://octet.design/journal/apple-brand-loyalty.

Ohio Department of Mental Health. 2010–2011. Annual Reports. Columbus, OH: ODMH (archived state reports on civil commitment and access).

OpenAI. 2022. "Introducing ChatGPT." OpenAI Blog, November 30, 2022. https://o penai.com/blog/chatgpt.

OSV News. "In this TikTok test of a baby formula emergency, 1 Catholic church really stood out." November 19, 2025. https://www.osvnews.com/in-this-tiktok-test-of-a-ba by-formula-emergency-1-catholic-church-really-stood-out.

Out of the FOG. 2017. "Terminal Uniqueness." June 26. https://outofthefog.website/ top-100-trait-blog/terminal-uniqueness.

Patel, Vemmy L., et al. 2023. "Low Availability, Long Wait Times, and High Geographic Disparity of Psychiatric Outpatient Care in the US." General Hospital Psychiatry 83: 101–107. https://doi.org/10.1016/j.genhosppsych.2023.05.001.

Patheos. "The Longest Journey You Will Make In Your Life Is From Your Head To Your Heart." June 30, 2019. https://www.patheos.com/blogs/mindfulchristianitytoday/201 8/07/the-longest-journey-you-will-make-in-your-life-is-from-your-head-to-your-heart.

Paris Martineau, "Maybe It's Not YouTube's Algorithm That Radicalizes People," Wired, October 23, 2019, https://www.wired.com/story/not-youtubes-algorithm-rad icalizes-people/.

Park, Brian Y., et al. 2016. "Is Internet Pornography Causing Sexual Dysfunctions? A Review with Clinical Reports." Behavioral Sciences 6 (3): 17. https://doi.org/10.3390/b s6030017.

Parkes, Walter F., and Lawrence Lasker. WarGames. Directed by John Badham. United Artists, 1983.

Pawlowski, Bogusław, et al. 2000. "Tall Men Have More Reproductive Success." Nature 403 (6766): 156. https://doi.org/10.1038/35003107.

Prison Policy Initiative. "Mass Incarceration: The Whole Pie 2025." March 11, 2025. https://www.prisonpolicy.org/reports/pie2025.html.

Psychology Today. "The Longest Distance in the World Is From the Head to the Heart." August 12, 2008. https://www.psychologytoday.com/us/blog/enlightened-living/200 808/the-longest-distance-in-the-world-is-the-head-the-heart.

Psychology Today. 2023. "Tribalism in the Age of Social Media." April 25. https://www.psychologytoday.com/us/blog/beyond-school-walls/202304/tribalis m-in-the-age-of-social-media.

Pew Research Center. "COVID-19 Vaccine Mandates and Public Opinion." 2022. http s://www.pewresearch.org/religion/2022/xx/xx/covid-19-vaccine-mandates.

Pew Research Center. 2023–2025. "Home Improvement and DIY Trends." Pew Research Center. https://www.pewresearch.org/social-trends/2023/xx/home-improvement-diy.

Pew Research Center. "News Use Across Social Media Platforms 2024." 2024. https:/ /www.pewresearch.org/journalism/2024/xx/xx/news-use-social-media.

Pew Research Center. "Reasons Adults Give for Not Having Children." July 25, 2024. https://www.pewresearch.org/social-trends/2024/07/25/reasons-adults-give-for -not-having-children.

Pierre, Joseph. "Morbid and non-morbid delusions: distinct patterns of social reinforce- ment." Schizophrenia Bulletin 47, no. 3 (2021): 678–687. https://doi.org/10.1093/schb ul/sbaa146.

Plato. 1892. Cratylus. Translated by Benjamin Jowett. In The Dialogues of Plato, vol. 1. Oxford: Clarendon Press. (Original work composed ca. 360 BCE; Heraclitus river fragment referenced at 402a.)

Post, Stephen G. 2005. "Altruism, Happiness, and Health: It's Good to Be Good." International Journal of Behavioral Medicine 12 (2): 66–77. https://doi.org/10.1207/s15327558ijbm1202_4.

PokerNews. "Hit Soft 17 in Blackjack." Accessed February 2026. https://www.pokernews.com/casino/casino-terms/hit-soft-17.htm.

Powerball. "Powerball Prize Chart." Accessed February 2026. https://www.powerball.com/powerball-prize-chart.

Precedence Research. 2025. "AI Companion Market Size, Share and Trends 2026 to 2035." December 22. https://www.precedenceresearch.com/ai-companion-market.

Preston, K., et al. "The Black Pill: New Technology and the Male Supremacy of Involuntarily Celibate Men." New Media & Society (2021). https://pmc.ncbi.nlm.nih.gov/articles/PMC8600582/.

Promises Behavioral Health. 2015. "Do You Suffer From Terminal Uniqueness?" May 29. https://www.promises.com/addiction-blog/do-you-suffer-from-terminal-uniqueness.

PsyPost. 2025. "Extraversion, Narcissism, and Histrionic Tendencies Predict the Desire to Become an Influencer." June 2. https://www.psypost.org/extraversion-narcissism-and-histrionic-tendencies-predict-the-desire-to-become-an-influencer.

Qualcomm. 2025. "Snapdragon 8 Elite Mobile Platform." Qualcomm. Accessed February 4, 2026. https://www.qualcomm.com/products/mobile/snapdragon/smartphones/snapdragon-8-series-mobile-platforms/snapdragon-8-elite-mobile-platform.

Quinn, Susan. Marie Curie: A Life. New York: Simon & Schuster, 1995.

Raitt, Bonnie. 1989. "Nick of Time." Nick of Time. Capitol Records.

Ramadhan, Roy N., et al. 2024. "Impacts of Digital Social Media Detox for Mental Health: A Systematic Review and Meta-Analysis." Narra J 4 (2): e786. https://doi.org/10.52225/narra.v4i2.786.

Rand, Ayn. 1957. Atlas Shrugged. New York: Random House.

Reagan, Ronald. 1987. "Remarks at the Signing of the Intermediate-Range Nuclear Forces Treaty." December 8, 1987. Public Papers of the Presidents of the United States: Ronald Reagan, 1987, Book II. Washington, DC: U.S. Government Printing Office.

Realbotix. 2026. "Realistic Humanoid Robots and Relationship-Based AI." Accessed February 2026. https://realbotix.ai/.

Reeves, Byron, and Clifford Nass. The Media Equation: How People Treat Computers, Television, and New Media Like Real People and Places. Cambridge University Press, 1996.

Religion Unplugged. "Woman's Church 'Baby Formula Test' Goes Viral, Exposing Compassion Gap." November 13, 2025. https://religionunplugged.com/news/kentuc ky-woman-church-baby-formula-test-goes-viral-exposing-gaps-in-compassion.

Reuters. "U.S. Vaccine Mandates Timeline." 2021–2022. https://www.reuters.com/wo rld/us/us-vaccine-mandates-timeline-2021-2022.

Reuters. "U.S. Vaccine Mandate Fallout: Reinstatements and Lawsuits." 2023–2025. https://www.reuters.com/world/us/us-vaccine-mandate-fallout-2023.

Reuters Fact Check. "Videos of people collapsing in China during COVID-19 outbreak." January 2020 (updated 2023). https://www.reuters.com/article/fact-check/videos-coll apsing-china-covid-19.

Reuters Fact Check. "Why COVID Vaccine Inserts Were Blank." 2021. https://www.r euters.com/article/fact-check/covid-vaccine-inserts-blank.

Reuters Institute. Digital News Report 2025. University of Oxford, 2025. https://reut ersinstitute.politics.ox.ac.uk/digital-news-report/2025.

Riordan, Michael, and Lillian Hoddeson. Crystal Fire: The Birth of the Information Age. New York: W.W. Norton, 1997.

Rose, Steve. n.d. "What is Terminal Uniqueness?" https://steverosephd.com/what-is-t erminal-uniqueness.

Royal Commission of Inquiry into the Terrorist Attack on Christchurch Masjidain on 15 March 2019. Report of the Royal Commission of Inquiry into the Terrorist Attack on Christchurch Masjidain on 15 March 2019. Wellington, New Zealand: Royal Commission of Inquiry, 2020. https://christchurchattack.royalcommission.nz/the-report.

Salimpoor, Valorie N., Mitchel Benovoy, Kevin Larcher, Alain Dagher, and Robert J. Zatorre. 2011. "Anatomically Distinct Dopamine Release during Anticipation and Experience of Peak Emotion to Music." Nature Neuroscience 14 (2): 257–62.

Samsung. 2025. "Galaxy S25 Ultra – Full Phone Specifications." GSMArena (or Samsung official site). Accessed February 4, 2026. https://www.gsmarena.com/samsung_galaxy _s25_ultra-13000.php.

Satia, Priya. Empire of Guns: The Violent Making of the Industrial Revolution. New York: Penguin, 2018.

Schüll, Natasha Dow. Addiction by Design: Machine Gambling in Las Vegas. Princeton, NJ: Princeton University Press, 2012.

Schweizer, Peter. 2012. Makers and Takers: How Wealth and Welfare States Are Transforming the World. New York: Doubleday.

Searcy Financial. "The Currents of Currency: Exploring the Connection Between Money and Water." June 30, 2025. https://searcyfinancial.com/blog/the-currents-of-currency -exploring-the-connection-between-money-and-water.

Simon, Herbert A. 1971. "Designing Organizations for an Information-Rich World." In Computers, Communications, and the Public Interest, edited by Martin Greenberger, 37–72. Baltimore: Johns Hopkins Press.

Social Security Administration. "What is FICA?" EN-05-10297 pamphlet. https://ww w.ssa.gov/people/materials/pdfs/EN-05-10297.pdf.

SoFi. "Understanding Fractional Reserve Banking." Updated 2024–2025. https://ww w.sofi.com/learn/content/what-is-fractional-reserve-banking.

St. Louis Fed. "What Price Convenience? The ATM Surcharge Debate." Regional Economist, July 1997. https://www.stlouisfed.org/publications/regional-economist/ju ly-1997/what-price-convenience-the-atm-surcharge-debate.

Stanford Center for Internet and Society. 2019. "The Christchurch Shooting Suspect Comes from an Extreme Online Culture." March 15. https://cyberlaw.stanford.edu/p ublications/christchurch-shooting-suspect-comes-extreme-online-culture.

Statcounter Global Stats. 2026. "Mobile Operating System Market Share Worldwide." January. https://gs.statcounter.com/os-market-share/mobile/worldwide.

Strategy+business. 2014. "Competitive Narcissism: A Marketing Lesson." August 12. h ttps://www.strategy-business.com/blog/Competitive-Narcissism-A-Marketing-Lesson.

Substance Abuse and Mental Health Services Administration (SAMHSA). 2012. Mental Health, United States, 2010. Rockville, MD: SAMHSA. https://www.samhsa.gov/dat a/sites/default/files/MHUS2010/MHUS2010.pdf.

Substance Abuse and Mental Health Services Administration (SAMHSA). 2025. "988 Suicide & Crisis Lifeline Performance Metrics: 2023–2024 Report." Rockville, MD: SAMHSA. https://www.samhsa.gov/data/report/988-performance-metrics-2023-202 4.

Surden, Harry. 2019. "Artificial Intelligence and Law: An Overview." Georgia State University Law Review 35 (4): 1305–1337.

Smith, J., et al. Forthcoming. "Effects of a Two-Week Digital Detox on Anxiety and Depression in Young Adults: A Randomized Controlled Trial." Journal of Behavioral Addictions.

Stahl, Stephen M. 2013. Stahl's Essential Psychopharmacology: Neuroscientific Basis and Practical Applications. 3rd ed. Cambridge: Cambridge University Press.

Susan Harmeling, "Virtue Signaling On Race Relations Only Hurts The Cause," Forbes, January 16, 2023, https://www.forbes.com/sites/susanharmeling/2023/01/16/virtue-sig naling-on-race-relations-only-hurts-the-cause/.

Tangney, June Price, and Ronda L. Dearing. 2002. "Humility." In Handbook of Positive Psychology, edited by C. R. Snyder and Shane J. Lopez, 411–419. New York: Oxford University Press.

Tang, Yi-Yuan, et al. 2022. "Mindful Attention Promotes Control of Brain Network Dynamics for Self-Regulation and Discontinues the Past from the Present." Proceedings of the National Academy of Sciences 119 (47): e2201074119. https://doi.org/10.1073/pn as.2201074119.

TechCrunch. 2025. "AI Companion Apps on Track to Pull in $120M in 2025." August 12. https://techcrunch.com/2025/08/12/ai-companion-apps-on-track-to-pull-in-120m-i n-2025.

Terik Booth. 2025. "What Does Crashing Out Mean: The Viral Slang That Captures a Generation's Limit." Medium, June 20. https://terikbooth.medium.com/what-does-crashing-out-mean-the-viral-slang-that-captures-a-generations-limit-40ce75b41936.

Thai, H., Lee, D. H., Kim, N., & Ebrahim, M. 2024. "How digital detox affects perceived stress, anxiety, depression, and wellbeing: A three-arm randomized controlled trial." Journal of Medical Internet Research 26: e55681. https://doi.org/10.2196/55681.

The Columbus Dispatch. "Ohio casinos to begin withholding jackpot winnings from parents owing child support." September 22, 2014. https://www.dispatch.com/story/news/2014/09/22/ohio-casinos-to-begin-withholding/23368304007/

The Dodo. "Dog Always Brings A Leaf To 'Buy' Himself Treats At The Store." September 16, 2022. https://www.thedodo.com/close-to-home/dog-buys-treats-using-leaf.

The Guardian. "Russell Brand's shift to anti-establishment commentary during COVID." October 2022. https://www.theguardian.com/culture/2022/oct/xx/russell-brand-anti-establishment.

The Guardian. 2006. "Seinfeld Actor Lets Fly with Racist Tirade." November 22. https://www.theguardian.com/world/2006/nov/22/usa.danglaister.

The Harris Poll. "LEGO Group Kicks Off Global Program To Inspire the Next Generation Of Space Explorers As NASA Celebrates 50 Years Of Moon Landing." July 16, 2019. https://theharrispoll.com/briefs/lego-group-kicks-off-global-program-to-inspire-the-next-generation-of-space-explorers-as-nasa-celebrates-50-years-of-moon-landing/.

The Institute for College Access & Success (TICAS). 2025. "Student Debt and the Class of 2024." Oakland, CA: TICAS. https://ticas.org/student-debt/student-debt-class-of-2024/.

The Lancet. "Natural Immunity vs. Vaccine-Induced Immunity: A Meta-Analysis." 2023.

The Mary Sue. "'The two girls nowhere to be found': Austin man sees two Walmart shoppers filming Angel Tree shopping video. Then he finds their full cart—abandoned." December 10, 2025. https://www.themarysue.com/walmart-angel-tree-influencer.

The New York Times. 2004. "From the Editors: The Times and Iraq." May 26. https://www.nytimes.com/2004/05/26/world/from-the-editors-the-times-and-iraq.html.

The New York Times. 2017. "How 'Doxxing' Became a Mainstream Tool in the Culture Wars." August 30. https://www.nytimes.com/2017/08/30/technology/doxxing-protests.html.

The New York Times, "'Rick and Morty' Fans Wanted Their Sauce. McDonald's Underestimated Just How Much," October 8, 2017, https://www.nytimes.com/2017/10/08/us/mcdonalds-szechuan-sauce.html.

The New York Times. 2022. "Six Killed in Chain-Reaction Crash on Missouri Interstate." March 17, 2022. https://www.nytimes.com/2022/03/17/us/missouri-highway-crash.html.

The New York Times. 2024. "UnitedHealthcare CEO Brian Thompson Is Fatally Shot Outside Manhattan Hotel." December 4, 2024. https://www.nytimes.com/2024/12/04/nyregion/unitedhealthcare-ceo-brian-thompson-shot.html.

The New York Times. "Vaccine Tattoos: The New Badge of Honor." May 2021. https://www.nytimes.com/2021/05/xx/vaccine-tattoos.

The Next Web. 2016. "Porn pioneers: How adult entertainment boosts technology." August 30. https://thenextweb.com/news/porn-pioneers-adult-entertainment-boosts-technology.

The Pulitzer Prizes. 2002. "Explanatory Reporting." https://www.pulitzer.org/winners/staff-53.

The Raleigh House. 2018. "Steps to Understand and Overcome Terminal Uniqueness." September 10. https://www.theraleighhouse.com/addiction-blog/how-to-overcome-terminal-uniqueness.

The Recovery Village. n.d. "Terminal Uniqueness and Recovery." https://www.therecoveryvillage.com/drug-addiction/terminal-uniqueness.

The Saint Newspaper. 2024. "All Hat and No Cattle: A Texan Insight into the Cowboy Aesthetic." March 7. https://www.thesaint.scot/post/all-hat-and-no-cattle-a-texan-insight-into-the-cowboy-aesthetic.

TheStreet. "Joel Osteen's net worth: The megachurch leader's wealth & income in 2025." July 13, 2025. https://www.thestreet.com/personalities/joel-osteen-net-worth.

The Verge. "The Rise of the Ratio: How Twitter Turned Rejection Into a Metric." March 2020. https://www.theverge.com/2020/3/xx/xx/twitter-ratio-explained.

The Washington Examiner. "Video shows Democrats ditching masks after press conference on COVID rules." November 20, 2020. https://www.washingtonexaminer.com/news/199482/video-shows-democrats-ditching-masks-after-press-conference-on-covid-rules.

Three Initiates [pseud.]. The Kybalion: A Study of the Hermetic Philosophy of Ancient Egypt and Greece. Chicago: Yogi Publication Society, 1908.

Tiersma, Peter M. 1999. Legal Language. Chicago: University of Chicago Press.

Time Magazine. 2016. "See the 'Loose Lips Sink Ships' Propaganda Posters of World War II." December 8. https://time.com/4591841/loose-lips-sink-ships-posters/.

"Too Much Information, Too Little Time: How the Brain Separates Important from Unimportant Things in Our Fast-Paced Media World." Frontiers for Young Minds, June 1, 2017. https://kids.frontiersin.org/articles/10.3389/frym.2017.00023.

Turkle, Sherry. 2011. Alone Together: Why We Expect More from Technology and Less from Each Other. New York: Basic Books.

Turkle, Sherry. 2015. Reclaiming Conversation: The Power of Talk in a Digital Age. New York: Penguin Press.

Twenge, Jean M. 2017. iGen: Why Today's Super-Connected Kids Are Growing Up Less Rebellious, More Tolerant, Less Happy—and Completely Unprepared for Adulthood. New York: Atria Books.

Typetone AI. 2023. "TL;DR: Origins, Popularity, and Benefits." August 16. https://www.typetone.ai/blog/tldr-summary-what-it-is-and-why-it-matters-in-the-digital-age.

U.S. Bureau of Engraving and Printing. "Paper & Ink." Accessed February 2026. https://www.bep.gov/currency/faqs/paper-ink.

U.S. Census Bureau. Historical poverty tables (various years, including 1963–2021 data referenced in analyses). https://www.census.gov/data/tables/time-series/demo/incom e-poverty/historical-poverty-people.html.

U.S. Department of Defense. 2024. "Fiscal Year 2025 Budget Request." https://www.defense.gov/News/Releases/Release/Article/3700000/dod-relea ses-fiscal-year-2025-budget-request/.

U.S. Department of Defense. "COVID-19 Vaccine Implementation." 2023 report. http s://www.defense.gov/Spotlights/Coronavirus-DOD-Response.

U.S. Department of Defense. "COVID-19 Vaccine Mandate Rescission and Reinstatement." January 2023. https://www.defense.gov/Spotlights/Coronavirus-DOD-Respo nse.

U.S. Department of Energy. n.d. "The War of the Currents: AC vs. DC Power." https://www.energy.gov/articles/war-currents-ac-vs-dc-power.

U.S. Department of Health and Human Services. 2023. Our Epidemic of Loneliness and Isolation: The U.S. Surgeon General's Advisory on the Healing Effects of Social Connection and Community. Washington, DC: HHS.

U.S. Department of Health and Human Services. "COVID-19 Vaccine Implementation." 2023. https://www.hhs.gov/coronavirus/vaccines.

U.S. Department of Justice, National Institute of Corrections. 2010. "Strip Searches in Jails." Washington, DC: NIC.

U.S. Department of State, Office of the Historian. "Nixon and the End of the Bretton Woods System, 1971–1973." Accessed February 2026. https://history.state.gov/milesto nes/1969-1976/nixon-shock.

U.S. Department of Veterans Affairs. "Montgomery GI Bill Active Duty (MGIB-AD)." VA.gov (historical rates and eligibility archived). https://www.va.gov/education/abou t-gi-bill-benefits/montgomery-active-duty/.

U.S. Department of Veterans Affairs. "Post-9/11 GI Bill." VA.gov. Updated 2025–2026. https://www.va.gov/education/about-gi-bill-benefits/post-9-11.

U.S. Department of Veterans Affairs and U.S. Department of Defense. 2013. VA/DoD Clinical Practice Guideline for the Assessment and Management of Patients at Risk for

Suicide. Washington, DC: VA/DoD. https://www.healthquality.va.gov/guidelines/MH/srb/.

U.S. Federal Reserve. "Currency in Circulation." Factsheet (updated 2025–2026). https://www.federalreserve.gov/paymentsystems/coin_currcirc.htm.

U.S. Geological Survey. "The Water in You: Water and the Human Body." Updated 2024–2025. https://www.usgs.gov/special-topics/water-science-school/science/water-you-water-and-human-body.

U.S. Government Accountability Office. Reports on military recruiting incentives and quotas (various 2010s–2020s). https://www.gao.gov.

U.S. Office of the Director of National Intelligence. "Declassified Assessment on COVID-19 Origins." October 2021 (updated 2023). https://www.dni.gov/files/ODNI/documents/assessments/Declassified-Assessment-on-COVID-19-Origins.pdf.

UnitedHealth Group. 2025. "UnitedHealth Group Reports 2024 Results." January 16. https://www.unitedhealthgroup.com/content/dam/UHG/PDF/investors/2024/2025-16-01-uhg-reports-fourth-quarter-results.pdf.

United Nations Office on Drugs and Crime (UNODC). Afghanistan Opium Survey 2022. Vienna: UNODC, 2023. https://www.unodc.org/documents/crop-monitoring/Afghanistan/Opium_cultivation_Afghanistan_2022.pdf.

United Nations Population Fund (UNFPA), State of World Population 2025 report (June 2025)

United States v. I. Lewis Libby, No. 1:05-cr-00394 (D.D.C. 2006). Court records and Fitzgerald Special Counsel Report, October 28, 2006.

Van Boven, Leaf, and Thomas Gilovich. "To Do or to Have? That Is the Question." Journal of Personality and Social Psychology 85, no. 6 (2003): 1193–1202. https://doi.org/10.1037/0022-3514.85.6.1193.

Veale, David, et al. 2015. "Am I Normal? A Systematic Review and Construction of Nomograms for Flaccid and Erect Penis Length and Circumference in Up to 15,521 Men." BJU International 115 (6): 978–986. https://doi.org/10.1111/bju.13010.

Verywell Health. "How Long Can You Survive Without Drinking Water?" July 16, 2025. https://www.verywellhealth.com/how-long-can-you-go-without-water-11741717.

"Voices on Independence: Four Oral Histories About Building Women's Economic Power." Smithsonian American Women's History Museum, October 25, 2024. https://womenshistory.si.edu/blog/voices-independence-four-oral-histories-about-building-womens-economic-power.

Walgrave, Stefaan, and Joris Verhulst. "The February 15 Worldwide Protests against a War in Iraq: An Empirical Test of Transnational Opportunities. Outline of a Research Programme." University of Antwerp, 2003. https://medialibrary.uantwerpen.be/oldcontent/container2608/files/Walgrave%20Verhulst%202003%20-%20The%20februari%2015%20worldwide%20protests.pdf.

Wang, Xiaojing, et al. 2023. "Overview on Brain Function Enhancement of Internet Addicts through Exercise Intervention: Based on Reward-Execution-Decision Cycle." Frontiers in Psychiatry 14: 9933907. https://doi.org/10.3389/fpsyt.2023.9933907.

Ware, Bronnie. The Top Five Regrets of the Dying: A Life Transformed by the Dearly Departing. Carlsbad, CA: Hay House, 2012.

Ware, Bronnie. "Regrets of the Dying." Blog post. Accessed [your date, e.g., February 2026]. https://bronnieware.com/blog/regrets-of-the-dying.

Watts, Alan. The Book: On the Taboo Against Knowing Who You Are. New York: Pantheon Books, 1966.

Wilson, Fred. 2010. "Takers and Makers." AVC (blog), October 6. https://avc.com/2010/10/takers-and-makers.

Wilson, Joseph C. 2003. "What I Didn't Find in Africa." The New York Times, July 6. https://www.nytimes.com/2003/07/06/opinion/what-i-didn-t-find-in-africa.html.

Wired. 2019. "A Brief History of Porn on the Internet." April 9. https://www.wired.com/story/brief-history-porn-internet/.

Wizard of Odds. "Roulette Basics – Rules, Bets, and Game Variations Explained." Updated July 1, 2025. https://wizardofodds.com/games/roulette/basics.

WKYT. "Somerset church uses numerous donations to help community after TikTok challenge." November 28, 2025. https://www.wkyt.com/2025/11/28/somerset-church-uses-numerous-donations-help-community-after-tiktok-challenge.

Wrangham, Richard. Catching Fire: How Cooking Made Us Human. New York: Basic Books, 2009.

Wolf, Maryanne. 2018. Reader, Come Home: The Reading Brain in a Digital World. New York: Harper.

World Economic Forum. 2025. "4 Imperatives for Improving Mental Health Care in 2025." January 13, 2025. https://www.weforum.org/stories/2025/01/4-imperatives-for-improving-mental-health-care-in-2025/.

World Economic Forum. 2025. "The Future of Jobs Report 2025." Geneva: World Economic Forum. https://www.weforum.org/publications/the-future-of-jobs-report-2025/.

World Health Organization. 2024. "Mental Health Crisis Intervention: Community-Based Approaches." Geneva: WHO. https://www.who.int/publications/i/item/9789240094826.

Worthington, Everett L., Jr., Joshua N. Hook, Don E. Davis, Daryl R. Van Tongeren, and Andrea J. Romero. 2016. "Humility: A Review and Synthesis." Journal of Positive Psychology 11 (6): 614–626. https://doi.org/10.1080/17439760.2016.1167935.

Yang, Andrew. The War on Normal People: The Truth About America's Disappearing Jobs and Why Universal Basic Income Is Our Future. New York: Hachette Books, 2018.

Zajonc, Robert B. 1968. "Attitudinal Effects of Mere Exposure." Journal of Personality and Social Psychology 9 (2, pt. 2): 1–27.

Zetter, Kim. "Hackers Finally Post Stolen Ashley Madison Data." Wired, August 18, 2015. https://www.wired.com/2015/08/happened-hackers-posted-stolen-ashley-madison-data/.

Zukav, Gary, and Linda Francis. The Heart of the Soul: Emotional Awareness. New York: Simon & Schuster, 2001.

Acknowledgements

The thing we tell of can never be found by seeking, yet only seekers find it. — Bayazid Bistami

This book exists because of dozens of people over the years, most of whom I will never be able to thank by name. Various Citizen Philosophers who I was in the right place at right time to encounter. Countless voices from recovery rooms. Strangers who were down for a deep chat at a bus stop. People I partied with in the before time. Authors whose books reshaped my thinking, many of them listed in the works cited at the back. The list is nearly endless.

I think back on everyone who has shaped this book and how I encountered them during the different eras of my life. I have always connected with unique minds, and sometimes I wonder what it would be like to gather them all into one room and watch those worlds collide. Writing this, I realize with some regret that I do not even recall many of their names. Some were just screen names. Others I met in the wild. All of them made an impact.

I have always been a seeker. Seeking other seekers.

— James

1999

The end is the beginning, and the beginning is the end. — Satguru Sivaya Subramuniyaswami

1999 was the year that the Cyberspace Psychosis infected the world. It was the first symptom, the first morning we woke up with a bit of a scratchy throat and a stuffy nose. Digitally.

We did not have an idea what we were really in store for.

I am a Xennial. That micro-generation from 1978 to 1982. We are the *Oregon Trail* Generation.[1] Which explains how we have avoided dysentery in the Territory, since that Map sure prepared us. Our unique position allowed us to grow up with an entirely analog childhood and live through a pervasively digital adulthood. We watched the whole thing happen from both sides of the screen.

Let's go back to 1999.

Remember that feeling? How excited everybody was? How optimistic and genuinely enthusiastic were we as a culture? We were looking forward to that New Year's Eve since 1982 when Prince invited us to the party. What a party it turned out to be. We stood on the threshold between two Ages.

The analogue past and our digital future.

Our healthy past and the Psychosis future.

---

1. The Oregon Trail was our generation's Kobayashi Maru.

Peter Jennings guided our nostalgia for *The Century*. He did it again a couple of weeks later with *The Century: America's Time*. Naturally, the American version ran longer. One thing the Empire was Absolutely intent on was making sure everyone knew the 21st century belonged to America. We were the world's only remaining superpower, and the Empire needed everyone to know it.

I basically ignored both of them since I was nineteen in 1999. Young, dumb, with no idea what I was doing[2], but I, like the rest of us, knew we were witnessing something special. The zeitgeist was Absolutely electric. Everything felt as if we were accelerating toward greatness. The future was barreling towards us with bright lights and blasting music, and we were all invited to the party.

Despite the overwhelming sense of optimism and momentum, a constant background hum lingered: Y2K. Legacy media was in full pearl-clutching mode, warning that computers would freeze, banks would collapse, planes would fall from the sky, the electric grid would fail, and the apocalypse would be upon us. Meanwhile, actual human beings cracked jokes about it and carried on with business as usual.

Y2K was a Triple A hijack attempt. This one emphasized Attitude, and the Empire sought to make us fearful of the future. They had seen the effects of the comment section on the Ocean Liners and they knew more and more people were migrating to the edge of the table and glancing around at things. So, in an effort to herd everyone to the center, they ran with fear. An entire media apparatus whipping itself into a frenzy over what was ultimately a nothing burger. If it were going to be a real problem, then Prince would have warned us about it.

Collectively, we were in uncharted Territory, and it felt like the weirdness was only getting started.

1999 was peak spectacle. Following up on Heaven's Gate, Monica Lewinsky, the U.S. stepping up as the world's police force, and those six months everybody got really into swing music.[3] 1999 was the culmination because it rolled several pivotal cultural milestones into a single year. One after another, like dominoes. All the craziness of the nineties compressed into the most dynamic twelve months ever.

---

2. Drugs. I was doing drugs.

3. Then it vanished like it never happened. If you were there, you know. If you weren't, I can't explain it either.

Then, in April, Columbine happened. Two kids shot up their high school in Littleton, Colorado, and the country fractured on impact. Thirteen murdered, twenty wounded, two suicides. Talking heads scrambled to explain it: guns, video games, antidepressants, Marilyn Manson, trench coats, anything. This didn't happen in an inner city. It happened in white bread affluent Colorado. It wasn't supposed to happen there. Something shifted. The weird kids got looked at differently after that, and zero-tolerance policies and active shooter drills followed not long after. A crack in the facade of collective innocence. A harbinger of worse times to come. But in 1999, even that couldn't dim the mood for long. The optimism was that strong.

Earlier that spring, *The Matrix hit theaters.*[4]

The Matrix was unique because of the cultural appeal. Before this, Sci-Fi only appealed to a certain segment of the population. This was not a space opera like *Star Wars* or *Star Trek*, and it was not in the same vein as *Total Recall* or *The Fifth Element* either. *The Matrix* was philosophical. It was provocative. And it was wildly popular. It forced the entire audience to think. To seriously consider the premise that your entire reality might be a simulation. Everything you've experienced might be an artificial construct. We could be living in a Virtual World and not even know it, maintained by machines siphoning off our body heat as a power source.[5]

The Matrix was a phenomenon, and its language became the backbone of our relationship with Cyberspace. It gave us *"Red Pill"* and *"Blue Pill"*. It gave us *"Glitch in the Matrix"* to explain odd happenings. *"What is real?"* became a mainstream question for the first time, asked by a guy with sunglasses training in kung fu with Cowboy Curtis. We even discovered there is no spoon.

The entire premise was deep and fascinating to discuss. The Red Pill represented consent. Morpheus didn't drag Neo out of the simulation. He offered a choice. Take the Blue Pill, live with your Relative Truth and go back to sleep. Believe whatever you want to believe. Take the Red Pill, open your eyes to the Absolute Truth and see just how deep it goes. Neo consented to learn the truth. The truth was bleak. Blackened skies, machines harvesting humans, slop for food, a hard life, no pleasure, no illusions to hide behind. The truth doesn't guarantee comfort just because you had the courage to look at it.

---

4. Neo literally woke up in a pod full of goo and discovered the grass was definitely not greener. If that's not the Virtual Reality Blues, nothing is.

5. Robert Monroe had given us a glimpse into the concept of loosh. IYKYK

I admire Cypher. The guy who took the Red Pill, saw reality for what it was, and said *no thank you.* He betrayed his entire crew to get plugged back into the simulation. He sat across from Agent Smith, savoring that steak he knew wasn't real, and said he didn't care. The Relative illusion tasted better than the Absolute truth. He had viewed the Territory, and he volunteered to go back to the comfortable lie. Ignorance is bliss. He saw the writing on the wall and wanted back inside. Who could blame him? Yes he was an asshole, but he was an *authentic* asshole. He saw the Territory and was not having any of it. He wanted to throw the entire Nebuchadnezzar under the bus, then back right over them firmly onto the Map.

The rebels would hop back and forth between the Map and the Territory by logging in. They would plug in and go online, exactly like the dial-up modems. When they needed to escape the simulation, they used payphones. Landlines. A mundane analog piece of technology that existed everywhere in 1999, and is nowhere to be found in the world of late stage Cyberspace Psychosis. We do not need them because there is no logging in and out for us. We are logged in all the time.

That exit from the digital world through a device that barely exists anymore. Think about that, when is the last time you saw an actual payphone? It was a sign of what was to come. The way out of the digital world was analog. That way out *doesn't exist anymore.*

The Matrix was the Map. Zion was the Territory.

The movie made the distinction neatly.

Another massive cultural pivot happened that summer when *American Pie* hit theaters. This is where the Empire drew the cultural line between Gen X and the Millennials.

I'm class of 1998. My graduation year's big high school movie was *Can't Hardly Wait.* The last great Gen X high school film. Preston Meyers, an awkward aspiring writer, spends four years secretly in love with Amanda Beckett, the popular girl. The movie had a wholesome quality. Sure, while the movie included some mature content, it implied it rather than celebrated it. The overall theme was genuine connection with a degree of wholesome satisfaction. Happy ending and all. It started with a Pop-Tart and ended with a kiss.

The class of 1999 got *American Pie.* The absolute opposite. Groundbreaking in its raunchy, in-your-face perversion.[6] Overt and obnoxious depravity. The point wasn't to connect with the love of your life. The plot was to get laid. Four guys make a pact to lose their virginity before prom. That's it. That's the plot. The basest desires fulfilled.

Buried in that movie, played entirely for laughs, was a scene where a teenage boy broadcasts a girl undressing via webcam to his entire class. We all know the scene. In 1999, we had never even seen a webcam. They were approximately as common as excellent decisions in a casino. The technology barely existed, and its introductory cultural moment was a sex crime. The future had arrived, and the future was Peeping Toms on parade.

That webcam was the most tech-forward glimpse in the entire film. I guarantee more people use webcams than fuck pies.

1980 was the last year of Gen X, and 1981 was the first Millennial year. Look at those two movies and you can see the cultural divide with your own eyes. The kids in *Can't Hardly Wait* are all Gen X. The kids in *American Pie* are millennials. In one, a Pop-Tart is an omen of a match made in Heaven. In the other, a teenager fucks a pie.

1999 gave us two culturally pivotal masterpieces of cinematic impact. One movie asks, "W*hat is real?*" and hands a generation a Map to question the simulation. The other movie asks, "H*ow can I get my dick wet?*", and gifted us the word MILF. One movie's rebels escape through payphones. The other movie's breakthrough tech is a webcam driven non-consensual voyeurism.

The Matrix proved we could see the cage. American Pie proved we'd rather stay in it.

All of it was happening while the entire country was counting down to New Year's Eve. We have never experienced another time where people were this fixated on a New Year. We came close in 2019 but that was a shadow of the 1999 hope. The anticipation was unlike anything before or since. Y2K had a good chunk of the population legitimately convinced the world was going to end when the clock struck midnight. They were so busy panicking about the machines breaking that they missed the machines winning.

---

6. Ok maybe not groundbreaking, anyone who had seen Meatballs or any of the Revenge of the Nerds movies knew sexualization wasn't exactly a foreign concept. American Pie just set the bar so much higher.

I grew up alongside Cyberspace. I remember Prodigy and CompuServe. I was on AOL sixteen hours a day while my family couldn't use the phone. I remember when AltaVista was the best search engine even though Lycos had the best commercials. Remember when different search engines were in competition with each other and would actually advertise to gain market share? Sigh. Good times. Now we just say *google it.*

In 1999, almost nobody had a cellphone. If you were cool, you had a pager. That was it. You made plans by calling a landline from another landline, and if the person wasn't home, you left a message on an answering machine and waited. You paid for things with cash. You got directions from a gas station attendant or a Rand McNally atlas. You went into a store to buy something, and if the store didn't have it, you drove to another store. Friction was built right in, and so was patience. Nobody thought of it as friction. That was just how things worked.

Today you can't buy a sandwich at some places without downloading their app. There is an app for everything. Parking meters. Dry cleaners. Restaurants that won't give you a menu unless you scan a QR code. Resistance was engineered out as surveillance was engineered in. No one offered us that choice. We just woke up one day as data points instead of people.

We cannot even get out of an app without it being a hassle anymore.

You cannot even unsubscribe from a service in Cyberspace without the insecurity popping up. These services sound like a desperate ex-girlfriend trying to set a world record for cringe. Many of us have experienced some version of,

"Are you sure you want to cancel?"

"What if I offer you 20% off an annual subscription?"

"But we had something special..."

"What if I change? What if I give you a whole month free?"

"Please don't leave me."

"Fine go, just tell me why! Here is the customer survey."

"Ok bye. I'm still going to email you every single day to remind you what you're missing."

It is the worst kind of rejection sensitivity playing out at the institutional level. The same neediness, the same inability to let go, the same desperate clinging to Attention. The Empire has become the "nice guy" of goods and services. They play nice on the surface but we all know they just want to fuck you. The Empire has the emotional maturity of a codependent partner who can't handle being told no.

In 1999, we had no idea it would get this bad. Our initial optimism from then is all but gone. No, not all at once. It has been a slow burn, in installments. Maybe it burned away in movements.

Every step of the way, we relied on Cyberspace a little more. Every step of the way, the Psychosis infected us a little deeper. The zeitgeist of 1999 didn't die in a single event. It died a death of a thousand cuts, each one a small migration into the screen.

Maybe it is time we migrated back.

Afterword

Well it is done. Here you have it. This book took everything I had to get written. I do not mean that materially. I had to dig deep within to get all of this completed. Overcoming myself to get it across the finish line.

The longest jump for anything seems to be the leap from 90%-100%, and the last ten percent of this book took me almost two months to complete. Most of that was line edits and other boring shit. It was a struggle to get through it, but we did it and we made it. By we I mean my staff of the cats: Texas, Whiskey, Ava, The Baron, and The Duchess, my AI agents, and Floof the Guinea Pig. The entire team here at PathWays Collective.

There is a lot of this book that I had to leave out. There was entire Movement called Cybersex that I just could not get to jive right. There were other quips, anecdotes, and passages that unfortunately didn't make the cut. Maybe I will publish them as a Volume 2. Or put some of them into essay form on my website. Who knows?

I want to thank each of you for taking this journey with me. I am grateful for you to have walked this path with me and I hope you enjoyed the scenery along the way. I would Absolutely love to hear from you! If something in the book touched you or helped you or gave you some clarity, tell me about it. If something in this book pissed you off so hard and you are still clenching your teeth about it, then I want to hear from you too. We can turn it into a conversation either way.

Right now our world is facing some of the biggest problems we have ever faced. It is going to be up to all of us, collectively, to figure out and then implement the correct solutions. Despite the digital darkness, there are bright lights shining all over, and when we shine together we are capable of anything.

Thank you again everyone for reading.

About the author

James Hickey is a meandering soul, writer, and podcaster who lives in Northeast Ohio with five cats and one guinea pig. He eats Chex Mix ™ with chopsticks, drinks his water with no ice, and graduated from the University of Life with a BS in charm, wit, and personality. He is the founder of PathWays Collective LLC, a consultancy specializing in Applied Neurodivergence, and hosts two podcasts: *The Sight Side*, on the neurodivergent experience in the workplace and professional innovation, and *Path of the Sober Seeker*, on sobriety and recovery through the lens of neurodivergence and personal evolution. He can be reached at pathwayscollective.net.

9 7 9 8 9 9 9 8 9 8 2 4 5 3